Plan and Market in Yugoslav Economic Thought

by Deborah D. Milenkovitch

Can a socialist state decentralize and still remain socialist? This is a real question in Yugoslavia, which started to reform its centrally planned model fifteen years earlier than other East European countries and has gone further in expanding the scope of market relations than other socialist countries have even contemplated. In Yugoslavia the progression has been from soviet-type planning to decentralization of current production decisions to decentralization of investment decisions to privatization of social property. The decision to establish workers' councils as the vehicle of decentralization has been of central importance.

Mrs. Milenkovitch analyzes the Yugoslav experience carefully and raises the intriguing question whether the changes are specific to Yugoslavia or whether there are common forces that will compel other socialist countries to abandon central planning of production and investment and ultimately induce them to reestablish ownership over productive factors. Though the book focuses on Yugoslavia, many of the economic problems discussed are common to other socialist nations and of keen interest to Western economists watching the socialist states experiment with new ways of meeting national economic needs.

"A very interesting combination of three different approaches ... history of economic doctrines, economic history (non-quantitative), and comparative economic systems. There does not exist any treatment of Yugoslavia that attempts to do what she has done successfully."—
Egon Neuberger

Mrs. Milenkovitch is assistant professor of economics at Barnard College.

Yale Russian and East European Studies, 9

YALE RUSSIAN AND EAST EUROPEAN STUDIES, 9

PLAN AND MARKET IN

YUGOSLAV ECONOMIC THOUGHT

by Deborah D. Milenkovitch

New Haven and London, Yale University Press, 1971

Set in Baskerville type
and printed in the United States of America by
Vail-Ballou Press, Inc., Binghamton, N.Y.

Distributed in Great Britain, Europe, and Africa by
Yale University Press, Ltd., London; in Canada by
McGill-Queen's University Press, Montreal; in Mexico
by Centro Interamericano de Libros Académicos,
Mexico City; in Central and South America by Kaiman
& Polon, Inc., New York City; in Australasia by
Australia and New Zealand Book Co., Pty., Ltd.,
Artarmon, New South Wales; in India by UBS Publishers'
Distributors Pvt., Ltd., Delhi; in Japan by John
Weatherhill, Inc., Tokyo.

Contents

Acknowledgments

This book could not have been written without the help of many friends and colleagues and without the support and cooperation of several institutions. Needless to say, the author alone bears full responsibility for the final product. Among those who have been most helpful, I should particularly like to thank: Alexander Erlich and Herbert Levine, who supervised the writing of my doctoral dissertation submitted to Columbia University in 1966, on which this book is based, for their assistance and encouragement; Benjamin Ward, who read the manuscript in an early stage and urged me to revise it for publication; Branko Horvat, whose valuable comments on the interpretation of Yugoslav events resulted in many improvements; Michael Montias, whose incisive criticisms resulted in increased clarity and accuracy at many points; Egon Neuberger, who forced me to rethink my definitions of plan and market and the requirements of systems that use both plan and market as coordinating devices; Svetozar Pejovich, who made me realize the crucial significance of a careful definition of property rights; and Aleksandar Bajt, Ivan Lavrac, Milan Mesaric, Jovan Raicevic, Milos Samardzija, and Jakov Sirotkovic, all of whom were kind enough to give me comments on particular parts of the manuscript.

Among the institutions contributing to the completion of this book, I should like to thank the following: the Woodrow Wilson Foundation, for making possible my first studies of the Yugoslav economy; the Ford Foundation, whose Foreign Area Training Fellowship supported my study and research for three years; the American Council of Learned Societies–Social Science Research Council, whose grant made possible a trip to Yugoslavia in the summer of 1968; the Barnard College Faculty Research Fund, which helped defray the typing expenses; and *East Europe,* for permission to extract some sections from my article published there.

My thanks also to Sin-ming Shaw and Anna Willman for assistance in research and to Kathleen McNally and Christine Dodson for assistance in preparation of the manuscript.

Last, but never least, my deep appreciation to my husband, Michael, for his assistance, his patience, and, most important, for his warm encouragement.

New York City   D. D. M.
1970

CHAPTER 1

Plan and Market as Organizational Options

I have entitled this study *Plan and Market in Yugoslav Economic Thought*. Some elaboration of the title may be useful. *Plan and market* refers to the question of how to organize the socialist society and the respective roles of plan and market in that organization. *Yugoslav* economic thought refers to Yugoslav views on the problems of economic organization in socialism. Although the focus is narrowly on Yugoslavia, many of the economic problems, as well as the Marxist-Soviet intellectual heritage, are common to other socialist nations. Finally, I have specified *economic thought* because, by and large, I am dealing with attitudes toward plan and market and not with actual economic organization. This does not mean that the actual system is ignored, but a full study of the economic organization in Yugoslavia remains to be done. I hope to devote attention to this topic in the near future.

This being said, it is apparent that I view plan and market in Yugoslav economic thought as only one part of an inquiry into the larger topic, the economic organization of socialism. We may, accordingly, start with some general comments on socialist economic organization and with a definition of "plan" and of "market."

ECONOMIC ORGANIZATION IN A SOCIALIST SOCIETY

The socialist society, whether Marxist or not, has several special characteristics. Socialist political-economic systems consciously select the ends toward which economic activity is directed. They select the means by which the ends are to be attained. The institution of private property, if not abolished, is significantly restricted.

The socialist society establishes explicit objectives that normally include not only the levels of consumption by individuals but other components such as the rate of growth and the income distribution. The method of organizing productive activity is also a conscious choice. The society must decide by whom, and on what basis, decisions about what to produce and how to produce it are to be made. The organizational options include a single, all-embracing state monopoly, producers' cooperatives, and a number of other possibilities.

If ends and means were completely distinct, the rational socialist society would select that method of organization putting society on its production possibilities frontier at the most desired point. But in socialist societies ends and means are not always completely distinct. The preferred organizational form may not always lead to the most efficient production and, if the organizational form were considered purely as a means, then it might be rejected. However, an inefficiency or higher cost may be tolerated as the price to be paid for achieving a social end, for organizational forms are often highly valued outputs of the system. Rationality requires that society explicitly weigh the cost of its preferred institutions; if the cost is sufficiently great, the organization preference may be sacrificed.

Two methods of economic organization have been historically most relevant for Marxist socialists. These may be called broadly "plan" and "market." Plan is used here to mean central determination of what and how to produce. In this method, decisions are based on central analysis of relevant information and are made from an economy-wide vantage point. In a physical analogy, planned decisions are made from the mountain top. From the peak of the mountain it is possible to survey the entire area, even though some of the detail may be lost and some few spots remain hidden. Market here means that decisions about what and how to produce are made from the viewpoint of the primary economic unit. Decisions are made on the basis of information about prices of inputs and of final products and on the basis of the detailed production data of the particular unit. Following the analogy, market decisions are made in the valley. Horizons are limited, but the quality and quantity of information is greater. The decision maker can base his conclusions on immediate, nontransferable information.

Plan and market methods correspond approximately to centralized and decentralized decisions. But the relation is inexact, as the following example shows. The center could collect the relevant data and determine, in relation to some set of ends, the efficient allocation of resources. Simultaneously, it could generate a set of "proper" prices that, when transmitted to the individual production units, would induce them to make that allocation, on the basis of independent decisions, envisioned by the planners. In this instance the decisions are, in a sense, decentralized. On the other hand, the center possesses all the information necessary to allocate resources directly, so the collection of information and the social vantage point employed are really central rather than local.

The important distinctions between plan and market are the quality of information available to the decision-making unit and the social vantage point from which decisions are reached. Both plan and market are methods of resource allocation, and either may be employed for any given set of economic objectives. It is not necessary to associate the use of the market mechanism with satisfying consumers' preferences or to associate planning with implementing leaders' preferences. This does not mean, however, that each method need be equally suitable in any given situation. In general, the usefulness of methods of economic organization depends upon a complex set of factors that may themselves vary over time. Specifically, the choice of economic organization will depend on the objectives of society and on the economic and technical conditions (factor supplies, production functions). As these conditions change over time—as indeed they must in a developing economy—the organizational methods most suitable may also vary. Thus one expects not constancy but change in the economic systems of socialist countries.

ECONOMIC REFORM IN SOCIALIST COUNTRIES

Soviet-type economies in the sixties have not disappointed our expectation of change. Defects in the classic organizational pattern have become apparent, and reforms are widespread in all countries. Further, most of these changes have resulted in an expansion of the scope of market phenomena. Despite important differences, the reforms involve a decentralization of decision making and an increase in the use of market signals. This is true whether the reforms merely revise the existing planning model to make use of more efficient information systems or to promote better adherence to plan objectives, or whether the reforms involve a major change in the system of economic organization.

Some of the forces behind these changes are clear. There is little doubt that for the purposes of accelerating economic development—or for any radical reorientation of the economic structure—a greater degree of central planning is necessary than for maintaining more balanced, less strained growth. The contrast between the economy on the verge of development and the more mature economy illustrates clearly how changes in both objectives and in the economic and technical conditions associated with the progress toward maturity might affect the choice of organizational method. The disadvantages of relying heavily on the market mechanism may be substantial for an underdeveloped country seeking rapid development, and the plan can offer many advantages. First, the plan serves to mobilize the population and to enforce a higher rate of savings than would otherwise have obtained. Second, because of the radical reorientation of resources required for economic development, discontinuities and externalities render the market mechanism inadequate to allocate resources. This is true for any radical change in the pattern of production but particularly true for underdeveloped countries with small, undeveloped markets. On the one hand, there may be monopolies. On the other, with few buyers and sellers, the consequences of enterprise decisions are less predictable. Under such conditions, the coordination of investment decisions can be a significant improvement. At the same time, at low levels of development, the planners' choices may be relatively simple. Certain needs appear to be obvious ("every nation needs a steel mill"), and planners need not consider an extensive list of the alternatives.

At a higher level of economic development, however, the disadvantages of the market are less important and the defects of the plan loom larger. The process of development itself serves to eliminate many of the very conditions that made the market work poorly. As development proceeds, supply elasticities increase, bottlenecks are eliminated, the number of producers and consumers of products increase, and radical shifts of productive capacities are less likely. Accordingly, the misallocation resulting from the use of the market may become less significant relative to the total volume of investment at higher levels of development. At the same time, the planning system itself may become dysfunctional. As technology becomes more complex and as supply bottlenecks are eliminated, the choices open to the planner multiply. It becomes far more difficult and vastly more costly to evaluate alternatives. Also, the planning bureaucracy may have developed its own information and decision-making biases that limit its usefulness. Bureaucracies usually resist change and are best adapted for producing the same old products in the same old way. But the process of development itself makes the old methods ever less suitable. Finally, if a sizeable investment goods sector has been constructed, emphasis will probably shift to products for consumption and the community may show greater concern about satisfying consumers. More affluent consumers are choosier consumers. No adequate substitute for satisfying consumers has been found to replace the market, least of all a burdensome bureaucracy. The need to satisfy customers is important not only in domestic trade but also for success in foreign trade.

Thus the very planning mechanism that may have been highly effective in bringing about economic development becomes counterproductive at a later stage in a more mature economy. By continuing to plan in the same manner, the community may be at a lower level of welfare than it could have attained through other methods of determining what and how to produce.

For all of these oft-cited reasons, once the foundations of an industrial society are laid, some shift in emphasis from plan to market is not surprising. This is not to suggest that such a shift represents the only direction in which the system can move to cope with new conditions. It may be possible to improve the process of plan construction and implementation. The development of data-processing capacities offers a rational, centrally planned alternative. It is also possible that far less radical changes in the basic Soviet planning model can eliminate its most important defects.

ECONOMIC REFORM IN YUGOSLAVIA

The Yugoslav economic system since its inception has experienced two radical economic reforms. Each has taken Yugoslavia a long way down the path from total plan to extensive use of the market. From Marx onward, in the socialist literature, the plan and the market had been traditionally viewed as mutually exclusive methods of resource allocation. For many years this "either-or" approach had characterized Soviet interpretations as well. When the Yugoslavs rejected the Soviet system and the Soviet analysis, they redefined the relation between plan and market.

Yugoslavia abandoned the Soviet-type planning model starting in 1950. In the first economic reform, the apparatus for the central planning of production was dismantled, enterprises became autonomous, and profit was reestablished as the motive force. Since 1960 Yugoslavia has made even more radical changes. The second major economic reform aimed at abandoning the central planning of investment and placing investment decisions under the control of autonomous, profit-seeking enterprises run by the workers. Decentralization of investment decisions has raised the further problem of the definition of ownership and the meaning of property rights in socialism, with the attendant implications for the distribution of income in the socialist state.

What stands out in the Yugoslav experience is that the Yugoslavs started to reform the centrally planned model about fifteen years earlier than did other East European countries, and that the Yugoslavs have gone further in changing the system than other socialist countries contemplate. Indeed, at this point, it can even be questioned whether socialism, in any meaningful sense, exists in Yugoslavia.

The Yugoslav experience raises the intriguing question of whether, and to what extent, we can generalize from the Yugoslav experience. Are these changes specific to Yugoslavia or are there common forces that will compel other socialist countries to abandon central planning and, ultimately, induce them to reestablish ownership claims over productive factors? This study traces the development of Yugoslav attitudes about plan and market in socialism and attempts to point to some key factors that seem to account for the changes in Yugoslav economic organization.

CHAPTER 2

Marx on Plan and Market

The Yugoslav intellectual heritage is Marxist, and thus it is necessary to consider Marx's views on economic organization. Several problems arise in discussing Marx's views on the socialist economy. Although Marx discussed precapitalist forms of economic organization illustratively and capitalist forms exhaustively, his treatment of the economics of socialism was not extensive. In addition, his writings extended over four decades, during which time he altered some of his views. He wrote at different levels of abstraction and at times he wrote for purely political purposes. As a result it is easy to find contradictions in Marx, and his own writings have spawned dramatically divergent views of the socialist society.

Nevertheless, a brief outline of the basic features of Marx's views on the economics of socialism seems possible. Despite his unwillingness to be drawn into a utopian description of the future, Marx made certain recommendations on the organization of the socialist society. More than that, as will be argued below, the entire thrust of his analysis of capitalism and of the market mechanism, taken together with his various statements on socialism, appear to support the view of Marx as a centralist who considered planning not only feasible but also superior to the market.[1] In any event, it is the centralistic Marx who was historically relevant for the Yugoslav Marxists. This chapter ex-

1. Although this conclusion is debatable, it seems to me that this view of Marx is more convincing. Most Yugoslavs, seeking Marxist legitimization for their own practice, contest it. Other Yugoslavs, to avoid the problem, underline Marx's failure to speak out explicitly on the subject of socialism.

9

amines Marx's views on three important problems that underlie this general conclusion: his views on producers' associations, his attitude toward plan and market, and his theory of value and the role of value in the socialist society.

PRODUCERS' ASSOCIATIONS IN THE SOCIALIST SOCIETY

In Marxist economic thought, the form of ownership of the means of production determines the motivation for productive activity, the allocation of resources generally, the pattern of economic development, and other phenomena. There are different interpretations of Marx's views on the critical question of ownership in socialism. According to one interpretation, society would own the productive resources and manage them according to centrally specified criteria. Others find in Marx hints of independent producers' associations that would own or at least manage the means of production directly and independently and engage in market transactions.

The problem is complex because "ownership" incorporates several economic relationships. Marx himself distinguished between the function of ownership and that of management.[2] However, at least three separate functions can be associated with a productive activity: (1) possession of title to the property (including the right to transfer or liquidate that property); (2) management of property in pursuit of certain objectives; and (3) the disposition of the proceeds of property. These three separate functions need not be vested in the same legal person.[3]

Marx was not entirely precise about the location of these

2. Karl Marx, *Capital*, 3 vols (Chicago: Charles Kerr and Co., 1906, 1909, 1909), vol. 3, chap. 23.

3. The institutional separation of management from title to property is familiar in the American corporation, as is the influence that management exercises over the distribution of net profits among retained earnings, bonuses, and dividends.

functions in the socialist society. In his one work that more than any other outlined the forms of the future society, *Critique of the Gotha Program,* Marx envisioned a "cooperative commonwealth, based upon the social ownership of the means of production." [4] "Social ownership" suggests that the title might be vested in the state or some other governing body as the representative of society as a whole. Engels took a clearer position on ownership, at least in the transitional stages: "The proletariat seizes political power and turns the means of production in the first instance into state property." [5]

Elsewhere Marx reinforced the centralist interpretation, speaking specifically of the centralization of the means of production as a rational form of organization. "The national centralization of the means of production will become the natural base for a society which will consist of an association of free and equal producers acting consciously according to a general and rational plan." [6] In this passage Marx specified a *single* association embracing all of society, and a *single* plan. Similarly, Engels' statement was unambiguous. The new social order, he said, "will first of all take the direction and control of industry and of all branches of production out of the hands of competing individuals and manage them by society itself . . . according to a common plan. . . . Thus it will discontinue competition and replace it by cooperation." [7]

The arguments showing that Marx favored centralization of the means of production under central national

4. Karl Marx, *Critique of the Gotha Program* (New York: International Publishers, 1933), p. 29.

5. Friedrich Engels, *Anti-Dühring* (Herr Eugen Dühring's Revolution in Science), 2d ed. (Moscow: Foreign Languages Publishing House, 1959), p. 386. Original in italics.

6. Karl Marx, *Sochineniia,* vol. 13, 241–42, as cited by Peter Wiles, *The Political Economy of Communism* (Cambridge: Harvard University Press, 1962), p. 358.

7. Friedrich Engels, *Principles of Communism,* trans. Max Bedacht (Chicago: The Daily Worker Publishing Co., n.d.), p. 15.

control seem more compelling than those that attempt to reveal Marx's support for a society composed of a number of autonomous productive associations. One type of statement that might be used to support producers' associations occurs in *Capital*. Marx postulated a distinction between social capital, in the form of stock companies, and private capital held by individuals. The formation of stock companies amounts to "the abolition of capital as private property within the boundaries of capitalist production." [8] The stock company "is a necessary transition to the reconversion of capital into the property of the producers, no longer as the private property of individual producers, but as the common property of associates, as social property outright." [9]

Producers' cooperative factories combine the forms of the stock company and worker ownership. They represent, though still within the capitalist form, "the first beginning of the new," as well as "all the shortcomings of the prevailing system." [10] Management in such a system is paid by the workers themselves. When associated labor becomes its own capitalist, the antithesis between capital and labor is overcome.[11]

However, Marx held that all types of stock companies, including producers' cooperatives, are transitional forms between the capitalist mode of production and the socialist. There is little support in Marx for self-owned or self-operated productive associations in socialism. It appears that Marx anticipated ownership and management by society as a whole and did not envision independent productive associations joined through the market. This conclusion follows even more decisively from the logic of his entire economic analysis of capitalism and the efficacy of the market.

8. Marx, *Capital*, vol. 3, p. 516.
9. Ibid., p. 517.
10. Ibid., p. 521.
11. Ibid.

PLAN AND MARKET

Marx and Engels distinguished between market and nonmarket methods of resource allocation. In premarket economies there is no exchange of products. This occurs either because there is no division of labor or because some principle, such as tradition, governs the allocation of work tasks and consumption possibilities. In a primitive economy, "the members of the community are directly associated for production; the work is distributed according to tradition and requirements and likewise the products to the extent that they are destined for consumption." [12]

Market methods of resource allocation

Marx began his economic analysis of capitalism with the concept of a commodity. A commodity is a reproducible good resulting from the application of human labor. It has use value. It is produced for the purpose of exchange on the market. Items that have no usefulness to anyone are not fully commodities, nor are nonreproducible items (scarce givens of nature), products of rare human talent, old stamps, etc.

The characteristics Marx ascribed to the commodity are relatively clear if not highly useful analytically. He gave a dual criterion for the production of commodities. One part requires the economic independence and self-interestedness of the unit producing for exchange. The second part requires private ownership of the means of production. Marx viewed both conditions as necessary for commodity production: "As a general rule articles of utility become commodities, only because they are products of the labor of private individuals or groups of individuals

12. Engels, *Anti-Dühring*, pp. 425–26.

who carry out their work independently of each other." [13]
In his chapter on commodities, Marx indicated that production with common ownership of the means of production was incompatible with commodity production. "Let
us now picture to ourselves . . . a community of free individuals, carrying on their work with the means of production in common. . . . The total product of our community is a social product." [14] The inference that social
product is not compatible with commodity is reinforced
when Marx adds, speaking of the same hypothetical case,
"we will assume, but merely for the sake of a parallel with
the production of commodities. . . ." [15] Engels also emphasized the private character of commodity production.
Commodities are "products made in a society of more or
less separate producers, and therefore in the first place private products." [16]

It appears, then, that neither Marx nor Engels gave serious consideration to the possibility, in socialism, of production for the market by nonprivate, self-interested, individualistic groups. For Marx and for Engels, independent production units and the resultant "anarchy" of the market
are as much a characteristic of private ownership as their
replacement by a plan would characterize the socialist
economy. "With the seizing of the means of production by
society, production of commodities is done away with. . . .
Anarchy in social production is replaced by conscious organization on a planned basis." [17] Social ownership of the
means of production was, for Marx and Engels, linked to
rational production according to a plan. (Of course, it
must be remembered that they believed socialism would
arise in relatively developed countries after capitalism had
ripened, matured, and entered into its advanced decline.)

13. Marx, *Capital*, vol. 1, p. 84.
14. Ibid., p. 90.
15. Ibid.
16. Engels, *Anti-Dühring*, p. 422.
17. Ibid., p. 390.

Marx clearly associated the socialist society with a plan and not with the spontaneous activity of individual producing units. His predilection for planning and his failure to consider market alternatives stemmed not only from his analysis of the advantages available under planning but also from his conviction that competitive production and market exchange are wasteful.

Commodity production requires that independent production units produce goods for the purposes of exchanging them on the market. The decisions about what to produce, how much, and how, are based on self-interest. In such an economy the "law of value" is said to operate. The "operation of the law of value" means that individual responses to the forces of supply and demand govern the ultimate allocation of resources. The law of value is but one method of allocating resources; plan and tradition are others. Where the law of value operates, the pattern of resource utilization and of final products in commodity production is determined by the interaction of the microeconomic decisions of the separate producing, consuming, and factor-supplying units. Marx saw anarchy and accident in such a method.

A major distinction between Karl Marx and Adam Smith lies precisely here. Smith saw an Invisible Hand regulating the individual units within the economy for the common good. Marx saw no apparent reason to think that the haphazard interaction of individual units would benefit society as a whole. The market adjustment process inevitably involves waste; planning could accomplish the same objectives more rapidly.

Marx discussed the market mechanism only in the context of capitalism. Many of the flaws he saw in the operation of the market—the effect of the declining rate of profit, the concentration of capital, business crises, the increasing misery of the working class—depend on the features of capitalism and the motivation of the productive units, rather than on the use of the market mechanism itself.

But Marx also had reservations about the suitability of the market adjustment process because he thought the market was an inadequate coordinator of supply and demand. He was sceptical about the ability of the market to attain the equilibrium price and quantity. Marx's fundamental distrust of this "anarchy" of the market drove him to advocate planning. "There is . . . no necessary, but only an accidental, connection between the volume of society's demand for a certain article and the volume represented by the production of this article in the total production. . . ." [18] Marx rejected the market for allocating resources because of his permanent vision of too many bales of cotton and not enough wheat.

Under what conditions are Marx's reservations about the ability of the market to attain equilibrium rapidly and without waste correct? Marx certainly did not provide a complete economic analysis of the efficiency of the market. Contemporary theory, however, offers qualified support for some of his general presentiments about the functioning of the market.

The satisfactory functioning of the market requires that the process of adjustment be such that each successive price and quantity be nearer the equilibrium price and quantity, and that equilibrium be attained with reasonable speed. Where changes in output can be brought about more or less continuously by varying factors of production, as Oskar Lange noted, "the process of adaptation is determined by a family of short-period supply (and cost) curves. With this type of adaptation, which may be termed Marshallian, each successive price is nearer the equilibrium price. . . . The Marshallian type of adaptation of supply seems to be the dominant one." [19]

18. Marx, *Capital,* vol. 3, p. 220.
19. Oskar Lange, *On the Economic Theory of Socialism,* B. Lippincott, ed. (Minneapolis: University of Minnesota Press, 1938), pp. 71–72, n. 20.

Scitovsky, Shaw, and Tarshis, in their study of mobilization of resources for war, noted certain circumstances in which each subsequent price and output may not approach equilibrium or which may otherwise be inefficient. The authors made two points about the dynamic efficiency of competitive markets. The first concerned response to the anticipated price of the final product; the second, response to the anticipated prices of the factors of production.[20]

Under certain conditions, the majority of producers may commit themselves irrevocably to new production plans on the basis of a price prevailing *before* any of their output according to those plans comes onto the market. As a result, competitive producers responding to market information alone may overrespond to the market price in the manner known as the "cobweb theorem." Such fluctuations in output and price occur "only if the span of time over which different producers' expansion plans have been spread is shorter than the 'gestation period' of these plans." [21] According to the authors, sudden major shifts in the structure of demand, such as those induced by mobilization for war, combined with long gestation periods and a pressure to complete expansion plans in a short period of time may make such overadjustment likely. Thus there are grounds for Marx's reservations, even though the authors concluded that such cases were not typical of the market adjustment process.

In times of peace, price changes are usually small and gradual and prompt producers to change their plans slowly and cautiously. That is why the practical importance of the cobweb theorem is probably small in the peacetime economy and is confined to farming, where special conditions make for long gestation pe-

20. Tibor Scitovsky, Edward Shaw, and Lorie Tarshis, *Mobilizing Resources for War* (New York: McGraw-Hill, 1951), Appendix 2, especially pp. 272–76.
21. Ibid., p. 274.

riods and for the concentration of production decisions within a short season.[22]

The authors noted a second source of dynamic inefficiency. Individual competitors respond to increases in demand for a product on the basis of present relative factor
prices. Their plans may involve a commitment to a technique of production that offers little opportunity for factor substitution and will not be efficient if different relative factor prices prevail. But if there are factors peculiar
to the industry, and if other competitors respond in a similar fashion, the resulting relative factor prices will differ
from those prevailing at the outset. Hence the choice of
techniques of the competitive producers may be unsatisfactory at the ultimately prevailing factor prices.

The greater the change in the structure of demand, the
greater the inefficiency of competitive market adjustment.
There are no problems of dynamic inefficiency in the stationary state,[23] and they are likely to be relatively unimportant in the economy in which changes in the structure
of demand are small and gradual. But where shifts in demands are of major importance, as in mobilizing resources
for war, or in the drastic reorientation of demand associated with an especially rapid program of economic development, the resulting inefficiencies of competitive response
to purely market information may be considerable.

The monopolist can estimate the effect of his activities
on both product and factor prices and hence respond more
efficiently. Competitive industries would show greater dynamic inefficiency than a monopolist in responding to
major shifts in demand. However, the inefficiencies and
waste of competitive producers due to insufficient knowledge about future product and factor prices can be reduced by providing, through the government or other

22. Ibid.
23. Ibid., p. 276.

methods, information about the production plans of competitors.[24] Thus, although Marx did not present a rigorous theoretical underpinning for his indictment of the market economy, contemporary economic analysis does provide theoretical support for some of Marx's reservations, especially under conditions of dynamic change.

Planned allocation of resources

The conclusion seems inescapable that Marx rejected both independent enterprises and market methods of production and resource allocation in socialism. He believed it would not be necessary to reproduce the defects of the market in the socialist society. The socialist economy would be centrally planned. The correctness of this conclusion depends on the assumption that the planned alternative would be superior to whatever defects were associated with the market mechanism.

Marx thought that in socialism it would be possible to establish directly the quantities to produce. "Only when production will be under the conscious and prearranged control of society, will society establish a direct relation between the quantity of social time employed in the production of definite articles and the quantity of demand of society for them." [25] Marx advocated planning because he thought it would be possible to establish the relationship between quantities demanded and quantities supplied without enormous difficulty.

Marx recognized that central planning requires the proper allocation of resources. "Society distributes labor-power and means of production to different lines of production." [26] The distribution of resources must correspond

24. Dynamic inefficiency of this type can also be reduced through speculation. Ibid., p. 273.

25. Marx, *Capital*, vol. 3, p. 221.

26. Ibid., vol. 2, p. 412.

to the requirements of the community. Apportionment of labor time "in accordance with a definite social plan maintains the proper proportion between the different kinds of work to be done and the various wants of the community." [27] Engels was more explicit. "The useful effects of the various articles of consumption, compared with each other and with the quantity of labor required for their production, will in the last analysis determine the plan." [28] Engels' vague premonition of the *problem* of efficient allocation was correct. It is necessary to compare "useful effects" both with one another and with the labor time necessary for their production. But he provided no criteria for measuring and ordering, that is, for comparing the "useful effects" with one another or with the necessary labor time.[29]

Under certain conditions the task of planning is considerably simplified. If demands are in the form of fixed quotas, if supplies of resources are given, and if there is no possibility of substitution of factors of production, prices are not necessary.[30] There is no problem of comparing useful effects and labor costs. The problem is one of technological efficiency and of consistency.

These are the simplifications employed in input-output analysis. Such a method at best assures consistency but not economic efficiency. It can maximize the output attainable in fixed proportions from the given technology and resources. There is no basis for comparing alternative methods of production or for comparing different output bundles in which goods are produced in different proportions. There is no optimization involved.

27. Ibid., vol. 1, p. 91.
28. Engels, *Anti-Dühring*, p. 427.
29. Lange, p. 133, n. 88. Lange also points out that a method of calculation in which labor costs are the only costs (where labor is the only scarce resource) "would be of little use for practical purposes." (Lange, p. 133, n. 88.)
30. Lange, pp. 67, 94.

MARX'S THEORY OF VALUE

Marx certainly did not perceive the problem of resource allocation in the restrictive terms of input-output analysis. He appeared to have assumed that the proper valuation of inputs was possible. If resources and outputs can be valued, then much of the task is accomplished. However, Marx provided no clear guide on the problem of valuation in socialism. Indeed, both Marx and Engels appeared to say that value was not relevant in the socialist society.

Definition of value

Marx defined *value* within the context of commodity production. He distinguished two different types of commodity producing societies, precapitalist (simple commodity production) and capitalist. In simple commodity production, production is carried on by a large number of isolated units producing for exchange on the market. The individual producer, typically an artisan, supplies his own labor. In the simplest case the producer may also supply his own materials and equipment. He uses his labor to make capital goods, to prepare materials, and to produce goods and services directly. Like Robinson Crusoe, such an individual is not concerned with the separate productivity of capital and labor. The producer allocates his labor time among alternative productive activities, and the total product appears to him as the product of his labor. Individuals enter those activities in which the result obtained per unit of labor time, their relevant resource, is greatest.

The producer need not make all of his own materials or his own capital. He may purchase them at a price. The fact of such purchase does not alter the essence of his maximizing principle: he still seeks to maximize the return to his labor input. But in this case the return to his labor input is the price obtained for the product less the expenditures on purchases of materials and capital equipment.[31] He still chooses an economic activity on the basis of return to his labor time.

In the long run, in either case, the mobility of individuals into different activities causes the product of all homogeneous labor to be equal in all activities.[32] As a result the relative prices of goods and services tend toward the ratios of total labor time necessary to produce a commodity or perform a service. Items requiring equal quantities of labor time would tend to sell at equal prices. In simple commodity production the worker receives the full value added by his productive activity. All value "originates" in labor and the proceeds of the labor return to the worker.

Marx then introduced capital into this highly abstract model. The new situation is capitalist commodity production. Capital, owned by individuals, is a separate factor of production. It has a mobility separate from and apart from that of labor. The crucial feature distinguishing capitalist commodity production is the dissociation of capital from the individual worker-producer. Owners of capital seek to employ their capital to best advantage, as do owners of "labor power." The capitalist's compulsion to accumulate causes him to seek the highest rate of return on his capital (equipment, materials, and advances for workers). This compulsion causes capital to flow into the sectors of the economy where the rate of return to capital is greatest. Competition among capitalists in the long run forces the rate of return to capital to be everywhere equal.

Prices under such conditions would tend, in the long run, not toward ratios of labor time, but toward the "price of production." The price of production is the long run

31. Marx, *Capital*, vol. 3, p. 208.
32. Assuming, for simplicity, with Marx, that all labor can be reduced by one method or another to some multiple of homogenous labor.

average total cost, including a uniform rate of profit on capital. The price of production thus permanently differs from the labor value price but differs in a systematic and calculable manner. Both labor value prices and the price of production are long run tendencies. Actual market prices fluctuate around the long run tendencies. "Value is the center of gravity around which prices fluctuate, and around which their rise and fall tend to an equilibrium." [33]

The role of value in socialism

Value, in the sense of long run, market-determined prevailing price, would obviously not exist in the absence of a market. In socialism there would be no independent producers, no competition, and no market; hence it followed that there would be no value. Engels said that in the future society "people will be able to manage everything very simply, without the intervention of the famous 'value.' " [34] But the banishment of value was only apparent.

Both Marx and Engels recognized that value, in its important sense, could not be dispensed with even in the socialist society. The "balancing of the useful effects and expenditures would be all that would be left, in a communist society, of the concept of value. . . ." [35] But their discussion appeared to suggest that value could be measured in units of labor time. Marx's statements seemed to emphasize labor unit bookkeeping.

After the abolition of the capitalist mode of production . . . the determination of value continues to prevail in such a way that the regulation of the labor time and the distribution of the social labor among

33. Marx, *Capital*, vol. 3, p. 210.
34. Engels, *Anti-Dühring*, p. 427.
35. Ibid.

the various groups of production, also the keeping of accounts in connection with this, become more essential than ever.[36]

And Engels said explicitly:

Society can calculate simply how many hours of labor are contained in a steam engine, a bushel of wheat. . . . It could therefore never occur to society still to express the quantity of labor put into products . . . in a third product . . . and not in its natural, adequate and absolute measure, time.[37]

To some, these statements implied that the socialist economy would have no prices, no money, and no financial calculations. Physical distribution of products and physical accounting of labor inputs would replace pecuniary calculations. Socialism would be a natural, moneyless economy. However, the natural economy is a planners' nightmare because of the millions of different physical units involved. Even if the planners were able to make a general plan on the basis of natural units and without monetary expressions, not all decisions could be made nor all allocations effected by planners. Some decisions would still be necessary at the enterprise or the consumer level. The decision process is unduly cumbersome if society insists on using natural units for comparisons instead of selecting a *numéraire*.

It might be supposed that the problem could be solved by attaching arbitrary weights by which items could be aggregated into useful bundles. One might select accounting units that served this purpose. While *any* set of weights will make aggregation possible, only that set of weights corresponding to opportunity costs will provide the information necessary for decentralized decision makers to

36. Marx, *Capital,* vol. 3, p. 992.
37. Engels, *Anti-Dühring,* p. 426.

make choices consistent with maximizing the established objectives.

Thus the problem of value is deeper than the cumbersomeness of physical units or the need to select some arbitrary set of weights. Even if labor were the sole input, the labor time necessary to produce the goods would not reflect an adequate set of weights. This is because the labor time necessary cannot be compared in any meaningful sense with "useful effects." At most it is possible to say that each of two goods have the same inputs of labor; whether the labor is more "usefully" employed in one or the other remains unanswered because we cannot compare the useful effects. But without a way of comparing "useful effects" it is not possible to follow Engels' advice: that the plan be determined by the comparison of the useful effects of alternative products with one another and with the quantity of labor necessary for their production.

Thus Marxist socialists have been compelled to search through Marx's writings to find a basis for the measurement of "value," an appropriate weight to attach to each commodity enabling both aggregation and comparison of costs and useful effects by decision makers. Although the quest for a measure of value has finally permitted the inclusion of costs other than labor (rent, interest), for the most part they have considered value to be a cost-determined magnitude. Their reasoning seems to be as follows. Given *any* measure of cost that is invariant with respect to output, planners can determine the quantities that will be demanded at a price that covers the costs. Then it would be possible to allocate resources so that market-clearing quantities of the goods would be forthcoming. This reasoning illustrates the way in which many Marxist socialists have inadequately perceived the relation between resource allocation and value. In a market economy, the valuation of terms on which the alternatives are offered is mutually and spontaneously determined, and the allocation of resources is accomplished automatically and spontaneously. Just as obviously, an economic system that removes the function of resource allocation from the domain of the market also eliminates the process whereby the coefficients of relative scarcity are automatically obtained. Planning would be relatively simple if the value coefficients existed independently of the resource allocation. Unfortunately, they do not.

Magnitude of value

In the search for the proper principles of pricing in the socialist economy, subsequent socialists returned to Marx's writings on commodity production. Marx's value theory constitutes a unified whole. Marx's several definitions of value appear to be mutually consistent, although, in the Ricardian tradition, value is a cost-determined magnitude. But it is not a simple-minded theory. Marx has long- and short-run concepts of value. He differentiated among pre-capitalist and capitalist forms of economic organization, and he recognized that both the prevailing price and the resource allocation depend on the maximizing principles of economic units.

"The value of a commodity," Marx said, is "the quantity of labor necessary for its production in a given state of society, under certain social average conditions of production, with a given social average intensity, and average skill of labor employment." [38] This statement provides the doctrinal foundation for the actual labor-cost approaches to price and value, and for socialist measurements of average costs of production for an entire branch of production. [39]

38. Karl Marx, *Value, Price and Profit* (New York: International Publishers, 1935), p. 33.
39. There are, of course, very practical administrative reasons for measuring the average costs of production in the Soviet economy. Such a measure shows the planners which firms are producing at higher than average costs.

But Marx also required that the commodity be produced as efficiently as possible. He rejected defining value as the actual labor expended. "What determines value is not the time taken to produce a thing, but the minimum time it could possibly be produced in, and this minimum is ascertained by competition." [40] His definition of value as the minimum cost of production contradicted his definition of value as the average cost of production.

Marx added a third requisite that gave stronger weight to the role of demand. "Every commodity must contain the required quantity of labor, and at the same time only the proportional quantity of social labor must have been spent on the various groups." [41] By focusing on the quantity of labor required to produce the amount of the commodity demanded by society, he raised the question of the role of effective demand in the determination of value.

Marx used all three formulations, often interchangeably. There are two possible explanations. (1) Within the framework of the major part of his analysis, long run competitive equilibrium, their meanings are *identical*. His concept of value in capitalism was classical: the long run average cost in competition. This meets all three conditions simultaneously. Demand and supply are balanced at a price that is equal to industry average costs. Average costs are the minimum necessary (given complete adjustment) and identical for all producers because competition forces all firms to produce at the minimum possible cost. (2) Alternatively, it is possible to dismiss his definition of value as the minimum time necessary to produce an object as an error. *The Poverty of Philosophy* is one of his earlier works. Marx modified his views on economic topics as his economic knowledge and sophistication increased.

40. Karl Marx, *The Poverty of Philosophy* (New York: International Publishers, 1963), p. 66.

41. Marx, *Capital*, vol. 3, p. 745. "Proportional" means that supply and demand are in equilibrium.

The short run and market value

Mark distinguished a special shorter run form of value, "market value." Market value differs from value in that it pertains to the world of less than complete adjustment.[42] Competition has not yet forced all producers to the same minimum cost position. There is incomplete adjustment of productive processes to some change in demand, supply, or technological conditions. Therefore, enterprises employ different methods that have different average costs per unit.

He distinguished three types of firms: those with less than average costs of production, those in which costs of production are equal to the average for the entire industry, and those whose costs of production exceed the industry-wide average. Normally, the majority of firms will be in the second category. And normally, market value is equal to the weighted average costs of production of the individual firms, that is, equal to industry average costs.

However, Marx did not say that market value is always identical with industry average costs. He specifically considered other situations. Should demand exceed supply at the industry average cost, market value would then be determined by the costs of commodities produced under the least favorable conditions. If supply exceeds demand at the industry average cost level, then market value is determined by the costs of the most favorably situated producers. "If the mass of the produced commodities exceeds the quantity which is ordinarily disposed of at average market values, then the commodities produced under the most favorable conditions regulate the market value." [43] In other words, in the short run, *market value is not determined by actual industry average costs.* The average cost of

42. Ibid., chap. 10.
43. Ibid., p. 211.

the minimum or maximum cost producers define the limits within which market value is located. Market price, the actual clearing price, is subject to no limits. In Marxist economic thought, value and price are not synonymous. Marx recognized perfectly well that, in a market economy, the actual market-clearing price at any moment is determined by the forces of supply and demand. Thus market price is subject to no limits. Market value, however, was conceived as a cost-determined magnitude. In the market economy, the magnitude of market value falls within the range of costs. But Marx did not entirely exclude demand from the determination of market value, as his analysis of the short run shows.

Marx recognized some of the essential features of demand and supply analysis. He explicitly recognized the income elasticity of demand.

> It would seem, then, that there is on the side of demand a definite magnitude of social wants which require for their satisfaction a definite quantity of certain articles on the market. But the quantity demanded by these wants is very elastic and changing. Its fixedness is but apparent. If the means of subsistence were cheaper, or money-wages higher, the laborers would buy more of them, and a greater "social demand" would be manifested.[44]

He also hinted at price elasticity of demand, both for final products and for factors of production. He observed that "if cotton were cheaper, the demand of capitalists for it would increase." [45] He also noted that "a rise of prices . . . cuts down the demand." [46]

Marx also differentiated between the long and the short run industry supply schedule. "For instance, if the de-

44. Ibid., p. 222.
45. Ibid.
46. Ibid., p. 225.

mand, and consequently the market-price, fall, capital may be withdrawn and the supply reduced." [47] "Vice versa, if the demand increases, and consequently the market price rises above the market-value . . . capital may flow into this line of production and production may be increased . . ." [48] He added that such a situation "may also bring about a rise in the market-value itself for a shorter or longer time, in some lines of production in which a portion of the desired products must be produced under more unfavorable conditions during this period." [49]

This latter notion was, in effect, a primitive description of a rising industry supply curve. Marx appears to have assumed that, in the short run, firms had individually constant cost curves, but that the costs of each firm differed. Thus the industry supply curve was rising. Market value, supply price, depends on the demand conditions, as shown in the accompanying diagram. Market value is still

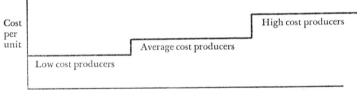

Marxian industry supply curve

deduced from costs, as is value. But since costs could now be considered as rising in the short run, at least, demand conditions determine the relevant level of costs. In this manner demand crept into Marx's analysis of value in cases of less than complete adjustment.

47. Ibid., p. 224.
48. Ibid., pp. 224–25.
49. Ibid., p. 225.

The socialist search for the proper form of pricing in socialism did not always perceive the basic unity of Marx's value theory. Socialist discussion includes interminable debates on which "form of value" is correct for the socialist society, citing various partial definitions of value: value in the long run, short run market value, value in simple commodity production, value in capitalist commodity production, value as the minimum necessary labor costs, value as the average necessary labor cost, and so forth. Some socialists rejected price calculations altogether and reverted to labor time measurements.

In the Soviet Union, especially, such discussions have as their purpose the establishment of uniform principles of pricing. But Marx certainly would have rejected any attempts to convert his analytical study of value into a basis of rules for administered prices. He recognized the absurd implications of nonequilibrium prices. Marx derided Proudhon for suggesting the same thing. Proudhon had inverted the logic: pick a price and this will automatically assure equilibrium! "Begin," he said, ridiculing Proudhon, "by measuring the relative value of a product by the quantity of labor embodied in it, and supply and demand will infallibly balance one another." [50]

It would be an exaggeration to conclude that Marx provided all of the essential elements for the proper determination of value. In fact, his exposition was quite confused, and he did not distinguish between "shifts in demand schedules" and "movements along a demand schedule." Nevertheless, Marx did provide some very sensible guidelines to analysis of demand and supply in Volume III of *Capital*. Further pursuit of this topic might have been fruitful for Marxist economists.

50. Marx, *Poverty of Philosophy,* p. 60.

CHAPTER 3

The Economics of Socialism in the
Soviet Union

A brief survey of Soviet political economy is important for
several reasons. First, the Soviet Union was the first state
to attempt to establish a Marxist economic and political
system. In the process of working out a system of economic
organization, it became necessary to reconsider the previously accepted Marxian principles of economic organization in socialism. In particular, it became apparent that
purely physical planning and allocation of resources was
not possible. Soviet political economy gradually recognized
this fact by revising the attitudes toward plan and market
methods of economic organization in socialism.

Second, the Soviet economic and political system had a
specific objective, rapid industrialization and economic
growth. This economic objective influenced the initial
choice of methods. In the late fifties the Soviet economy
entered a new stage of relative economic maturity. As the
economic conditions and also the economic objectives of
the system altered with maturity, Soviet writers began to
consider alternative methods of economic organization.
The Soviet Union tentatively and cautiously began to introduce reforms. Analysis of the changing requirements of
the maturing economic system and of the relative usefulness of particular methods of economic organization aids
in understanding Yugoslav attitudes toward plan and market. It is of interest to consider whether the differences
between Soviet and Yugoslav attitudes toward the market
are differences of timing or of substance and to consider

whether other Soviet-type economies are likely to adopt the Yugoslav pattern of economic organization.

Finally, a familiarity with Soviet political economy, especially in the Stalinist phase, is indispensible for understanding the initial Yugoslav method of economic organization and the interpretation of political economy. Yugoslav economic thought and practice from 1945 to 1948 were virtually indistinguishable from those in the Soviet Union.

EARLY SOVIET POLITICAL ECONOMY

Throughout the twenties, a fruitful and relatively free decade in Soviet economic thought, debate raged over the form of the socialist society, particularly its economic organization.[1] Prior to the Russian Revolution, many Marxists had agreed that socialism implied a planned economy in which resources would be allocated in physical terms. In the euphoria after the success of the revolution, some followers of Marx anticipated the transition to the purely naturalistic economy they thought he had predicted. The Party Program of 1919 and Bukharin's *Economy of the Transition Period* in 1920 epitomized these hopes. "As soon as spontaneity is replaced by a conscious social regulator," Bukharin argued, " 'commodity' becomes simply 'product' " and the economic features of commodity production—price, profit, financial calculation—can pass out of existence.[2] These ideas were paralleled in practice by

---

1. On Soviet political economy in the twenties see Adam Kaufman, "The Origin of 'The Political Economy of Socialism,' " *Soviet Studies* 4, no. 3 (Jan. 1953): 243–72; Alexander Erlich, *The Soviet Industrialization Debate, 1924–1928* (Cambridge: Harvard University Press, 1960); N. Spulber, *Soviet Strategy for Economic Growth* (Bloomington: Indiana University Press, 1964).

2. N. Bukharin, *Economy of the Transition Period*. Translation cited from Kaufman, p. 248.

the physical allocation and procurement system known as War Communism. War Communism, however, was merely a temporary expedient.

During the twenties the Soviet Union reverted from War Communism to a market economy. The New Economic Policy, introduced in April 1921 at the Twelfth Party Congress, inaugurated a mixed economy of heterogeneous sectors, socialist and capitalist. It was neither a purely capitalist commodity economy nor a purely socialist economy, but combined elements of both. A new theory of the economy of the transition period, based on the presence of two distinct and incompatible types of production, came into vogue. It held that commodity production continued in the agricultural sector (then still in private hands), while the products of socialist industry had ceased to be commodities and had passed into the higher stage of social product.[3]

The theory of the dual economy soon gave way before the Plan.[4] At the Sixteenth Party Congress in 1930, Stalin said that the Soviet Union was only laying the foundations for socialism. Six years later, on introducing the 1936 constitution, Stalin declared that the first phase of communism—socialism—had on the whole been achieved. With the collectivization of agriculture, private ownership became insignificant. The liquidation of the kulaks and the transfer to the kolkhoz meant the destruction of the last

3. V. I. Lenin, "Nakaz STO mestnym sovetskim uchrezhdeniiam," in *Sochineniia* (4th ed., Moscow) 32 (1932): 362; cited in Mllos Samardzija, "Problems of Commodity Production in Socialism and Economic Theory in the USSR Today," *Socialist Thought and Practice*, no. 4 (Dec. 1961): 99.

4. For a discussion of Soviet political economy from the inception of the plan era up to Stalin's death, see J. Miller, "A Political Economy of Socialism in the Making," *Soviet Studies* 4, no. 4 (Apr. 1953): 403–33; Ronald L. Meek, *Studies in the Labour Theory of Value* (New York: International Publishers, 1956); Samardzija, *Socialist Thought and Practice*, no. 4 (Dec. 1961): 87–118.

roots of capitalism, and with it, of commodity production. The economic "laws" peculiar to commodity production, the law of value and the resulting law of the average rate of profit, were "abolished." The supremacy of planning in the thirties and the focus of attention on technical and engineering problems (as well as the purge of economists) pushed economic topics from the scene. Socialism became synonymous with centralized natural planning. The role of the market was restricted to the distribution of part of consumers' goods and, to some extent, to the recruitment and mobilization of labor.

During the decades that followed, Soviet political economy has reconsidered the role of the market and of the law of value. At a relatively early stage Soviet leaders recognized that, even in the planned economy, it was not feasible to ignore the market totally. Egalitarian wage ideals gave way to highly differentiated payments.

In 1941 the topic of political economy reappeared, and a draft of a new text on that subject (the first since 1928) was begun. In 1943 the official silence was broken. An important unsigned article appeared, "Some Questions in the Teaching of Political Economy." [5] That article reversed the trend started in the thirties toward the naturalistic economy that was subject to no economic laws. The article stated that the socialist economy is also subject to the operation of economic laws.[6] These laws were held to differ, however, from the economic laws of capitalism. According to the article, capitalist economic laws are chaotic in operation.

The economic laws of socialism, on the other hand, "operate as recognized laws consciously applied and uti-

5. *Pod Znamenem Marksizma,* no. 7–8 (1943). A translation appeared, "Teaching of Economics in the Soviet Union," *American Economic Review* 34, no. 1 (Sept. 1944): 501–30. The article is assumed to have been written by, or with the approval of, Stalin.

6. "Teaching of Economics," p. 511.

lized by the Soviet state in the practice of socialist construction." [7] These laws were the "objectively necessary" policies for attaining socialism. The article identified other objective necessities of socialist development: the distribution of consumption shares according to work done and the economic principle of financial accountability.[8]

According to the article—and this represented a major change from the official position in the thirties—some economic laws of capitalism, in particular, the law of value, nevertheless continue to exist in socialism. Other laws of capitalism, such as the average rate of profit, do not. The discussion of the law of value was obscure. In Soviet usage in 1943, the meaning of the operation of the law of value was narrow and it seemed to refer to any individualistic response to price.[9] *Any* financial signal that affected the demand for, or supply of, resources, products, or factors, was taken as an operation of the law of value. The fact that labor was paid in money, convertible into consumer goods, according to the amount of work done, was considered an example of the operation of the law of value, presumably because the rates of pay (real wages) affect the desire to work (supply of labor).

Similarly, setting prices to "deviate" from value meant using financial signals consciously, setting prices on other

7. Ibid., p. 514.
8. Ibid., pp. 516–17. Original in italics.
9. Or indeed even to the existence of such categories. Ostrovitianov argued that the existence of money and of trade in the Soviet Union meant that value and the law of value continued to exist. "Up to very recently the view prevailed among Soviet economists that, despite the existence of trade and money, the law of value had been done away with in the Soviet economy. Such a statement of the question suffered from a deep internal contradiction. It is impossible to recognize the presence of trade and money and at the same time to deny the existence of value. To do so is equivalent to granting the form and denying the content inasmuch as the content of the money form is value. The price of commodity is nothing but the value expressed in money." K. Ostrovitianov, "Ob osnovnykh zakonomernostiakh razvitiia sotsialisticheskogo khoziaistva," *Bol'shevik*, no. 23–24 (Dec. 1944): 56.

than their normal basis, to encourage or discourage the supply or use of a resource or product. In general, "the Soviet state sets as its goal the establishment of commodity prices based on the socially-necessary costs of their production." [10] The "costs of production serve as the starting point in the setting of prices." [11] But actual "prices of commodities are set with certain deviations from their values." [12]

Two reasons were given for such "deviations": (1) Prices were set "corresponding to the particular objectives of the Soviet state," [13] presumably on an arbitrary basis to encourage the consumption of some articles and to discourage the consumption of others, both in final consumption and in the use of inputs in production. (2) Prices also deviated from the costs of production because of disparities between the demand of society for items and "the quantity of commodities of various kinds which can be sold under the existing scale of production," [14] that is, given the size of existing capacities and resources allocated to their production. Market-clearing prices were established, although the existence of a large gap between cost and market price did not induce additional supplies of the commodity.[15]

The law of value was said to operate in a "transformed" manner in socialism. This meant that the plan, and not the atomistic responses of individuals to financial signals, determined the basic composition of output and the allocation of resources. Although the role of the law of value as an allocator was quite limited, prices were manipulated

10. "Teaching of Economics," p. 511.
11. Ibid.
12. Ibid., pp. 523–24.
13. Ibid., p. 524.
14. Ibid.
15. Such arbitrary "deviations" of price from value are quite different from the uniquely determined and calculable differences between labor values and the price of production. See Chap. 2.

to induce the consumption of the quantities determined by the state.

According to the 1943 article, commodities continued to exist in socialism. Monetary payments permitted the purchase of different quantities of goods on the market. Accordingly, goods that entered into private consumption were classified as commodities. Only with the attainment of full communism would consumption goods be distributed without regard to money payment. Only then would purchase and sale of goods, financial incentives—and thus commodity relations and the law of value—entirely cease.

Stalin's *Economic Problems of Socialism in the USSR* in 1952 provided the next major reinterpretation of the political economy of socialism.[16] He revised the interpretation of economic laws. According to Stalin, some economic laws transcend social systems. For example, the laws of commodity production transcend the capitalist system and are applicable whether there is simple or capitalist commodity production. Other laws, such as the average rate of profit, are peculiar to capitalism and do not survive it. Economic laws are the reflection of objective processes that take place independently of the will of men. He rejected the notion put forth in the 1943 article that economic laws can be "transformed." According to Stalin in 1952, economic laws cannot be created, transformed, or abolished, but only perceived, studied, and utilized.[17] Economic laws are like natural forces. Man cannot abolish floods but he can utilize water and control the results.

Stalin defined the basic law of socialism as "the securing of the maximum satisfaction of the constantly rising material and cultural requirements of the whole of society through the continuous expansion and perfection of socialist production." [18] In order to work toward that ob-

16. Joseph Stalin, *Economic Problems of Socialism in the USSR* (Moscow: Foreign Languages Publishing House, 1952).

17. Ibid., p. 11.

18. Ibid., p. 33.

jective, a socialist economy must allocate resources only on the basis of the "law of balanced (proportionate) development of the national economy." This law supersedes the law of competition and anarchy of production under capitalism.[19] The law of the balanced development of the national economy determines the proper proportions between the capital goods and consumer goods sectors of the economy. Stalin stated as a flat law that giving primacy to the means of production is necessary for the continuous expansion of the economy. "The national economy cannot be continuously expanded without giving primacy to the production of means of production." [20] This requires "a continuous expansion of all social production, with a relatively higher rate of expansion of the production of the means of production. The relatively higher rate of expansion of production of means of production is necessary not only because it has to provide the equipment both for its own plants and for all other branches of the national economy, but also because reproduction on an extended scale becomes altogether impossible without it." [21] In other words, Stalin asserted that in order for the level of national income to rise, for the economy to grow continuously, the capital goods sector must be expanded at a relatively faster rate than the consumer goods sector.

This argument is valid only under certain conditions and is not valid in the general form in which Stalin stated it. If "continuous expansion" means simply a positive rate of growth, this can be attained without the expansion of the capital goods sector at a more rapid rate than the consumer goods sector, unless the capital-output ratio is increasing at a relatively rapid rate. If "continuous expansion" means maintaining a constant rate of growth, Stalin's conclusion is valid only if the capital-output ratio is rising.

19. Ibid., p. 11.
20. Ibid., p. 22.
21. Ibid., p. 51.

If, because of the type of technology introduced or because of the relatively more rapid expansion of those sectors of the economy that have relatively high capital-output ratios, increasing inputs of capital are necessary to produce constant increments to output, then the relative size of the capital goods sector must increase to maintain existing rates of growth. However, Stalin did not assert that this was the case.

If the incremental capital-output ratio is constant, then an increase in the relative share of the capital goods sector is only necessary in order to increase the rates of growth. In general, the larger the size of the capital goods sector relative to the economy as a whole, the higher the rate of capital formation a given economy can sustain without recourse to foreign trade. Therefore, an autarchic socialist economy that wanted to accelerate the rates of growth would have to increase the capacity of the capital goods sector. While a case could be made for Stalin's conclusions, provided the appropriate conditions hold, Stalin himself did not qualify his statement that "continuous expansion" requires the primacy of expansion of the capital goods sector. In the form in which Stalin stated it, his conclusion is not correct.

According to Stalin, planning had to supersede the allocation of resources by the law of value. Full operation of the law of value presumably would have shifted resources to the more profitable consumer goods sector at the expense of heavy industry. The law of value could not allocate resources in the socialist society because the resulting sectoral distribution would destroy the possibility of continuous growth.[22] This is what Stalin meant when he said that the law of value has no "regulating" function in the socialist society.[23] It does not allocate resources among major economic sectors.

22. Ibid., p. 22.
23. Ibid., p. 18.

Stalin added that, nevertheless, the law of value "influences" production. Stalin's example, if not his general exposition, showed that the law of value did indeed influence the supply of factors. Stalin distinguished between the influence of the law of value on articles in *circulation* and on *production*. In the former case, in the distribution of existing goods, "the law of value, preserves, within certain limits, of course, the function of a regulator." [24] But the operation of the law of value extends also to production, where it "has no regulating function in our socialist production, but nevertheless influences production." [25] He implied a connection between real wage rates and supplies of labor: "Consumer goods, which are needed to compensate labor power expended in the process of production. . . ." [26] And he explicitly stated the importance of the influence of cost accounting, profitability, and production costs on production.[27] Hence the principle of financial accountability assists in conserving resources and hence to improve productive efficiency. He also pointed out that an inaccurate (too low) setting of the price of cotton would result in inadequate cotton production. He complained that, if a certain proposal for the price of cotton had been accepted, "we should have ruined the cotton growers and would have found ourselves without cotton." [28] While the terms of trade between farm and town are not the only determinant of the supplies forthcoming, the law of value is one of the factors which influence that output. In this sense the law of value influences production, even in socialism. This was regarded as a temporary necessity. When agricultural property became fully social property, the law of value presumably would cease to influence the supply of

24. Ibid.
25. Ibid., pp. 18–19.
26. Ibid., p. 19. In this case, the meaning was very close to that of the 1943 article, despite the fact that the verbal formula had altered.
27. Stalin, p. 19.
28. Ibid., p. 22.

agricultural products. The supply would be fully planned, like all state sector goods.

In Stalin's formulation, commodities still existed. He distinguished two types of property in socialism: state property and collective farm property. Transfer between the two sectors constituted exchange. By this definition, change of ownership became the criterion for commodity production. Goods within the state sector did not change ownership and were not commodities. They were, therefore, not subject to the operation of the law of value. Production was determined exclusively by the plan.

With Stalin's passing from the scene in 1953, the restraints on economic discussion slowly relaxed. The official repudiation of Stalin and his policies in 1956 opened the gates to new ideas.[29] In late 1956, a conference of economists held that Stalin was in error in confining the law of value and the designation of commodity to consumer goods and the products of cooperatives. Goods transferred *within* the state sector were now declared to be commodities and the law of value universally applicable.[30]

With this dictum, Soviet political economy completed its reversal on commodity production in socialism. Originally, it had been alleged that commodity production did not exist in socialism. Even in the transition to socialism, when two types of ownership, private and state, had co-existed, Lenin had maintained that the products of the state sector, including those exchanged with the peasantry,

29. On post-Stalin developments, see Vsevolod Holubnychy, "Recent Soviet Theories of Value," *Studies on the Soviet Union*, 1, no. 1 (1961): 47–72; Alfred Zauberman, "The Soviet Debate on the Law of Value and Price Formation," in Gregory Grossman, ed., *Value and Plan* (Berkeley: University of California Press, 1960); "Revisionism in Soviet Economics," in L. Labedz, ed., *Revisionism* (New York: Praeger, 1962); Maurice Dobb, "The Revival of Theoretical Discussion among Soviet Economists," *Science and Society* 24, no. 4 (fall 1960): 289–311; Samardzija, *Socialist Thought and Practice*, no. 4.

30. Report of the conference in *Voprosy Ekonomiki*, no. 2, 1957.

were not commodities.[31] With the abolition of private property in the thirties, commodity production was alleged to have vanished altogether. But starting in the forties, commodities and the law of value gradually reappeared, first in consumption goods and then in the products of agricultural cooperatives. Finally products that circulated only within the state sector were declared commodities, thus reversing Lenin completely. The universality of commodity production [32] was generally accepted and the time horizon for the elimination of commodity production was indefinitely extended.[33] Academician Strumilin gave commodity production in socialism his formal blessing. "Commodity relations have undoubtedly survived the socialist revolution and have entered our new, Soviet way of living for good." [34]

SOVIET ECONOMIC REFORM DISCUSSIONS

The extension of the law of value meant that economic categories of value, profit, price, and the concept of eco-

31. "A state product—a product of a socialist factory, which is exchanged for a peasant product, is not a commodity in the political-economic sense of the word. . . . It ceases to be commodity." Lenin, *Sochineniia* 32, p. 362, as cited by Samardzija, p. 99.

32. In socialism, of course, labor power could not be a commodity, and cannot therefore be exploited.

33. Aleksandar Vacic makes especially clear how the domain of commodity production has gradually extended in socialist thought. Initially, commodity relations were thought to be a feature of the capitalist economy and were not expected to endure into socialism. Subsequently, it became necessary to divide socialism into at least three phases: transition from capitalism to socialism, construction of full socialism and transition from socialism to communism. Soviet doctrine has gradually extended the time horizon for market operations, so that now the market is an integral feature of full socialism or even of the transition to communism. *Uzroci robne proizvodnje u socijalizmu* (Belgrade: Naucna knjiga, 1966).

34. S. Strumilin, "Zakon stoimosti i planirovanie," *Voprosy Ekonomiki*, no. 7 (1959): 132.

nomic calculation were again significant.[35] Since 1956 there has been considerable discussion in the Soviet Union about these questions. Should central planning be supplemented by a mechanism through which enterprises would make some decisions? How is price related to central and peripheral decisions about what and how to produce? What is the relation between financial success indicators and enterprise activity?

Soviet discussions of, and proposals for, economic reforms focused on two topics: the principles of pricing and the methods of plan implementation. Although the topics are logically related, the discussions have been separate, taking place at different points in time, with different participants, and at different levels of abstraction. A further difference is that the price reform discussions have been rather fruitless, while a number of reforms have been made in the methods of plan implementation.

Price reform

It is useful to survey the Soviet notions on the proper formation of prices in order to contrast them with Yugoslav approaches to socialist price formation. Three distinct approaches dominated the Soviet price reform discussion.[36]

35. It was not easy to shed the earlier views. In 1964 Academician Arzumanian said: "One gets the impression that we are still talking about commodities, money, and similar categories as categories inherited from capitalism, as categories with which one should part as soon as possible. However, socialism, as experience has shown, cannot exist without those categories." Meeting of the Special Session of the Presidium of the Academy of Sciences of the USSR on Contemporary Soviet Economy, reported in Belgrade *Politika,* July 5, 1964.

36. Soviet positions on price reforms have been discussed in a number of articles that fully document the articles and books in which Soviet authors presented their views. See Morris Bornstein, "The Soviet Price Reform Discussion," *Quarterly Journal of Economics* 78, no. 1 (Feb. 1964): 15–48; Robert Campbell, "Marx, Kantorovich, and Novozhilov: *Stoimost'* versus Reality," *Slavic Review* 20, no. 4 (Oct. 1961): 402–18; Zauberman, *Value and Plan.*

One approach defended existing practice. A second approach advocated uniform principles of price formation based on the distribution of surplus value. The third approach emphasized the concept of opportunity cost.

Turetskii, Gatovskii, Ostrovitianov, and Maizenberg argued that prices have many other functions than equating supply and demand.[37] Prices are utilized by planners to promote diverse objectives: to provide (planned) profits to the enterprises for the purposes of stimulating productivity, to encourage the introduction of new technology, and to implement social policy. In lieu of a theory of price formation, these authors suggested a practical guide: price was to be composed of branch average costs of production plus a markup on average costs, plus a turnover tax, the incidence of which was highly varied. These authors emphasized that the problem of pricing is complex, and they questioned the usefulness of applying uniform rules for price formation by adding to the costs of production.

Attacking the arbitrariness of the pragmatic approach, a second group sought unitary principles according to which it could "distribute the surplus product." The principles would be applied equally to consumers and producers goods, thus eliminating the two-tiered price structure characteristic of Soviet prices and radically altering relative prices throughout the economy.[38] Three proposals were made for unitary principles: the labor value price, the prime cost price, and the price of production.

The labor value price would distribute surplus according to current labor costs. The advocates of the value price were Strumilin and Kronrod.[39] They favored the value

37. See Bornstein, pp. 24–25 for detailed references.

38. "Distribution of the surplus product" refers to the principles according to which the sales price exceeds the costs of (present and past) labor; $c + v$ constitute the total labor costs per unit. The third element in the equation shows what "addition" shall be made.

39. See Bornstein, p. 29, for detailed references.

price on two grounds. Doctrinally, it is based on the proposition that only human labor creates new value. Hence
only living labor can create surplus value as well.

$$\text{value price} = c + v + v \cdot M/V$$

where c is the branch average materials cost per unit, including depreciation,[40] v the branch average wage cost per
unit, V the total wage bill for workers in "material production," and M the total surplus value to be distributed.

In addition, value prices would encourage the introduction of advanced methods and capital equipment. The use
of such prices would cause labor-intensive goods to be relatively expensive and capital-intensive goods to be relatively
cheap. Thus value prices would contribute to the introduction of more capital equipment and the increase of the
productivity of labor, insofar as decisions were based on
price considerations.

An alternative proposal related surplus to branch average costs.

$$\text{prime cost} = c + v + (c + v) \cdot M/(C + V)$$

where $c, v, M,$ and V are as before and C is the total value
of materials and depreciation in material production.
Kondrashev argued that, while live labor is the sole source
of value, live labor creates more "surplus value" when it is
equipped with more capital.[41] This proposal attempted to
take that into account by applying the markup not only to
present labor, but to previous labor (material costs and
depreciation) as well.

The price of production, based on Marx's analysis of
capitalism, would distribute surplus on the basis of capital
invested.

40. Branch average costs of production are simply the average cost for
producing a given commodity, where the average is taken on the basis
of all firms producing that product.
41. Bornstein, p. 31, for detailed references.

$$\text{price of production} = c + v + k \cdot M/K$$

where c, v, and M are as before, k is the branch average fixed and working capital per unit, and K is the total capital in material production. The productivity of labor depends on the amount of capital with which it is equipped. The differences in surplus product depend not on the labor, but on the capital. Hence the supporters (Malyshev, Sobol', Vaag, and Atlas) argued, the surplus is attributable to the capital.[42]

Of the three methods of distributing surplus value, the value price undervalues capital-intensive goods most. To the extent that prices govern decisions and profits are the objective, the value price would encourage the use of artificially cheap capital in place of artificially expensive labor. The prime cost is subject to the same criticism but in lesser measure. Capital-intensive goods are artificially cheap because there is no interest charge on the capital stock. Thus, under either method (labor value or prime cost pricing), a piece of capital equipment that took x hours to produce and lasts one year would be included in costs and price at the same rate as a piece of capital equipment that took $10x$ hours to produce and lasts ten years.

An example illustrates the relation among the prices. Assume that two products are produced by different methods. Product I is labor-intensive; product II is capital-intensive.

	Product I	Product II
Labor expenditures (v)	200	100
Depreciation and materials (c)	100	200
Capital stock (k)	300	600

In each case, $c + v$, or 300, is one part of the price. But the amount of surplus added will differ. The example shows how the surplus would differ.

42. Ibid., pp. 31–32 for detailed references.

	Product I	Product II
Labor value price	$200\ M/V$	$100\ M/V$
Prime cost price	$300\ M/(C + V)$	$300\ M/(C + V)$
Price of production	$300\ M/K$	$600\ M/K$

If we use the labor value prices, the labor-intensive product is more expensive than the capital-intensive product. Using the prime cost method, we find that the prices of the products are identical. However, if we use the price of production, the price of the capital-intensive product is higher.[43] In the last case, capital-intensive goods, which are scarce, would be used more efficiently, to the extent that price plays a role in resource allocation, than under pricing methods that impute no cost to the use of scarce capital.

In addition to conceptual difficulties of the pricing principles proposed, they would seem to imply that prices remain fixed over some period of time. The establishment of any arbitrary set of prices ignores demand and supply and does not establish equilibrium. Unless the prices are changed frequently, quantities demanded of some items can exceed or fall short of the quantities supplied. Where demand exceeds supply, resources will have to be allocated by some nonprice criteria. Nonprice criteria emerge consciously or unconsciously to fill this need. But as soon as nonprice criteria determine the allocation of resources, it becomes less important what accounting prices are used.[44]

All definitions of price that proceed from cost categories miss the point. Preoccupation with price formation as such obscures the recognition that it is the relative quantities which are of concern and that pricing rules are, or should

43. This example is oversimplified. In a full working-out of the problem, one would have to take into account that the prices of the labor and capital inputs would also be attained by different methods, thus not the same in each case. This is known in Marxian economics as the "transformation problem."

44. Bornstein, p. 35.

be, merely tools for obtaining the correct quantities. For this reason, Soviet approaches to opportunity costs are more productive than the cost-price approaches. Novozhilov and Kantorovich have both developed notions of opportunity costs.[45]

Novozhilov sought the conditions for minimizing the necessary labor inputs in the production of a specified bill of outputs. He argued that the availability of a scarce resource to factory X reduces the labor inputs necessary to produce the specified output in that factory, but requires labor inputs in factory Y where the scarce resource is not made available. The additional labor input in factory Y (the next best use of the resource) over what would have been necessary had Y received the given scarce resources must be included in the estimation of the costs of production in X. These "inversely related costs" are the opportunity costs of scarce nonlabor inputs expressed in terms of additional costs incurred elsewhere (the technical rate of substitution between labor and nonlabor inputs in the production of a given output). By selecting that production process which minimizes the total costs of each partial decision (where costs include the inversely related costs), the specified output is produced with minimum total labor costs.

Kantorovich sought to find the methods of production that, given the available resources and production techniques, maximize the quantities produced of a given assortment.[46] If we are given any set of available inputs, technical possibilities, for each objective (for example, maximizing the outputs in specified proportions), there is an efficient employment of resources. In this case the opportunity costs are calculated in terms of output foregone (marginal rates of transformation between goods at equilibrium). The opportunity costs, "shadow prices," and the

45. Bornstein, pp. 33–34. See also Campbell, pp. 402–18.
46. Bornstein, p. 40.

efficient allocation of resources differ for each output mix, each set of technical conditions, and for each set of available inputs. These shadow prices could be used for planning; they might also be employed as operational prices at the enterprise level. Central authorities could compute the allocation of resources on the basis of their desired output, available resources, and technical methods. They would obtain efficient allocations of resources and "shadow prices." They could issue physical commands to implement the allocation or they could control resource use by price. Producing units could operate independently as profit maximizers in response to equilibrium prices determined simultaneously for the whole economy.

The opportunity cost approaches comprehend the essential unity of resource allocation and price determination, and they mark a major step forward in Soviet economic thought. Both the Kantorovich and Novozhilov proposals stopped short, however, of suggesting that planning of desired outputs—the specification of what to produce—should be determined on the basis of opportunity costs.

Plan implementation and enterprise autonomy

The discussion of the problems of plan implementation was more fruitful. There are real difficulties in the centrally planned economy, and Soviet discussions revealed a concern with improving the system.

The Soviet method of economic organization is deficient both in plan construction and in plan implementation. The reforms focused on improvements in the implementation of the plan. However, the problems of the Soviet method of organization as a whole become clearer if we briefly consider both types of deficiencies.

Plan construction
Soviet methods of plan construction do not provide any explicit methods for assuring that the output combinations

planned will provide the leaders with the highest possible level of satisfaction. In order for leaders to select that combination which places them on their highest attainable indifference frontier, they must compare their marginal rates of substitution among objectives with the marginal rates of transformation of the objectives in production. This could be done if planners prepared estimates of the maximum quantities attainable of several different product mixes.[47] In that case leaders could select among alternative product mixes on the basis of opportunity costs. However, current Soviet planning methods do not appear to follow such a procedure to permit the selection of the preferred combination of outputs.

Second, the methods employed can assure at best reasonable consistency. They do not consider all possible methods of producing a given output. The method of material balances, like input-output techniques, estimates resource requirements for a specified output on the basis of fixed input coefficients. The materials necessary for the specified output are compared with supplies of the materials that are forthcoming. By various adjustments, needs for materials are brought into balance with availabilities.

Planners use aggregate characteristics of production in a particular industry to calculate the average resource requirements for a specified output. Information about specific differences among firms is lost; the resulting directives may be inefficient by requiring differentiated plants to adhere to industry-wide averages. Using such input norms, the method of balances seeks to assure that adequate quantities of inputs are forthcoming for intersectoral balances. In addition, the process of material balancing is not carried through sufficient iterations to generate a completely consistent allocation of resources. The inconsistency of resulting directives to the production units limits

47. Richard W. Judy and Herbert S. Levine, "Toward a Theory of Value in Centralized Economic Planning," paper presented at the Econometric Society Meetings, Dec. 1960.

the possibility of the simultaneous fulfillment of all directives and may produce an infeasible plan.

Thus there is nothing in the material balances method which excludes the possibility that, using the same inputs but different production methods, it would be possible to produce at least as much or more of each and every good. If the plan is also infeasible, it may not even be possible to attain planned targets, even though they lie well within the production possibilities frontier.

Implementation of the plan

The impediments to rational implementation of the plan at the enterprise level are probably more serious. Ideally, enterprises receive signals in the form of physical indicators that more or less completely determine their use of inputs, technical methods, and quality and assortment of outputs. The objective of the producing unit is to fulfill all (consistent) parts of its physical plan. The producing unit is rewarded according to its adherence to the instructions transmitted. If the instructions are consistent, if the supplies are forthcoming, and if the incentive system is sufficient to ensure compliance, then the enterprise should be able to fulfill the tasks assigned to it.

If the directives sent to the producing units are inconsistent, if the supplies are not forthcoming, or if the directives do not completely determine all details, the producing units will have to make some decisions. There are serious defects in the pricing system on the basis of which the firm must decide. In addition, the incentive system of the firm is improper in its focus.

There are two basic requirements for enterprise decisions to contribute to the attainment of leaders' objectives. First, the enterprise criterion for making decisions must be consistent with those objectives. But when there are multiple objectives and there is any doubt about their simultaneous achievement, the problem arises of which commands to ignore. Second, the prices upon the basis of which the decisions are made must be scarcity prices. There is an inadequate knowledge of the rates at which leaders are willing to sacrifice one objective in order to achieve another.[48] Even if the maximizing principle of the enterprise is consistent with the leaders' objectives, if the prices to which the enterprises respond are an inaccurate measure of opportunity costs, the resulting decisions at the enterprise level do not contribute to attaining the leaders' objectives.

Soviet economists started in the late fifties to discuss the allocation of tasks, the signal system, and the incentive system upon which the Soviet economy operates. Various proposals suggested limited decentralization of the existing command economy, and in September 1965 significant reforms were announced. The plan would continue to specify quantity, assortment, price, and the date of delivery. The multiple norms (cost reduction, labor, and other input norms per unit of output) would be abandoned, and the enterprise would be free to select and combine its own inputs. The enterprises would be rewarded on the basis of a single financial indicator, realized profits (from actual sales) in relation to capital. Therefore, the enterprise would seek to produce only what it could sell and to minimize all kinds of inputs so as to minimize costs. Provided that plan specifications were met, enterprise performance would be evaluated and rewarded in terms of the single financial indicator.

The Soviet reforms are partial. They concern the maximizing principle of the enterprise and its criterion for decisions. To the extent that the prices to which the enterprises respond do not measure opportunity costs, the resulting allocation of resources remains inefficient, although perhaps not as inefficient as under the previous system.

48. See Neil S. Weiner, "Multiple Incentive Fee Maximization: An Economic Model," *Quarterly Journal of Economics* 77, no. 4 (Nov. 1963): 603–16.

CHAPTER 4

Origins of the Yugoslav Economic System

Yugoslav economic thought in the postwar period developed slowly over two decades. Within this time period it is possible to identify, provisionally, five periods of development. The first period, comprising the immediate postwar years, was one of dominant Soviet influence and emulation of the Soviet model. It lasted from 1945 to 1949. The second period, dating from sometime in 1949 and lasting to 1953, saw the rejection of Soviet thought and practice and the search for an alternative. The Kidric economic solution, advanced at this time, was destined to be temporary. The third period, which began around 1953, saw the evolution of the general features of the Yugoslav "new economic system" that were put into practice starting in 1954 and whose basic forms have been retained to the present. The task of elaboration was completed by 1958, and the results were embodied in the Party Program of that year. The fourth stage, especially from 1961 to 1965, was marked by a bitter conflict over regional aspects of the development policy and was climaxed by the defeat of the centralizers. The subsequent phase, dating from 1965, while still showing the strains of the centralization-decentralization conflict, raised fundamental questions about ownership and distribution in the Yugoslav economic system.

PERIOD OF SOVIET INFLUENCE

The Yugoslav socialist state came into existence on November 29, 1945. Soviet influence initially dominated both Yugoslav economic thought and Yugoslav economic practice until the Cominform Resolution of June 28, 1948. Soviet influence was so complete that the Yugoslavs hastened, well before their comrades elsewhere in Eastern Europe, to nationalize the means of production and to commence with central planning. Yugoslav leaders regarded the Communist Party of the Soviet Union as the sole authority on the interpretation of Marxism. In addition, the Soviet Union had a monopoly of practical experience in planning the socialist economy.

Soviet political economy as a theoretical guide

Early Yugoslav writing echoed Soviet explanations of the political economy of socialism along the lines of the still authoritative 1943 article.[1] That article had stressed the fundamental difference between the basic economic laws governing capitalism and those governing socialism. Capitalist systems were held to be governed by the law of value, while socialism was governed by its own laws. The law of value continued to operate in socialism but in a "transformed" manner. The state utilized the law of value for its planning purposes.

The Yugoslavs dutifully proclaimed the plan to be the socialist form of resource allocation. Boris Kidric, the principal architect of the early postwar economic structure, president of the Economic Council and of the Federal Planning Commission, provided the authoritative interpretation of the Yugoslav economy. He discussed the Yugoslav economy in three major works prior to the Yugoslav decision to abandon Soviet tutelage in this field.[2] The third statement, made in January 1949, is interesting be-

1. "Teaching of Economics in the Soviet Union," *American Economic Review* 34 (Sept. 1944): 501–30.
2. Boris Kidric, "Karakter nase privrede," *Komunist* 1, no. 6 (Nov. 1946); *Privredni problemi FNRJ* (Zagreb: Kultura, 1948); and "Karakter robnonovcanih odnosa u FNRJ," *Komunist* 3, no. 1 (Jan. 1949): 36–56.

cause it shows both the seeds of the new ideas and the extent to which Kidric was still tied to Soviet doctrine.[3]

The transitional economy

According to Kidric, the Yugoslav economy was then in the process of transition from capitalism to socialism.[4] The Yugoslav transitional economy was dualistic; it had elements of socialism and of capitalism. The dual economy is characterized by two forms of ownership, two types of property relations, and two forms of the law of value.

Much of Yugoslav agriculture had remained in private ownership. According to Kidric, where there is private property, the principles of production are those of commodity production. Private property meant that isolated production units pursued their own economic interests in response to financial indicators provided by the market. Such units operated according to the law of value, that is, in response to the forces of supply and demand. The law of value in the private sector did not operate as it would have in a capitalist economy. The socialist aspect of the system, characterized by the plan, limited the unregulated operation of the law of value. Specifically, the plan established agricultural tasks through contracts and obligatory deliveries. The effect of the law of value in the private sector was thus limited.

The products of the socialist sector were also commodities.[5] There were two forms of socialist property, social-cooperative and state. The social-cooperative sector had remnants of commodity production and the law of value. Unlike his Soviet mentors, Kidric recognized the existence of commodity production and the operation of the law of value *within* the state sector (a position not accepted in the Soviet Union until 1956). "Within state

3. Kidric, *Komunist* 3, no. 1 (Jan. 1949): 36–56.
4. Ibid., p. 36.
5. Ibid., p. 44.

property there exist . . . economic firms as independent economic units with their own economic accounting. This factor also conditions exchange and the existence of commodity-monetary relations, that is, the operation of the law of value." [6]

However, the operation of the law of value and the commodity-monetary relations in the state sector differed fundamentally from those in the private and socialist-cooperative sectors.[7] The organization of production in the state sector had radically altered with the advent of socialism. Capitalist economic units were independent. They were connected with one another only indirectly, through the market. In socialist Yugoslavia the economic units were *financially* independent. But their connections were no longer indirect and through the market, but direct, through the plan. "Indirect social ties of producers were replaced by direct social ties based upon socialist property and its planned management." [8] The plan distributed resources and tasks among branches of production. For this reason commodity production in the state sector was not the same as commodity production in capitalism.[9]

The plan and the market
While the law of value operated in socialism, it was the plan that established the dimensions and directions of activity.

> The law of value exists and operates actively in our economic system. But it ceases to be the basic law of socialist economic development. . . . The basic socioeconomic law of our development became social planning which, among other things, means the deliberate and expedient use of the objectively existing

6. Ibid., p. 45.
7. Ibid., p. 36.
8. Ibid., p. 45.
9. Ibid., p. 46.

law of value, known to us and governed by us. . . .
Now [the law of value] becomes a mighty weapon of
planning, a means of carrying out the tasks of socialist
construction which were thought out in advance and
established by the plan.[10]

The contradiction between the plan and the law of
value had several dimensions. The "market" and the
(untransformed) law of value represented the economic
methods of capitalism. Consumer sovereignty determined
what would be produced. Individualism and anarchy
reigned in production. The quest for profits was the motive force. By contrast the "plan" was the basic method of
socialism. It implied the sovereignty of society (as interpreted by leaders) and the direct planning of production.
Plan fulfillment was the objective.

Both "plan" and "market" had several meanings. As a
result, the discussion about the proper relationship between plan and market was frequently confused. The
"market" was initially rejected for the construction of
socialism for three types of reasons.

1. Construction of socialism was the primary task of the
transitional period. Leaders' preferences, and not the
wishes of individuals, had to determine the basic economic
objectives. The plan was identified with the primacy of
leaders' preferences, while the market appeared to imply
the ruling of consumers' desires. In this sense the conflict
between plan and market was very real, and the adoption
of the planned method signified the primacy of leaders'
preferences.

2. Marxists believed that it was possible to plan output
and to organize production directly. It was not necessary
to rely on the individualistic and anarchistic mechanism
of the market. In this sense plan and market were competing methods of resource allocation. Most Yugoslav leaders

10. Ibid., p. 53.

believed that the direct method was superior to the indirect method of the market. The market inevitably entailed lack of coordination, anarchy, confusion, and waste.

3. The market and the methods of capitalism were rejected because they were tied to the profit motive. The market and the law of value required an incentive, a motive force. In capitalism it was the pursuit of profits. But pursuit of profits was not a suitable objective for the socialist society. Focus on short run profit maximization would not necessarily produce the best decisions. Furthermore, profit maximization was alleged to induce a capitalist mentality.

In his discussion Kidric had touched upon an idea that he developed more fully later. He suggested that socialism transformed all market relations from the end, or objective, of economic activity into a means of achieving socialist goals.[11] Kidric was beginning to distinguish among the several meanings attributed to "plan" and "market." That ability permitted him later to conclude that the plan could establish the basic objectives, while the market could serve as a means of implementing the plan. Kidric did not yet fully perceive that the use of the market was not identical with a return to the capitalist economy.

Despite overwhelming similarities, some slight differences between the Soviet and the Yugoslav formulations were apparent already at this date. Kidric recognized commodity production within the state sector. He suggested that the market might serve as a means for attaining the objectives of society. The significance of these barely perceptible differences was not apparent for a number of months. At any rate, such minor differences in formulation did not detract from the basic identity of Soviet and Yugoslav thought. Orthodoxy of doctrine was paralleled by orthodoxy of practice.

11. Ibid., p. 47.

Soviet model as a practical guide

In the first postwar years, Yugoslavia, more than any other Eastern European satellite nation, copied Soviet institutions and practices. The Yugoslavs, because of the strength of Tito's domestic support, had been able to adopt the socialist forms earlier than the other Eastern European nations, which were still maintaining facades of coalition governments. In contrast to other Eastern European countries, communist control of Yugoslavia was achieved without Soviet support.

The economic system of the initial postwar years, established in 1947, later became known as the period of "administrative planning." The tasks of the immediate postwar years were reconstruction and basic economic development, followed by rapid industrialization. These goals were alleged in retrospect to have required the centralized, authoritarian, and detailed planning system.

Soviet practice was the ideal if not always the practical model. All basic means of production in industry and transport were nationalized, as were banks, commerce, and insurance. The major part of Yugoslav agriculture, however, remained in private ownership. There are numerous Yugoslav accounts of the operation of the economy in this period.[12] The means of production were owned by society but they were controlled by the state administrative system. In Yugoslavia, the founder of the enterprise (federal, republic, or local authority) held formal title to property and with it the right to transfer capital from enterprise to enterprise and to dissolve enterprises. This same body had the right to dispose of any profits resulting from the opera-

12. The description which follows is drawn from France Cerne, "Planning and the Market in Yugoslav Economic Theory," (Berkeley: University of California, Center for Slavic and East European Studies, July 1962), mimeo.

tions of its enterprises. Management, however, was under the control of ministries that planned production in physical terms with respect to quantities and assortments of goods produced. The ministries and their agencies supervised the choice of technical methods, the allocation of raw materials, the type of investment outlays, and planned output and price and profits.

The entire economy operated according to a comprehensive state plan. Individual enterprises received annual production targets stated in value and physical terms, along with production norms for inputs, quotas of workers, and of raw materials. Enterprises transferred their products to specified buyers (or ministries) at assigned prices and earned planned rates of profits. Supply contracts specified the amount of goods, delivery dates, recipients, and prices. Prices in interfirm transfers served mainly for accounting purposes. Market relations among enterprises were administratively regulated. Only trading enterprises could engage in direct sales to consumers. Consumption was rationed partially or entirely. Occupational choice was limited. Labor quotas were allocated to factories according to labor force balances, along with other factors of production, at rates of payment established by the state.

The management of the firm had limited responsibilities and rights: to combine the factors of production provided so as to achieve the assigned output targets and cost reduction norms, to make insignificant repairs and unimportant administrative expenditures, and to dispose of the director's funds. Economic decisions at the enterprise level were highly restricted.[13]

13. In many respects, the Yugoslav firm in this period resembled the Soviet firm described by David Granick, *Management of the Industrial Firm in the USSR* (New York: Columbia University Press, 1954); Joseph Berliner, *Factory and Manager in the USSR* (Cambridge: Harvard University Press, 1957).

Despite the close identity of outlook and similarity of practice, Yugoslavia came to reject the Soviet model. In 1950 the Yugoslav government set the economy on a new course. Tito's speech on June 26, 1950, called for the establishment of workers' councils to manage all factories.[14] The changes in economic structure began with the "law on management of economic enterprises and higher associations by workers' collectives" passed the following day. The law was but the first of many that over the next three years transformed Yugoslavia from a Soviet-type command economy into market socialism.

Market socialism ran counter to the entire Yugoslav postwar heritage. The question is how the Yugoslavs were brought to such an abrupt change and rejection of Soviet doctrine and practice. The causes for the change in economic doctrine and policy appear to be diverse.

Political and ideological factors

Political conflicts had developed between the Yugoslav and Soviet communist parties as early as 1945 (and even earlier during the war years). To some extent the conflicts were the inevitable consequence of the divergent interests of two nation-states. The economic policies pursued by the Soviet Union toward Eastern European countries in

14. Josip Broz Tito, *Workers Manage Factories in Yugoslavia* (Belgrade: Jugostampa, 1950), the text of his speech. Actually, workers' councils had been introduced experimentally in the fall of 1949 in some factories. (See Benjamin Ward, "From Marx to Barone: Industrial Organization in Postwar Yugoslavia," Ph.D. dissertation, Department of Economics, University of California, Berkeley, 1956, for the most comprehensive discussion of the actual progress of the Yugoslav system and dates at which specific changes were made.)

these years, as well as Soviet attempts to infiltrate the military and intelligence apparatus of Yugoslavia, aggravated the situation. For its part, Yugoslavia was very self-consciously the only full-fledged socialist state in Eastern Europe in the immediate postwar years and expected a special relation with the Soviet Union. These grievances mounted slowly over the years.

Tensions between the two communist parties reached a peak early in 1948 when the Soviet party sharply criticized certain Yugoslav policies. The critique was directed mainly at party matters but it did touch on Yugoslav agricultural policy and accused Yugoslavia of lagging in collectivization.[15] After a few months of worsening relations, reflected in the correspondence between the two parties, Stalin acted abruptly. The climax came in the form of the Cominform Resolution of June 28, 1948, which expelled Yugoslavia from the communist family of nations. It came, possibly, as a shock to the Yugoslav party leadership, many of whom believed that their disagreements with the Soviet Union could be resolved.[16]

In the course of the next year, the Yugoslav communist party made a number of moves to rectify the conditions to which the Soviet party had objected.[17] Yugoslavia went even further in imitation of the Soviet model, particularly in hastening the rate of collectivization. Not until late

15. For two interpretations of these events, see George W. Hoffman and Fred W. Neal, *Yugoslavia and the New Communism* (New York: Twentieth Century Fund, 1962), chap. 8; A. Ross Johnson, "The Dynamics of Communist Ideological Change in Yugoslavia: 1945–1953," Ph.D. dissertation, Department of Public Law and Government, Columbia University, 1967. Johnson's account of the ideological developments, especially during 1949, has been very useful.

16. Hoffman and Neal, chap 8. Johnson argues, however, that the interparty correspondence of spring 1948 made the permanent nature of the split quite clear to the Yugoslav leadership. It was strategic for the leadership to avoid a doctrinal dispute initially, while strengthening its own position; Johnson believes this motive accounts for the actions observed (pp. 360ff.)

17. Hoffman and Neal, chap. 8.

1949 did the Yugoslav party leadership advocate a different line. It is in this total context of the complex of political factors that the Yugoslav quest for a new economic system must be viewed.

The immediate public response of the Yugoslav party to the Cominform Resolution was to ignore it. At the Fifth Congress of the Communist Party of Yugoslavia held in July 1948, Stalin was even praised. In January of 1949 the decision was made to collectivize agriculture.

In March of 1949 Milovan Djilas, departing from the general party line at that time, called for a halt in the Yugoslav denials of Soviet charges and for a statement of the positive aspects of Yugoslav policies.[18] His plea met no immediate response. In July 1949 Milentije Popovic attacked the nature of economic relations among socialist states, declaring it to be entirely unsocialist.[19] This criticism was reiterated by Djilas in September of the same year.[20] But it was Mose Pijade who first raised the question of the *internal* relations, that is, of defects in the Soviet organizational system. In a series of articles in the fall of 1949 he concluded that such errors as were apparent in Soviet external relations could only arise from faulty internal relations.[21] The first completely open statement that the Yugoslav difficulties lay in defects in the Soviet internal order appeared only at the end of December of 1949.[22]

Thus it was late 1949 before the Yugoslav party leaders

18. Milovan Djilas, "Aktuelna pitanja agitacije i propagande," *Partijska izgradnja* 1, no. 1 (Mar. 1949): 15–16, as cited by Johnson.

19. Milentije Popovic, "O ekonomskim odnosima izmedju socijalistickih drzava," *Komunist* 3, no. 4 (July 1949): 98–160.

20. Milovan Djilas, "Ljenin o odnosima medju socijalistickim drzavama," *Komunist* 3, no. 5 (Sept. 1949): 1–56.

21. Mose Pijade, "Veliki majstori licemerja," *Borba*, Sept. 22, 29; Oct. 5, 6, 1949, as cited by Johnson, p. 143.

22. Makso Bace, "O nekim pitanjima kritike i samokritike u SSSR-u," *Komunist* 3, no. 6 (Nov. 1949): 125–67, as cited by Johnson, pp. 142–45. He notes that this issue of *Komunist* was published at the end of December.

questioned openly the internal organization of the Soviet system. During the course of 1950 this developed into an extensive critique of Soviet centralization of political and economic decisions and the dominance of the bureaucracy; in March 1950, Djilas made the first major speech attacking the Soviet Union.[23]

The Yugoslav communist party had emerged from the experience convinced of the correctness of its own stance. It followed that the Soviet party was in error. Even to admit such a possibility represented a radical change in outlook.[24] But the Yugoslavs went even further. If the cause of Stalin's errors appeared to be excessive bureaucratization, then the correction of the error would lie in finding an alternative to the bureaucratic organization of the state. This led the Yugoslavs to reconsider their own economic and political organization.

Edvard Kardelj, as early as July 1949 had outlined the seeds of a new interpretation of the transition period from capitalism to communism based on the withering away of the state.[25] He referred to such Marxist-Leninist classics as *The Paris Commune*[26] and *State and Revolution*[27] for support, for it is in these works that popular participation, soviets, and workers' management of factories appear. The development of "socialist democracy" required the withering away of the state and the development of special forms of organization based on mass participation. He noted in

23. Milovan Djilas, "Na novim putevima socijalizma," *Borba,* Mar. 19, 1950 (text of a speech delivered Mar. 18 to the students and professors of Belgrade University).

24. The awe in which Stalin and the Soviet party was held is illustrated in Milovan Djilas, *Conversations with Stalin* (New York: Harcourt, Brace and World, 1962).

25. Edvard Kardelj, "O narodnoj demokratiji u Jugoslaviji," *Komunist* 3, no. 4 (July 1949): 1–83.

26. Karl Marx, *The Paris Commune* (New York: New York Labor News Co., 1920).

27. V. I. Lenin, *State and Revolution* (New York: International Publishers, 1943).

his article that workers' consultative meetings already existed. "The undeveloped, spontaneous form must be developed further into a continuous form of direct cooperation of the workers in the management of our enterprises." [28]

There were thus three threads to the ideological change in Yugoslavia: (1) a negative criticism of the bureaucratic organization of the Soviet Union; (2) a positive appraisal of participatory forms of government (including the association of direct producers in the management of enterprise), whereby the state apparatus would wither away; and (3) a new analysis of the roles of plan and market in socialism. But it was not immediately clear how these elements fit together.

Having rejected the Soviet example, the Yugoslavs sought to weave together a new political and economic system. The two major strands of the incomplete economic theory were management of enterprises by workers and decentralization of the economic system with increased reliance on market relations. Although originating independently, the two notions were bound together in logic. If the workers were to have something to manage, there had to be some meaningful autonomy of decision making at the enterprise level.[29] These elements suddenly coalesced in early 1950. According to Djilas' account,

> One day—it must have been in the spring of 1950 —it occurred to me that we Yugoslav Communists were now in a position to start creating Marx's free association of producers. The factories would be left in their hands, with the sole proviso that they should pay a tax. . . . I soon explained my idea to Kardelj and Kidric while we sat in a car. . . . Without leaving the car, we thrashed it out for little more than

28. Kardelj, *Komunist* 3, no. 4: 56.
29. See Jiri Kolaja, *A Polish Factory* (Lexington: University of Kentucky Press, 1960), for a study of workers' management without autonomy.

half an hour. . . . A couple of days later, however, Kidric telephoned me to say that we were ready to go ahead at once with the first steps. . . . A little later, a meeting was held in Kardelj's cabinet office with the trade-union leaders, and they proposed the abolition of the workers councils, which up to that time had functioned only as consultative bodies for the management. Kardelj suggested that my proposals for management should be associated with the workers councils. . . . Shortly there began the debates on the issues of principle and on the statutory aspects, preparation that went on for some four or five months. Tito, busy with other duties and absent from Belgrade, took no part in this and knew nothing of the proposal soon to introduce a workers council bill in the parliament. . . . Kardelj and I, convinced that this was an important step, pressed him hard. . . . The most important part of our case was that this would be the beginning of democracy, something that socialism had not yet achieved; further, it could be plainly seen by the world and the international workers' movement as a radical departure from Stalinism. Tito paced up and down, as though completely wrapped in his own thoughts. Suddenly he stopped and exclaimed: "Factories belonging to the workers —something that has never yet been achieved!" . . . A few months later, Tito explained the Workers' Self-Management Bill to the National Assembly.[30]

The initial moves in the direction of liberalizing the economy were tentative and cautious. The newly established workers' councils remained largely without economic power. There was little immediate progress toward changing the nature of the planned economic relations. The gestation period lasted from 1950 to the end of 1951.

30. Milovan Djilas, *The Unperfect Society: Beyond the New Class* (Harcourt, Brace and World, 1969), pp. 219–22.

During this time the structure that the planned economy was to take and the instruments to secure its operation were being formulated. One reason for the long delay, doubtless, was the enormity of the changes involved. It, was a long step from a centralized command economy to the restoration of the market. Essential to the operation of a market was a price system that was free to respond to market forces. This was established, in several stages. In January 1951 the new law on the Formation and Determination of Prices of Consumer Goods provided for free price formation for nonrationed commodities. In March, industries under the supervision of local governments (industries of local significance) had most of their prices freed. In September, prices of most remaining consumer goods were freed and consumer rationing was eliminated in the latter part of 1951 and early 1952. In June 1952 there was a further liberalization of the retail prices of consumer goods. In the industrial sector, in the late summer of 1951 new prices were established for raw materials and semifabricates; in January 1952 the prices of manufactured goods were allowed to adjust to the new raw material prices, and in June 1952 the raw material prices were allowed to seek their own level, with, apparently, a few exceptions such as steel. It is in this context of liberalization that the Law on the Planned Management of the National Economy passed at the end of December 1951, established the temporary arrangement known as the "system of accumulation and funds," bearing the imprint of Kidric's thought. This lasted only two years; at the beginning of 1954 major changes came into effect, completing the transition to a market economy.

Economic factors

If the roots of the shift in Yugoslavia's economic system were to be found in disappointment in the Soviet system

with respect to the economic and social conditions it per-
petuated, the actual rejection of Soviet forms was precipitated by economic chaos, especially in the years 1950 to
1952. The accompanying table illustrates the disastrous

Index of National Income and Production,
1947 = 100

Year	National income	Industrial production	Agricultural production
1948	123	127	117
1949	131	136	119
1950	117	136	87
1951	129	127	128
1952	109	124	85
1953	130	140	122

Source: *Statisticki godisnjak FNRJ,* 1962 (Belgrade: Savezni zavod za statistiku, 1962), p. 92.

performance of the economy. National income in 1952 was
scarcely above 1947 levels despite five years of planning
and very high rates of investment. Industrial production
showed no increase in 1950 over the previous year and
actually declined in 1951 and 1952. Agriculture is a special
case and will be considered below.

Certainly, these economic conditions gave impetus to
the demand for major economic reform. Yet the causes of
poor performance need to be further examined before any
conclusions can be drawn about the relation between the
system of central planning and the performance.

The first Yugoslav five-year plan, for the years 1947 to
1951, was highly ambitious.[31] It envisioned that national
income in 1951 would be double that of 1939. Agricultural
output was to increase to 1.5 times the 1939 level. For the
industrial sector the plan envisaged a fantastic increase to
five times the prewar level. Despite these ambitious goals,

31. *Five Year Plan of the Federal People's Republic of Yugoslavia* (Belgrade: Jugoslovenska knjiga, 1947).

realization of planned targets proceeded fairly well in 1947 and 1948. Industrial output expanded 53 percent and 24 percent, respectively, due in considerable measure to the initial underemployment of industrial capacities.[32] National income in 1948 was 99.8 percent of that planned.[33]

The planners had underestimated the resources necessary for continued increases and overestimated the domestic resources available, as well as aid from the Soviet Union. The new investments now to be undertaken had long planning periods and contributed to inflationary pressures before their products came onto the market. The small amount of investment allocated to the agricultural sector made fulfillment of agricultural objectives unlikely. The prognosis for continued rapid growth at levels foreseen in the plan was poor.

As a result of this situation, the effect of the Cominform Resolution was especially severe. There were two economic consequences of the rupture. The first was direct: the blockade of trade with Yugoslavia by the members of the socialist camp. The second, indirect consequence was the Yugoslav decision to collectivize agriculture. Both of these events, as well as droughts in 1950 and 1952, had such severe repercussions on Yugoslav levels of economic activity that it is virtually impossible to reach any meaningful conclusions about the effectiveness of centralized planning as an economic system in Yugoslavia. This hinders our ability to understand what economic grounds may have prompted the Yugoslavs to adopt a new system. It also makes comparisons with the subsequent changes in East Europe and the Soviet Union difficult.

The Cominform blockade required a major reorientation of foreign commerce. The levels of trade activity

32. C. Bobrowski, *La Yougoslavie Socialiste* (Paris: Cahiers de la fondation nationale des sciences politiques, no. 77, 1956), chap. 3.

33. Boris Kidric, chairman of the Planning Commission, *Yugoslavia: Progress of the Five Year Plan* (Washington, D.C.: Embassy of the Federal People's Republic of Yugoslavia, 1949), p. 39.

dropped sharply. Trade with the countries of the socialist camp came to a virtual standstill by the summer of 1949. Whereas in 1947, before the blockade, 48.3 percent of Yugoslav imports came from the Soviet Union, Czechoslovakia and Hungary, in 1950 trade with those three countries was virtually nonexistent. Yugoslav foreign trade shifted to Western and other nations, but the volume of trade diminished. By 1950 the total value of imports was only 75 percent of that in 1948, but the incidence was uneven.[34] Western assistance in providing credits and, later, aid kept Yugoslav imports from declining more disastrously.[35] The blockade reduced Yugoslav supplies of some essential raw materials and eliminated its sources of certain specialized machinery and replacement parts.[36]

While investment continued at high levels, little additional production was forthcoming, in part because of the nature of the investments undertaken but also because of production bottlenecks resulting from the disruption of trade.[37] However, whether the effects of trade disruption were as severe as the Yugoslavs usually suggest (attributing

34. *Statisticki Godisnjak FNRJ, 1959* (Belgrade: Savezni zavod za statistiku, 1959), p. 175. According to the figures given, the value of imports of raw materials dropped in 1950 only to 93 per cent of those in 1948, and imports of machinery and transportation equipment only to 95 per cent of those in 1948. Major drops were registered for manufactured goods, various finished products, and chemicals.

35. The first United States loan of $20 million was announced in Sept. 1949. Forty million dollars more was approved by spring 1950, while to meet the severe drought of the summer of 1950, a $50 million grant was appropriated. This marked only the start of American assistance to Yugoslavia. John C. Campbell, *Tito's Separate Road* (New York: Harper and Row, 1967), chap. 2 and appendix table, p. 171.

36. The index of value of imports by branch of activity shows more significant decreases. For mining and manufacturing as a whole, the index for 1950 was 73 (1948 = 100); for coal, 61; ferrous metallurgy, 65; nonferrous metallurgy, 68; nonmetals, 79; metal industry, 81; electric industry, 72; chemical industry, 55; paper industry, 64; and textiles, 66. However, the petroleum derivatives industry index was 108 and rubber, 119. *Statisticki Godisnjak FNRJ*, 1959, p. 175.

37. Bobrowski, chap. 4.

to it in great measure the poor performance of the years
1948 to 1952) is dubious, and other major factors need to
be considered in explaining the poor economic performance.

At least in part due to the criticism by the Soviet communist party of Yugoslav policy in the countryside, Yugoslavia decided in 1949 to collectivize agriculture. This
measure was taken despite successful harvests in 1947 and
1948 and despite the fact that the obligatory grain purchase plan for 1948 was fulfilled by 134 percent (a fact
which presumably precludes a parallel with Soviet collectivization which was based upon an alleged lag in grain
collections).[38] It is now widely admitted in Yugoslavia that
the collectivization of agriculture was a mistake and was
based upon political and not economic motives.

The collectivization drive began after the harvest of
1949, and reached its peak by mid-1951 with slightly less
than 20 percent of the arable land and the number of
households.[39] The effect of the policy on output is difficult
to interpret because of the variable climate in these years.
The year 1950, when the drive was at its height, was one
of severe drought, and output fell drastically. In 1951,
when weather conditions were favorable, the percentage of
land under collectivization was at its peak, and output was
high. 1952 saw another drought, and in 1953 when the
peasants were permitted to leave the collectives, output
was the same as in 1951.

It simply is not possible on the basis of aggregate data to
reach any conclusions about the effects of collectivization.
The policy was probably inefficient. The stated reasons for
collectivization are to increase output by the more rational
organization of agriculture. Yugoslavia was not in a position in these years to produce the agricultural machinery

38. Kidric, *Yugoslavia: Progress of the Five Year Plan*, p. 38.
39. A decree of July 1951 permitted limited withdrawal from the cooperatives.

and other industrial products that might have raised output in agriculture. (The unstated reasons for collectivization are to acquire a greater portion of the agricultural output, at minimal cost, for use outside the agricultural sector.) In any event the policy was unpopular with the peasantry; in 1953, for this reason or in keeping with the greater liberalization in other fields, peasants were permitted to leave collectives and did so in large numbers.

Finally, the performance of the agricultural sector was not without effect elsewhere in the economy. If we examine industrial output by sector, we find the greatest drops in output in those sectors dependent on agricultural raw materials.[40] The heavy industry sectors continued to grow.

Given the disastrous economic conditions observable from 1950 on, it was reasonable to seek a change in the economic system even if the failures were not immediately and obviously the product of the system of economic organization. But this does not tell us what role economic considerations played in the ensuing changes. Nor is it clear whether decentralization was rational for Yugoslavia at this time. If the shortcomings in the economy were primarily due to supply bottlenecks (as would follow from the Cominform blockade and the agricultural failures), then centralization of an appropriate type could assure that the high priority sectors acquired the scarce resources necessary to fulfill critical output targets.[41]

In recent years, a rationale for the economic reforms observed in Soviet-type economies has been established. According to these arguments, central planning is rather well

40. Wood, paper, textiles, leather goods, food processing, and tobacco. *Jugoslavija 1945–1964: Statisticki pregled* (Belgrade: Savezni zavod za statistiku, 1965), pp. 144–45.

41. On the other hand, it could be argued that Soviet-type centralization is too inflexible to cope well with supply uncertainty, leading to excess inventory accumulations rather than the efficient allocation of temporarily scarce resources.

suited for mobilizing the economy for development but its very success in delivering the economy to the middle levels of development—at which productive conditions, factor supplies, technology, and preferences may change—makes it no longer useful.

In the initial stages of development, planning is useful for several reasons that were noted earlier. It can raise the rate of savings. Because of the radical reorientation of production required for economic development, discontinuities and externalities render the market mechanism inadequate to allocate resources, while the plan can coordinate such decisions. At the same time the planning process may be carried out in a relatively simple manner, concentrating on certain obvious tasks without considering an extensive list of alternatives. These considerations refer principally to the advantages gained by investment planning. There are additional factors that make the planning of production and administrative allocation useful. At early stages of development, acute bottlenecks limit production. Soviet-type planning and incentive systems that rely on exhortation, threat, bonus, and promotion to attain physical output targets may initially be effective in raising output.

Soviet-type planning becomes less useful as development proceeds. Once bottlenecks are broken, the emphasis on quantity alone ceases to be rational. Taut planning and quantitative indicators introduce aberrations that make no sense at higher levels of development: systematic understatement of capacities and overstatement of input needs; insufficient incentive to produce the desired assortment, to meet customers specifications or to innovate; and little pressure to minimize costs.

At the same time, planning of the type previously practiced becomes either very costly, impossible, or inefficient. The process of information collection mushrooms. As technology advances and as supplies of factors become more elastic, the choices open to the planners multiply. There are alternative methods for completing any given task. The range of choices with respect to product and method of production becomes staggering. The comparison of all possible output combinations and production methods would be prohibitive. Millions of persons would have to be employed in the preparation of the plan. On the other hand, less costly planning methods fail to consider all alternative outputs and production methods. As a result the methods employed in production may be inefficient and the combination of goods actually produced may be suboptimal.

The costs of planning may be further compounded by the existence of general systematic errors of a planning bureaucracy. Such a bureaucracy resists change and is best adapted to producing the same old products in the same old way. The information system may also generate systematic biases in the information on which planning is based.

In the process of development, then, the market mechanism becomes a more attractive method of economic organization. The initial disadvantage of the market becomes less significant as the adjustment process becomes more marginal in character. The market provides a stimulus for satisfying customers (domestic and foreign) in assortment and quality, and also for the generation of new products. The market provides information more efficiently and permits it to be processed in disaggregated form at the local level, eliminating the need for much of the bureaucracy.

Although something of this sort may be a plausible explanation for East Europe in the sixties, its relevance to Yugoslavia in the fifties is not immediately apparent. Certainly Yugoslavia in 1950 was a very underdeveloped country. It is not clear why Yugoslavia would have "outgrown" the advantages of a centralized economy so early, and so much earlier than other countries at broadly similar levels of development. The Yugoslav answer is that similar conditions were present in all Eastern European countries but that only Yugoslavia was sufficiently free from rigid Stalinism to be able to take this step. This argument would be more convincing if one could point to a slowdown in the growth rate of East European countries dating from the early fifties. As a rule it was only in the sixties and only in the more advanced countries that difficulties began to appear.

Yugoslavia might have had rational grounds for decentralization because of its isolation from the socialist camp. In a large country or trading area, the disadvantages of central planning would be offset for some time by the greater economies of scale that could be realized through central planning, while in a smaller country there could be no such offset. Further, the isolation of Yugoslavia forced it to trade in the more demanding world markets that require quality and up-to-date items, aspects for which centrally planned systems are not particularly well suited, it seems.

It is not clear, then, what economic motives accounted for the Yugoslav reorientation of economic outlook.[42] While it may be true that economic factors made the decentralization advantageous or even "inevitable," these reasons are not compellingly obvious. There is no denying the severe economic situation by 1952, but the nature of the disaster is not clearly related to the economic system as such and it is not immediately obvious that a change from centralization to decentralization was the answer.

42. The cynic finds still another rationale for the Yugoslav changes. In this view, central planning never existed at all in Yugoslavia, only an enormous Balkan bureaucracy. Abolition or significant reduction of the bureaucracy was bound to be an improvement.

It is also possible to argue that central planning was never abolished but was retained until much later on (or even to the present day). While this is probably true with respect to investments, the organization of decisions about output within the framework of existing capacities did change significantly.

Furthermore, the Yugoslavs did not merely decentralize. They selected a particular type of economic organization based on worker-managed factories that constituted an integral part of the general social and legal framework. The search for motives for economic change cannot be restricted to economic factors alone, and noneconomic reasons may have played a major role.[43]

A CHANGE IN DOCTRINE

The proposed changes in the organization of the economy constituted a radical departure from the practice and from the commonly accepted interpretation of Marxist economic thought. Accordingly, it was necessary to develop a new theory of the transitional economy. A major preoccupation of Yugoslav writers at this time was to provide a Marxist explanation of the change.

Socialist commodity production

Kidric was the first to devise a theoretical model of decentralized market socialism and a new doctrine.[44] He sought to demonstrate that the envisioned changes were a correct interpretation of Marx, as well as to provide a guide for the practical problems of economic organization.

Kidric's demonstration of the consistency with Marx rested on the concept "socialist commodity production." Kidric gave the name "socialist commodity production" to the system in which the means of production were socially

43. One purely political explanation focuses on the need to reduce the bureaucracy because the party members loyal to the Soviet Union in the ongoing conflict were mainly in the central apparatus, while the communists at the village, factory, and commune level were more loyal to Tito.

44. Boris Kidric, "Teze o ekonomici prelaznog perioda u nasoj zemlji," *Komunist* 4, no. 6 (Nov. 1950): 1–20.

owned but where production was carried on by individual socialist enterprises. The socialist enterprise was an economic-legal entity making decisions about production.

Kidric outlined the characteristics of the socialist enterprise: (1) operation on the principle of economic accountability, (2) the right to manage fixed and circulating capital entrusted to it by society, (3) the right to carry out investment specified by the plan, (4) the right to participate in planning, and (5) the right to dispose of the part of the enterprise income arising from economizing and to distribute these funds to investment and to individual bonuses.

The identification of socialist enterprises that engage in "socialist commodity production" was a bold step and an innovation in Marxist economic thought. It has been argued above that Marx associated commodity production with private ownership and that he did not conceive of a system in which property would be socially owned but where producing units would operate independently of one another.[45] The Yugoslav dilemma was doctrinal. Was socialist commodity production—the Yugoslav name for their system—compatible with Marx's analysis?

To demonstrate compatibility, Kidric elaborated the new Yugoslav doctrine about the transition to socialism. In the lower stage of the transition to socialism, socialist property assumes the form of state property. In the higher stage, social property is under the management of freely joined direct producers. There is an historical progression. In the transition from capitalism to communism, the state "appears first in the capacity of collective manager, and simultaneously as the factual and legal owner of the means of production. . . ."[46] But state socialism, no matter how much it began to resemble some kind of "state communism" could represent "only the first and the shortest step

45. See Chap. 2 above.
46. Kidric, *Komunist* 4, no. 6 (1950): 5.

of the socialist revolution." [47] The correct (and inevitable) path of development of socialism required the "transformation" of state socialism into free associations of direct producers or socialist commodity producers. If state socialism were retained longer than required, it would become "state capitalism of the 'pure' type (without ownership by middle classes but with a parasitic bureaucratic class)." [48]

The notion of the transition was outlined by Djilas in his series of articles in late November 1950.[49] At the beginning, the state must use its power to nationalize the means of production.[50] State ownership over the means of production is necessary as long as productive forces are undeveloped and disproportions exist.[51] But by its success in overcoming disproportions, the need for state management is reduced. Herewith begins the struggle with the bureaucratic forces. The role of the state is, on the one hand, progressive (especially in the struggle against capitalist elements and in the organization of simple commodity producers, above all in agriculture) but, on the other hand, it gives birth to bureaucratic tendencies. Unlike the Soviet Union, where the bureaucratic tendencies had won and socialism of the lower stage based on state ownership had been transformed into state capitalism, Djilas maintained that Yugoslavia was still engaged in the struggle. [52]

In the free association of direct producers that was the next stage of socialism, relations among commodity producers were those of exchange, according to Kidric. The

47. Ibid.
48. Ibid., p. 6.
49. Milovan Djilas, *Savremene teme* (Belgrade: *Borba,* 1950). Originally published in *Borba* (Nov. 19, 20, 26, and 29, 1950). Page references given here to the book.
50. Ibid., p. 46.
51. Ibid., p. 48.
52. Ibid. However Kardelj, in his speech of Dec. 29, 1950, "Nova Jugoslavija u savremenom svetu," called the system in the USSR deformed socialism, not state capitalism.

basic aggregate outlines of production were, however, determined by the plan. Commodity exchange was not the basic force that established the ends of productive activity in socialism; it was only the means for carrying out the plan.[53]

Kidric conceded that Marx had not foreseen the possibility of socialist commodity production in the transition to communism. Kidric presented socialist commodity production as an indispensable stage in the process of transition from capitalism to communism, but a fleeting phenomenon. Socialist commodity production itself was valid only for a limited period of time in the transition from capitalism to communism.

Kidric believed (with Marx) that market forms of exchange would be ultimately abolished. Socialist commodity production was not the vehicle by which the economy would enter into communism.

> "Pure" socialism, which is necessary for the direct transition to communism and which was foreseen by Marx and Engels in their main works, and commodity exchange, exclude one another not only dialectically but, strictly speaking, absolutely.[54]

Kidric's theory of the transition to socialism merely postponed the abolition of the market until a higher stage of economic development was attained.[55]

53 The idea that Kidric had briefly noted before became the basis of his new scheme. The real dimensions of the changes he advocated were seen in his division of the decision-making process into two levels, basic and operational planning.

54. Kidric, *Komunist* 4, no. 6 (Nov. 1950): 6.

55. As radical as the Kidric theses appeared at the time, subsequent practice went far beyond them. The enterprises became more free than Kidric had ever suggested. Unfortunately, Kidric did not live to see these developments—he died in 1953.

Proposals for economic reorganization

Kidric also made concrete proposals for economic reorganization. The key to his view of the economy was the distinction between "fundamental" and "operative" planning. Fundamental, or basic, planning was the responsibility of the state organs. It established desired macroeconomic relations. Basic proportions were consciously planned—not the result of individualistic decisions. This constituted the explicitly socialist element of the system. Operative planning took place at the enterprise level. It was influenced by the macroeconomic relations of the plan and the economic instruments (fiscal and monetary policy) and by the economic pressures of the market.

The distinction between the two types of planning amounted to a redefinition of the crucial relation between the plan and the market. Although Kidric was never ready to give the market a full role in resource allocation, he recognized that the establishment of social objectives and the selection of means to attain them were different activities. The plan could establish the objectives, but the market and the independent activities of the enterprise might contribute to the attainment of the goals. Plan and market were no longer in absolute contradiction. In addition, his proposals would permit an element of consumer sovereignty in determining the composition of output. "If the enterprise, following its own interest, were forced to take care of assortment and quality of output, it would produce the commodity in such assortment and of such quality as the market demanded." [56]

Kidric's proposals made it possible to combine leaders' preferences about macroeconomic objectives with consumer preferences to determine the composition of output

56. Kidric, "O nacrtima novih ekonomskih zakona," *Komunist* 5, no. 4–5 (July–Sept. 1951): 7.

of consumer goods industries. In addition market relations among firms would replace the centrally determined system of plan objectives, norms, and contracts. In that way enterprises would receive supplies more adapted to their needs and would be able to produce at minimum cost.

Kidric established three aggregative indices to guide the economy: minimum utilization of capacity, value of basic investment construction, and average rate of accumulation and funds.[57]

Minimum utilization of capacity

In the original version of central planning the enterprises were subordinate, in a hierarchic structure, first to general directorates and then to ministries. Ministries were significantly reorganized with the first law on workers councils of June 1950; in June 1952 the general directorates, the direct organs of control over the enterprises, were abolished. At about the same time, mid-1952, the supply allocation plan, another prominent feature of centrally planned economies, was also abolished and replaced by direct contracts between buying and selling firms. The prices of most items, both final goods and many raw materials, were freed by this time. The enterprises therefore had a great amount of new freedom to operate, at least within the limits of existing capacities.

Not fully trusting the market mechanism, the leaders felt that some kinds of limits on enterprise freedom were necessary. The Law on Planned Management of the National Economy of December 1951 provided for a federally determined minimum rate of capacity utilization. Because there was no longer any output plan to determine the product mix of the individual firm, it was necessary to calculate for each firm what value of output (mix unspecified) was equivalent to the minimum rate of capacity utili-

57. For additional discussion of these proposals, see Bobrowski, pp. 175–89; Ward, "From Marx to Barone," chaps. 3–6.

zation. In fact, calculations were not made for all firms, so some operated without targets at all. There were neither positive nor negative rewards attached to fulfilling the value of output target. Enterprises had a great deal of lee-way in determining the composition and level of output, and supply and demand factors could influence the assort-ment produced.[58]

Value of basic investments

The aggregate rate of investment was centrally deter-mined. Investment funds were allocated centrally by in-dustrial sector and geographic region through the General Investment Fund, rather than, as previously, directly through the Budget.

The rate of accumulation and funds

The principle of taxation was the most controversial of the Kidric proposals. The state calculated the total planned wages fund, that is, the amount of money neces-sary to pay (at standard rates) the number of workers necessary to produce the output specified by the require-ments of the minimum capacity utilization.

The state then specified the total value of expenditures on investment (accumulation) and social consumption (funds). The ratio

$$\frac{\text{total expenditures on investment and social consumption}}{\text{wages fund}}$$

was the "average rate of accumulation and funds." The significance of the rate of accumulation and funds went beyond establishing a ratio between social expenditures and private consumption. It also provided a basis for price determination and for taxation of the enterprise.

Social expenditures represent the "surplus product" of

58. Ward, pp. 190ff.

society. Labor produces the total product of society but workers receive only part of the product in the form of wages. The remainder is the surplus product of society. Total product of society is equal to the wages (consumption fund of the workers) plus accumulation and social funds.

The value price of an individual commodity is the average socially necessary costs of production plus the amount of surplus product the commodity embodies. Socially necessary costs include direct labor inputs and indirect labor inputs—depreciation of capital equipment and the materials used up in production. Kidric defined the value price to be the "total average socially necessary costs of production, transportation, and selling," [59] multiplied by the average rate of accumulation and funds. Kidric's variant of value price differed from the normal version of value price in Marxian economics. Using the symbols as before, c is the branch average materials cost per unit, including depreciation; v the branch average wage cost per unit; V the total wage bill for workers in material production; M the total surplus product to be distributed; and C the total value of materials and depreciation in material production. From Chapter 3 we recall:

$$\text{value price} = c + v + v \cdot M/V$$

and

$$\text{prime cost} = c + v + (c + v) \cdot M/(C + M)$$

Kidric specifically included transport and trade costs for the commodity in question. His version of the "rate of surplus product" is M/V but he applies this to total material costs $(c + v)$ and not just to live labor costs (v). Thus, if c' and v' represent costs of production including transport and trade,

$$\text{Kidric value price} = c' + v' + (c' + v') \cdot M/V$$

59. Kidric, *Komunist* 4, no. 6: 13–14.

Kidric recognized that these value prices would not be market-clearing prices in Yugoslavia at that time. The plan still strongly influenced the relative quantities of different types of goods produced and these goods were, subject to some exceptions, to be sold at market-clearing prices. As yet there was no question of making major adjustments of the relative quantities produced on the basis of a large gap between price and cost.

He believed that ultimately long run market-clearing prices would be identical with value prices through the adjustments of relative quantities. "As the development of the material forces of production of the socialist economy brings the economy nearer to the harmonious satisfaction of needs, . . . deviation of planned price from value price . . . tends to disappear." [60] For the interim period he advocated "planned prices." Planned prices were to be established along lines similar to Soviet practice or prior Yugoslav experience. The price level of consumer goods was quite high, while the price level in producers' goods was considerably lower.[61]

The basic taxable category was enterprise income. This was gross receipts less material expenditures and depreciation. Enterprise income was subject to a tax and the remainder was at the disposal of the enterprise for distribution to wages and bonuses, reinvestment, housing, and other enterprise activities for the workers. The size of the tax rate was not uniform but was established virtually for each enterprise. The objective appears to have been to establish tax rates that would leave all enterprises in equivalent positions with respect to income. The income available for distribution by the enterprise (after payment of all costs of production and taxes) should constitute, for all firms, an equal percentage of its direct labor costs. A simplified example illustrates the principle:

60. Ibid., p. 15.

61. The prices of some consumer goods were freed and attained market-clearing prices.

	Product of enterprise A	Product of enterprise B
Planned price	100 dinars	76 dinars
Materials and depreciation (c) per unit	20	20
Income before taxes per unit	80	56
Planned wage cost per unit (v)	50	50

Assume that the objective is to make income after taxes (the payment fund available for distribution by the enterprise) equal to the planned wages fund plus 10 percent. In this example, it would require 55 dinars residual, per unit, after taxes. The tax rate on income for enterprise A would be 25/80. The remainder, 55/80, or 55 dinars, would be left for the payment fund. The tax rate for enterprise B, 1/56, leaving 55/56 of 56 dinars, or 55 dinars, for the payment fund.[62]

Application of these rates of tax to planned income would leave each enterprise with a sum of 10 percent above planned labor costs to distribute to incentive payments and various other projects.

The rates of accumulation and funds, or taxes, often determined individually, were applied to actual enterprise income (a variable not laid down in the plan) to determine tax obligations. The remainder after taxes stood at the disposal of enterprises for bonuses, collective consumption, and reinvestment. The actual amount available to the enterprise depended on the actual costs and revenues of the enterprise. But because the rate of tax on enterprise income was constant for each enterprise, the firm was encouraged to minimize its costs and thus maximize its income, before taxes or after taxes.

When planned prices were considerably higher than the average costs of production, the rate of tax was to be high. When planned prices were very near the average cost of

62. It was usually expressed in a somewhat different manner in Yugoslavia. Payment fund = income/$(1 + AF)$, where AF was the rate of accumulation and funds. In this case for enterprise A, the rate of accumulation and funds would be 25/55 (expressed in its percentage form).

production, the rate of tax was to be low. Despite the fact that the rates varied from branch to branch, and within the branch often from enterprise to enterprise, they provided an incentive for cost reduction. The amount of funds available for enterprise distribution was a fixed proportion of the enterprise actual income. Thus, if the enterprise cut its costs, the workers stood to gain by it. The amount of money to be distributed varied as a function of enterprise income and not as a function of the number of workers. The system did result in a reduction of the number of workers.[63]

The system also had several disadvantages. The income of the enterprise and, consequently, the funds available for distribution varied with any shift in the price of the final product. Thus, if the prices of final products rose, it would increase the amount of enterprise funds available to workers in those branches in which prices were rising. The effect would be to increase workers' incomes without necessarily calling forth an increase in the production of the more expensive item.[64]

Similarly, if the price of the nonlabor inputs fluctuated, the income of the enterprises would be highly variable. It would induce the enterprises to use different factor combinations if relative prices shift. But if the level of all input prices rose, it would mainly effect a considerable squeeze on enterprise funds for distribution. Further, changes in

63. Igor Weitzmann, *Das System der Einkommensverteilung in der sozialistischen Marktwirtschaft Jugoslawiens* (Berlin: Duncker and Humblot, 1958), p. 43.

64. This is because workers are interested in the volume of enterprise funds relative to the number of workers, and not in the absolute size of the residual. See Chap. 8 for a further discussion of producers' cooperatives.

The capitalist entrepreneur, on the other hand, wishes to maximize total profits, which he does by producing that output at which marginal revenue is equal to marginal cost. An increase in price will mean that marginal revenue now exceeds marginal cost, and the capitalist will add to total profits by expanding output.

prices of factors or final products would have a highly differentiated effect on each enterprise: it would be affected in different measure, depending on its particular rate of tax.

But there was a fundamental problem in the system itself. The objective was to provide an equal starting position for all workers. If the planned prices covered virtually all goods and were held constant over long periods of time, then it might have been possible to achieve the original objective and provide a stimulative effect. However, such prices would not remain equilibrium prices (if they ever had been). On the other hand, any change in price of the final product could mean windfall gains or losses to the workers without having much effect on the quantities produced. Changes in prices of factors, especially in the level of factor prices, as was likely in inflationary conditions, could also mean windfall gains or losses. In order to achieve the objective of equal starting positions, it would be necessary to recalculate the rate of accumulation and funds for each firm at frequent intervals as the prices of the factors of production and of the final products changed.

In addition, the provision for differing rates of tax for each enterprise (but where the rate was constant with respect to the level of income the enterprise attained) meant that the incentive to reduce costs was quite different in different enterprises. In all cases workers had an incentive to maximize enterprise income, but the marginal increment to enterprise funds for distribution resulting from a given reduction in costs depended on the rates established for the individual enterprises. Obviously, the incentive to cut costs was less strong if the rates of accumulation and funds were very high.

A full year and a half had passed between the call for the new system in June 1950 and the substantive changes in economic organization. Kidric's system was put into practice starting in January 1952. The system of accumulation and funds, although it had significantly extended the freedom of the enterprise, for the reasons noted above was not completely satisfactory, either in accomplishing the desired income distribution or in stimulating productivity.

Although Kidric's scheme was a major break with the Marxist heritage and the past practice, and although he envisioned expanding the role of the market, he remained basically a *central* planner.[65] This was clear in his articles in 1951 and 1952.[66] He emphasized the transitory character of commodity production in socialism and recognized only limited freedom for the enterprise. He objected to proposals to extend the market and to increase the independence of the firm. These would rely on microeconomic initiative and develop the quest for profit.

> The average rate of profit as a principle of economic operation represents a pure contradiction in the socially planned management of the economy. . . . Introduction of that principle in the new economic system would mean . . . a step into anarchy of distribution and socialist reproduction.[67]

65. "Notwithstanding some of his new ideas of economic decentralization, he remained the defender of planned economy, though less rigidly centralized, and was not the advocate of a competitive socialist model that after his death some political leaders and economists held him to have been." (Cerne, p. 11.)

66. Kidric, *Komunist* 5, no. 4–5 (July–Sept. 1951): 1–27; "O nekim teoretskim pitanjima novog privrednog sistema," *Komunist* 6, no. 1–3 (Jan.–Mar. 1952): 42–49.

67. Kidric, *Komunist* 6, no. 1–3 (Jan.–Mar. 1952): 42.

CHAPTER 5

Yugoslav Market Socialism

The Kidric proposals and the system of accumulation and funds introduced in 1952 proved to be only temporary. Yugoslav economic thought entered a new stage almost immediately with the introduction of those reforms. The years from 1953 on saw further discussion of the twin objectives of workers' management and decentralization of the economic system. This discussion produced an extended justification, a new organizational plan and, starting in 1954, significant changes in the economic system. The remainder of the decade was devoted to developing a workable system embodying these principles.

DOCTRINE OF THE NEW ECONOMIC SYSTEM

It had been apparent from the first statements on the changing economic forms that the Yugoslavs did not have a very precise idea of the type of economic system they were striving to establish.[1] Generally, however, the Yugoslavs were pleased with the response to the loosening of administrative controls over the enterprises. The limited degree of enterprise autonomy and the free play of market

1. The entire political theory of the "new communism" developed rather slowly. "The doctrinal bases of Titoism emerged by bits and pieces, chiefly in the pronouncements of individual leaders, over the period of a decade. Beginning from a negative position—opposition to Soviet ideas —and charting unexplored territory, the various theoretical observations were sometimes so cautious as to be vague. Reflecting the emerging and changing Titoist system, they were sometimes contradictory and had a pragmatic quality not always easily distinguishable from confusion." Hoffman and Neal, p. 157.

forces had worked sufficiently well for the Yugoslavs to consider more sweeping changes in the economic regime. The remaining restraints were felt to be a burden and a limitation on the capabilities of the economy.[2] The Yugoslavs sought to escape the inadequacies of their system by removing many remaining administrative controls. A predisposition for more liberal economic measures was noticeable and many writers were excited over the possibility of a largely free market.

> While the first period of Yugoslav economic thought was characterized by the dominant role of the state in the economy, and the neglect of the role and place of the market mechanism, the second period was characterized by the greater, and occasionally idealized role of the market and the market mechanism.[3]

Not all Yugoslavs became immediate advocates of the market. Ideologically, it had proved difficult enough for Yugoslav Marxists to abandon the previously orthodox interpretation of the political economy of socialism. Yugoslav writings between 1951 and 1953 still exhibited considerable confusion as to whether it was "Marxist" to speak of socialist commodity production.[4] Yugoslavia needed a

2. "The system of the rate of accumulation and funds was in substance a typical compromise between the ever-growing forces of socialist democracy and the old state administrative system in the management of our economic affairs." (Milentije Popovic, "Povodom nacrta uredaba o privrednom sistemu," *Nasa stvarnost* 7, no. 9 (Sept. 1953): 5.

3. Dusan Pirec, "Ekonomska teorija planske privrede," *Nasa stvarnost* 16, no. 5 (May 1962): 600.

4. France Cerne, "Planning and the Market in Yugoslav Economic Theory," provides several examples on p. 12.

There was little doubt in the minds of Soviet economists about the orthodoxy of the Yugoslav experiment. "There exist foreign economists who, contrary to the facts, consider the law of value as the regulator of production. Some of them (among them some Yugoslav economists) consider socialism not as a planned, but as an anarchical economy, as the totality of isolated forms, where each operates independently in market competition in internal and even on foreign markets, establishes indepen-

concise ideological explanation for the even more liberal policies now advocated, an explanation in terms of the Marxist dialectic.

These notions were being worked out in 1952 and 1953, and, with only slight changes, were retained. The Program of the Yugoslav communist party (known officially as the League of Communists since 1953), adopted at its Seventh Congress in 1958,[5] was the authoritative statement of the principles of the Yugoslav socioeconomic system. It marked agreement on the basic principles.

State capitalism

A new historical interpretation, a new logic, and a new set of working principles were necessary to explain the extensive liberalization envisioned. Milentije Popovic, among others, undertook to make such a statement.[6] He started from a discussion of state capitalism.[7] He drew a parallel between the individual capitalist and the state capitalist. In both cases the "owner" appropriates the three significant functions of ownership: holder of title to the property, manager of property and disposer of the profit or surplus value arising from the use of property. Thus the state, even the socialist state, could be a monopolistic

---

dently prices and in dependence on market competition, determines the volume and the structure of investment." L. M. Gatovskii, "Ob uspol'-zovanii zakona stoimosti v sotsialisticheskom khoziaistve," *Kommunist*, no. 9 (1957): 40.

5. *Yugoslavia's Way. The Program of the League of Communists of Yugoslavia.* Trans. Stojan Pribichevich (New York; All Nations Press, 1958).

6. See the following articles by Milentije Popovic: "Sta drzavni kapitalizam znaci u drustvenom razvitku," *Nasa stvarnost* 7, no. 2 (Feb. 1953): 3–34; *Nasa stvarnost* 7, no. 9 (Sept. 1953): 3–33; "Povodom diskusije o privrednom sistemu," *Nasa stvarnost* 8, no. 1–2 (Jan.–Feb. 1954): 9–50.

7. Milentije Popovic was not the first to use the concept of state capitalism. As we have seen, this concept was introduced in late 1950 by Djilas, *Borba*, Nov. 19, 20, 26, and 29; and used by Kidric, *Komunist* 4, no. 6 (Nov. 1950): 6.

owner, and the economic system of that type was state capitalism.[8]

State capitalism had two important consequences: bureaucratization of the state machinery with consequent bureaucratization of economic life and reduction in human freedom; and the exploitation of the worker by taking the product of his labor away from him. Both aspects were important. Capitalism of whatever form exploits the worker by taking from him the product of his labor. State capitalism thus exploits the worker because the worker is not in a position to dispose of the product.

In the Program adopted at the Seventh Congress of the League of Communists of Yugoslavia in 1958, it was agreed that state ownership had been necessary in the initial stages of the transition to socialism. Yugoslavia had narrowly averted state capitalism by keeping state ownership only as long as objectively necessary. President Tito had stressed the historic ending of one phase when he introduced workers' councils into law in 1950. "From now on . . . the state ownership of the means of production—factories, mines, railways—is passing on to a higher form of socialist ownership. . . ." [9] The Program completed the formal argument. "Socialization of the means of production can take various forms in its course from indirectly social or state ownership—characteristic of the first phase of socialist development—to more and more direct and actual social ownership, under increasingly direct management by emancipated and freely associated working people." [10] Socialist development proceeds by stages through revolution, nationalization and confiscation of property, and state ownership and management of resources to a gradual return of control to direct producers and to so-

8. Milentije Popovic identified not only the Soviet Union but also Yugoslavia as state capitalist. This part of his analysis was not generally accepted in Yugoslavia.

9. Tito, p. 3.

10. *Yugoslavia's Way*, p. 129.

ciety itself. In this way the state apparatus withers away and true social ownership is attained.

Social ownership

The central problem was to define social ownership. The following bundle of property rights (which may be restricted or unrestricted) is associated with private ownership:

1. Right to use property for personal production and consumption.
2. Right to use property personally for market production and to sell the produce and retain the proceeds.
3. Right to rent property to others and to receive income therefrom.
4. Right to keep property without using it.
5. Right to alter the nature of property.
6. Right to use up or deplete property.
7. Right to sell physical property.
8. Right to liquidate a going concern.
9. Right to sell shares of income of a going concern.

The problem was to determine which specific rights over property were to be exercised by society and which by the workers in the enterprise.

Popovic, in his approach to social ownership, focused on the relation of the worker to the means of production and to the product of his labor. He sought to identify the conditions that would put an end to the dehumanized bureaucracy of state capitalism. The resolution of the conflict between capital and labor, he argued, could only lie in placing capital—the means of production—under the management of workers themselves. The means of production must be managed by the association of direct producers.[11] This in itself was not novel; Tito had emphasized management by workers themselves three years earlier.

11. Milentije Popovic, *Nasa stvarnost* 7, no. 2 (Feb. 1953): 18.

But Popovic's interpretation of the requirements was more far-reaching than Tito had suggested.

> Free association of producers must be understood as an association of producers which produces commodities and exchanges its products in a socialist market for the products of other associations, freely and independently. That means that the association of producers must have a certain minimum of productive individuality and independence, freedom to manage the products of its labor and to exchange them on the market.[12]

Producers must be free from the arbitrary intervention by the state apparatus and commodity production must proceed under the laws of the market. "The freer are commodities in the process of production, the more independent the economic laws of society, to that extent man is . . . also freer and more independent."[13] Therefore, factory workers must assume the management of really independent enterprises. Enterprises must have the right to use and to manage the means of production at their disposal. That freedom to manage, in Popovic's view, extended only to decisions about production within the framework of current capacities; as for investment, the wider community of elected representatives must make such decisions.[14]

Popovic argued that the right of the workers to dispose of the product of labor is equally necessary, along with the freedom from intervention by the state, to end exploitation. It is necessary not only to return to the worker the management of the means of production but also the fruits of his labor. "The individual producer again owns the product of his labor—through his collective."[15] The right

12. Ibid.
13. Ibid.
14. Ibid., no. 9 (Sept. 1953): 11.
15. Ibid., no. 2 (Feb. 1953): 19.

of the producer to the entire product, albeit a collective right, is a "natural right." [16] "Not even a 'force above society' nor the force of society has the right to take it away. . . . All other rights of producers follow from this one." [17]

Socialist commodity production, characterized by the decentralization of economic operations and control of the economic activities of the independent enterprises by the workers themselves, would restore to the producer the product of his labor. Socialist commodity production would enable the worker to "decide on the allotment and distribution of the social product and to appropriate directly a part of the social product which he produced in socially organized production." [18]

The concept of ownership was unclear in socialist commodity production because the important property rights were divided between the state as representative of society and the enterprise, and Popovic concluded, "in our country it is not possible to speak of ownership. It simply does not exist." [19] The effective negation of ownership followed from the establishment of another set of property rights vested in the workers in the enterprise:

> Social ownership as an economic category is not vested in any holder. No one holds the titular right of social ownership, not even the federation or other politico-territorial units, nor economic organizations and autonomous institutions. But . . . the law recognizes a special property right which it calls "the right to use." [20]

The content of the right to use consists in the right whereby the holder is authorized to *use* and *dispose*

16. Ibid., pp. 20–21.
17. Ibid., p. 20.
18. *Yugoslavia's Way,* p. 129.
19. Milentije Popovic, *Nasa stvarnost* 8, no. 1–2 (Jan.–Feb. 1954): 18.
20. "Development of Forms of Ownership in Yugoslavia," *Yugoslav Survey* 4, no. 12 (Jan.–Mar. 1963): 1686.

of property in social ownership in accordance with
law.[21]

Popovic also argued that it followed from the abolition
of ownership that "there is no profit. . . ." [22] Accordingly,
the question ceased to be "to whom the profit?" Elimination of ownership as an economic category and as a basis
for receiving income would mean the elimination of payments to individuals as owners of capital. Labor would
become the sole criterion for the distribution of social
product. Accordingly, Sergije Krajger argued that the accounting concept of "profit" should be done away with
altogether and replaced by the "net income" of the enterprise.[23] The wage would be abolished—and with it, wage
relations and exploitation. He also pointed out that direct
producers manage as well as work, thus payment for their
labor would include an implicit payment to their "entrepreneurship."

The "right to use" in Yugoslav law represents a new
bundle of property rights and is the key legal concept in
Yugoslav decentralization, as Pejovich has pointed out.[24]
Definition of the right to use divides the property rights
associated with private ownership between the state and
the enterprise. Referring to the property rights enumer-
ated a few pages above, the right of *usus fructus* is encom-
passed by rights 1, 2, and 3. The Yugoslav "right to use"
was significantly broader, containing rights 1, 2, 3, 4, 5,
and 7, but not 6 (right to use up property), 8 (right to
liquidate a going concern), or 9 (right to sell shares of income of a going concern). The Yugoslav firm could acquire

---

21. Ibid. Italics supplied.

22. Milentije Popovic, *Nasa stvarnost* 8, no. 1–2 (Jan.–Feb. 1954): 18.

23. Sergije Krajger suggested this explicitly in "Dohodak preduzeca u
nasem sistemu," *Nasa stvarnost* 7, no. 2 (Feb. 1953): 47–67.

24. Svetozar Pejovich, "Liberman's Reforms and Property Rights in
the Soviet Union," *Journal of Law and Economics* 12, no. 1 (Apr. 1969):
155–62.

productive property by producing it itself, by purchasing it from other firms, or by government grant. Once it acquired the productive property, the firm was obligated to maintain the value of its productive property (book value) by amortization payments and replacements. The firm could alter the form, but not the value, of social property. The enterprise was not permitted to depreciate or use up the value of property, to liquidate the enterprise,[25] or to sell shares in its earnings.[26] The property rights denied the firm remained vested in society. Society retained the rights to liquidate social property and to determine to whom shares of enterprise income could be assigned. Subject to these limitations, the firm may use social property for market production and it can receive the proceeds of its sales. For this right the firm pays a fee in the form of interest on the book value of enterprise assets.

The prices of many goods had already been freed from controls, and direct contact between buyer and seller had replaced the previous planned movement of goods through ministerial channels. Now a number of additional changes followed from the analysis of social ownership. Investments were to be provided by repayable, interest-bearing loans for which enterprises compete, rather than through budgetary grants. Major changes were made in the enterprise accounting system, putting costs on a more rational basis and emphasizing a threefold division of enterprise receipts.[27] The new accounting system, established by the law on the distribution of the total revenue of enterprises (December 24, 1953) recognized three claims upon the gross receipts of the firm: production costs, obligation to society (taxes), and the residual enterprise income. Under

25. In the event of bankruptcy, the social claim on book value of assets has priority over other claims on enterprise assets.

26. Initially at least. A modification was permitted, for limited periods of time, by the economic reforms of the mid-sixties.

27. See Ward, "From Marx to Barone," pp. 213–66 for discussion and analysis of the 1954 changes.

the revised accounting system, costs consisted of material costs, depreciation, interest and principal payments on borrowed capital, indirect business (turnover) taxes, location rent, wages and salaries,[28] social security and housing fund contributions, and a tax on working and unamortized fixed capital. In principle, workers were to decide upon the use of the residual income left after payment of taxes.

Social controls

The new model freed the enterprises from many restrictions. The working collective was to have the right to determine not only the current production but also to invest retained earnings, to borrow from banks and to decide about future changes in productive capacities. "Factories to the workers" would at long last be a reality.

The slogan "factories to the workers" has a long tradition in the syndicalist movement, but not until the Yugoslav experiment did the essentially syndicalist concept of workers' management find a warm welcome in Marxist socialism.[29] Despite the apparent resemblances of their system to syndicalist concepts, the Yugoslavs deny the connection. Yugoslavs argue that their system could *not* be interpreted as "giving the factories to the workers outright, along with the right to appropriate total output (less a certain contribution to society)." [30]

28. Until 1957, federally established minimum wages were included in the contractual costs, while bonuses and supplements came out of the residual income at the disposal of the enterprise. Since 1957, personal income has been a residual item and not a cost. All workers' income depends upon the residual income of the enterprise. A base wage is guaranteed by the state should enterprise income be insufficient to pay the base wage.

29. Marx rejected anarchistic and syndicalist tendencies. See George Lichtheim, *Marxism, An Historical and Critical Study* (New York: Frederick A. Praeger, 1961), especially "Marxism, Anarchism, Syndicalism."

30. Cerne, p. 10.

In a cooperative society some degeneration of socialism would inevitably take place. The means of production in enterprises would no longer be common
property, for the rest of society would have neither
the right to manage the economy nor the right to
dispose of the national product. Thus, state ownership would be transformed not into direct public
ownership but into some quasi-ownership by working
collectives.[31]

Apart from doctrinal disputes, the economic issue involved is important. Without specific forms of social intervention, firms operating under conditions of workers'
management would behave as if they were owners of capital. It is not clear that their behavior benefits society. This
might be true for several reasons. First, noncompetitive
market structures might develop. Monopolistic pricing
practices would be at odds with the welfare of society. Second, independent enterprises would hinder the coordination of enterprise investment decisions. Independence
might mean that significant external economies or other
divergencies of private and social calculations would not
be accounted for. Third, if workers were to determine the
rate of investment, the resulting rate might be less than
the politically desired rate. Finally, the maximizing principles of a producers' cooperative and, therefore, the effects on resource allocation are far from clear.[32]

On the one hand, social control was indispensable to
avoid these difficulties. On the other hand, if bureaucracy
was to be replaced by self-governing associations, what
kinds of social control were permissible? The solution was
sought in social control by the community, the forms of
which were often complex. The political-economic system
that came into effect with the 1953 Constitution had two

31. Ibid.
32. See Chap. 8 below.

bases: workers management of the primary economic units and political self-government at the commune, republican, and federation levels.[33] Government organs not only established the explicit framework within which the independent enterprises operated, they also exercised other types of influence to assure that the enterprises were responsive to the interests of society. The linking of the interests of the enterprise and of society was accomplished in a number of ways, as will be seen. These links formed an integral, although often implicit, part of the system. It is not surprising, then, that when many of these forms of social control were removed in the mid-sixties, that the old problems of assuring the consistency of enterprise actions with the preferences of society reappeared.

OPERATION OF THE ECONOMIC SYSTEM

The following discussion presents a sketch of the operation of the system and development of social controls in the period 1954 to 1960. In 1961 major economic reforms were introduced, which changed the situation.

There were four basic features of the Yugoslav economic system of decentralized market socialism: (1) an economic plan, (2) market methods of resource and product allocation, (3) production by independent enterprises, and (4) management by workers whose incomes are a residual. This combination of features distinguished Yugoslav market socialism from free enterprise economies and from command economies, from syndicalism and from other models of decentralized socialism.[34]

33. See Charles P. McVicker, *Titoism, Pattern for International Communism* (New York: St. Martin's Press, 1957), and Hoffman and Neal on the ideological and political aspects of the governmental system.

34. There is more than a casual resemblance between this system and the various models of market socialism developed in the thirties. However, as far as I have been able to ascertain, those models had no direct

The plan and the economic instruments

The plan established the basic macroeconomic proportions. Basic principles of economic development and not
myriads of detail were considered the proper subject matter for political determination. The plan transferred decisions about the rate of capital formation, the distribution
of investment funds among economic and geographic sectors, and the size of collective consumption expenditures
to the political sphere. On the basis of these broad political
decisions, the plan forecast production possibilities. It ex-
trapolated from previously attained levels on the basis of
known changes in the size and structure of the labor force,
capital stock, and other factors affecting the nation's production possibilities.[35] The plan ceased to be a directive
or a set of administrative orders. While the plan as such
had no binding force, it was not conceived as a vague
directive nor as a provisional hypothesis. Plan objectives
were to be obtained by a variety of economic instruments:
credit policy, fiscal policy and the regulations specifying
the accounting methods of the enterprise, and certain
direct controls.

---

impact on Yugoslav thought at this time. Those who were prominent in
developing the new system were not acquainted with formal Western
economics. For more detailed study of the operation of the Yugoslav eco-
nomic system in the fifties, see Ward, "From Marx to Barone." Also, Egon
Neuberger, "Central Banking in Semi-planned Economies: Yugoslav Case,"
Ph.D. dissertation, Department of Economics, Harvard University, 1957,
Harry Schleicher, *Das System der betrieblichen Selbstverwaltung in Jugo-
slawien* (Berlin: Duncker and Humblot, 1961); and Weitzmann, *Das
System der Einkommensverteilung in der sozialistischen Marktwirtschaft
Jugoslawiens.*

35. See Albert Waterston, *Planning in Yugoslavia* (Baltimore: The
Johns Hopkins Press, 1962); Branko Kubovic and Vidosav Trickovic,
National and Regional Economic Planning in Yugoslavia (Belgrade:
Federal Planning Bureau, 1961); and Jaroslav Vanek, "Economic Planning
in Yugoslavia," in Max Millikan, ed., *National Economic Planning* (New
York: National Bureau of Economic Research, 1967).

Credit policy

Credit policy determined the total amount of investment to be made in a given year. Planners estimated the investment funds anticipated from retained earnings of enterprises and amortization funds. They also estimated the distribution of investment funds to be provided by regional political authorities. This aggregate and its structure could then be compared with the amounts specified in the plan. The difference could be provided by credits from the national banking system. Credit policy was selective, allocating funds by geographic regions and industrial sectors. Essentially, it created noncompeting capital markets within which funds were allocated among enterprises on the basis of a number of criteria.[36] The result was that "the central government has full control and decision-

36. The actual allocation of investment funds is subject to numerous influences. At one time the Yugoslavs attempted to allocate a certain portion of investment funds within sectors through investment auctions. A relatively small part of available funds was auctioned off to the highest bidders. See Egon Neuberger, "The Yugoslav Investment Auctions," *Quarterly Journal of Economics* 72, no. 1 (Feb. 1959): 88–115. This method was abandoned for a number of reasons. One reason was that it proved unsatisfactory to have factory management bid, often unrealistically, for investment funds.

In its place, the Yugoslavs returned to the use of multiple criteria: expected rate of return, financial stability of the enterprise, riskiness of investment, contribution to foreign trade balance, portion of funds supplied by the enterprise, etc. As Wellisz has emphasized, a consistent ranking of scarcities requires the expression of qualitatively different entities in common terms. When multiple criteria that are not directly comparable are employed, there is no general application of the principle of economizing. Stanislaw Wellisz, *The Economies of the Soviet Bloc: A Study in Decision-Making and Resource Allocation* (New York: McGraw-Hill, 1964), p. 179.

Some writers, including Gorupic, appeared to recognize the necessity of a single quantitative term. "Differential advantages and disadvantages of each alternative . . . may be quantitatively established, where possible, by means of a single variable that summarizes several variables under a common denominator." Drago Gorupic, "The Investment Decision in Our System of Capital Formation," *Eastern European Economics* 2, no. 3 (spring 1964): 33.

making power over investment outlays, both by means of economic policy on distribution and, as a last resort, by means of direct decisions on allocation." [37]

> In providing directives for banking credit operations, the plans most frequently lay down credit quotas for investment in definite sectors of the economy or in definite economic targets, establish the rates of interest or dates of repayment of credits, fix the minimum of enterprises' own participation in investment projects, etc. However, all these directives and frameworks still leave the banks a wide scope for decisions regarding the direction and conditions of the allotment of resources.
>
> In this way the central social bodies possess an important means for influencing the final allocation of social resources . . . without having to decide on every individual investment.[38]

Fiscal policies

The major tasks of fiscal policy are to counteract the inflationary impact of government expenditures on social consumption and of government investment and to achieve the desired distribution of income. On the basis of forecasts of the social product, central authorities calculated the fiscal revenues necessary and set the tax rates accordingly. The major sources of revenues were the turnover tax and the taxes on the enterprises. The major enterprise taxes were the capital tax on enterprise working and unamortized fixed capital (book value), the tax on wages, and the tax on enterprise profits. It has been estimated

37. Milos Samardzija, "The Market and Social Planning in the Yugoslav Economy," *Quarterly Review of Economics and Business* 7, no. 2 (summer 1967): 43.

38. Vojislav Rakic, "Fundamental Characteristics of the Yugoslav Economic System," in Radmila Stojanovic, ed., *Yugoslav Economists on Problems of a Socialist Economy* (New York: International Arts and Sciences Press, 1964), p. 137.

that the combined taxes listed accounted for approximately one-third of national income.[39]

The taxes on the enterprise as well as the regulations governing the enterprise accounting system were designed to influence enterprise behavior. The capital tax raised the cost of capital and encouraged firms to economize in its use. At various times taxes (occasionally progressive) were imposed on the bonus payments by the enterprise to discourage excessive payments to individuals and to encourage retaining profits for investment purposes. Regulations governing the enterprise accounting system also attempted to give the enterprise an incentive to operate efficiently and in accord with social objectives. The difficulties in establishing such a system can be seen from observing the changes in the laws on distribution of enterprise income. For example, after workers in 1952 had initially used their freedom to raise personal incomes, in 1953 a progressive tax on bonuses to wages from enterprise funds was imposed. The rates were prohibitive beyond a very low percentage of actual wages.[40] In 1954 legal limits were set by the local government on the share of net profits that could be distributed to bonuses, and the enterprise funds distributed to bonuses were small in 1954, representing only 5.17 per cent of the base wage.[41] In addi-

39. J. M. Fleming and Viktor R. Sertic, "The Yugoslav Economic System," *International Monetary Fund Staff Papers* 9, no. 2 (July 1962): 213. They estimated the percentage composition of fiscal revenues for 1959 as follows:

Type of tax	Percentage of total fiscal revenues
Capital tax	18
Profits tax	31
Turnover tax	24
Wage bill tax	11
Local tax	11
Taxes outside the social sector	5

40. Weitzmann, p. 45.
41. Ibid., p. 52.

tion, actual wage scales were no longer established by the enterprise (which had exercised considerable authority in 1953) but were subject to approval by a commission representing the enterprise, the trade union, and the communal people's committee. In 1955, because of the poor effect on productivity, the system of wage payments was again altered. Wage scales continued to be established as in 1954, but the enterprise workers' council was permitted to set labor norms, which influenced the actual pay received.

In 1956 the system was again revised. Communal determination of local tax rates and bonus limits had left insufficient funds to the enterprise for bonuses or for investment. The portion of enterprise funds to be distributed to wage bonuses was established by federal regulation on the basis of the ratio of distributed profits to total wage payments in the previous year, with a small increase permitted.

In 1957, in another move to increase incentives, costs were redefined to exclude personal incomes. Now personal income came entirely out of the residual income of the enterprise. As before, gross profits were subject to a tax. From net profits a maximum of 50 percent could go to personal incomes and a specified percent were to go to local government and to the housing fund. The remainder was paid into enterprise accounts for the reserve fund, working capital, and collective consumption.

In 1958 the restrictions on the distribution of net profits were removed and instead was established a progressive but not prohibitive tax rate on personal earnings as a share of total net profits. The next major change came in 1961 and will be discussed below.

These changes suggest the difficulties in trying to find a suitable system that would give workers incentive, cause them to bear the risk of poor decisions, induce them to produce efficiently and profitably, and convince them to reinvest rather than take high wage increases.

The market

Credit and fiscal policy did not suffice to provide the kind of social control desired. Two other types of control existed: direct limitation of the market mechanism (through price controls and quantitative restrictions) and "moral suasion," the indirect influence exerted on the enterprise.

Market structure

It is through the market that specific resources are allocated. The logic of the Yugoslav system relies heavily on the functioning of the market. Individual profit-seeking enterprises respond to the signals of the market and in so doing produce best and most cheaply those products for which society has the greatest need. To function properly, there must be adequate competition in product and factor markets.

In the initial stages of their experiment the Yugoslavs were quite enthusiastic about the beneficial effects of competition. When the system was first introduced, large state enterprises were broken into numerous, competing, and autonomous enterprises. This was sometimes carried to extremes. For example, the maintenance of railroads became the task of autonomous collectives; railroad maintenance became chaotic. While large numbers of firms are doubtless beneficial in some areas, especially in retail sales and light consumer goods, the Yugoslavs soon found it was not suitable for all activities in the economy.[42] On the other hand, in many cases competition never existed at all. In the event of outright monopoly the government uses price controls. For other products the threat of imports

42. Official pressure for more rational integration of enterprises came only in 1962. (*The Fourth Plenum of the Central Committee of the League of Communists of Yugoslavia*, Belgrade, Jugoslavija, 1962).

from abroad at lower prices is supposed to induce domestic producers to price competitively. However, the precarious Yugoslav balance of payments position has prevented the import of sufficient quantities of goods to exert a significant influence on the price and output policies of domestic producers.

The Yugoslav system presumably would not demonstrate the type of dynamic inefficiency that arises from inadequate knowledge of the plans of one's competitors, purchasers, and suppliers. Yugoslav enterprises have at their disposal knowledge about the anticipated levels of demand as a result of the planning process. The economic chambers serve to transmit information about the investment plans of its members, so as to avoid duplication of facilities or other errors arising from ignorance of the intentions of other producers.

Price controls

The markets for goods and services were subject to substantial control. The objectives of price policy were to protect consumers from monopoly pricing, to control the general price level in times of inflation, and to influence the price structure with respect to specific commodities. Prices had been freed from controls in 1951 and 1952 in principle (on steel products and some other items in short supply, they had apparently never been free) but inflationary pressures caused a reinstitution of controls and, in May 1954, price ceilings were officially imposed on some other scarce materials. By 1955 forty materials comprising 50 percent of the total value of industrial raw materials and semifabricates were subject to price ceilings.[43] This meant an abandonment of the principle of freely formed domestic prices. Other forms of price regulation established in subsequent years required that firms obtain per-

43. J. M. Montias, "Economic Reforms and Retreat in Yugoslavia," *Foreign Affairs* 37, no. 2 (Jan. 1959): 293–305.

mission to raise prices and that they justify such requests with documentation of rising costs of production. In 1960 communal councils were authorized to set prices for certain foodstuffs and services. Producers' prices for most industrial goods were controlled and the upper limit of the markup in retail merchandising was also set by law, so that virtually all prices became subject to control. Since the mid-fifties the methods and extent of price control expanded, culminating in the general price freeze of March 1965.

In addition to direct price controls, authorities have additional power over prices by manipulation of turnover taxes to absorb excess purchasing power. The incidence of turnover tax is greatest in manufactured consumer goods. A system of differentiated coefficients was applied to imported and exported goods until 1961. The coefficients were similar to a turnover tax for imported items and provided subsidies for certain exports.

Other interventions in the market

The most important restriction on the market was in the allocation of capital. The allocation of resources for investment purposes was significantly affected by various devices including credit policy but not restricted to it. Other types of intervention altered relative price relations for the purpose of affecting the investment volume that could be carried out through retained earnings. Price controls prevented clearing prices for some commodities and evoked nonprice methods of allocation. In areas in which prices were representative of scarcities, turnover taxes removed part of the surplus from the disposal of the enterprise, which otherwise could have used the funds to expand capacities. By either device, the surpluses available to the firms were controlled and the flow of autonomous investment funds was restricted. At the same time there was a liberal use of subsidies, tax rebates, premia, and interest-free credits that affected the ability to invest, and even to operate at all. Often the price ceiling was at such a low level that subsidies were necessary if the industry were to begin to cover its costs. Subsidies also camouflaged various other operations that were unprofitable for quite different reasons.

In short, various types of intervention sought to insure that the market economy would operate in harmony with social interests. Instead of assuring harmony, these interventions were nearly fatal to the market mechanism itself.

The enterprise

The autonomous enterprise, managed by workers, is the basic unit of the Yugoslav economic system. The Yugoslav enterprise is a legal entity. It is free to contract for raw materials and intermediate materials, for capital equipment and workers, and to compete (within the limits set by the central credit policy) for capital funds. It determines its product, production methods, and output levels. In principle it is free to establish prices for its products. The Yugoslav enterprise is supposed to operate much like the free enterprise.[44] It makes decisions about production and investment in the light of its own self-interest.

The enterprise is responsible not only to the workers, but to society. In part its responsibility to society is secured by the joint political-economic influence over enterprise decisions. In part, it is secured by taxes and regulations. The enterprise operates within a framework of complex legal and fiscal regulations. The enterprise is subject to stringent financial controls. It must maintain separate accounts at the bank for various funds (amortization fund, workers' housing fund, reserve fund, current expenses, etc.). Funds once set aside can only be used for the pur-

---

44. Except in the event of bankruptcy, in which case the enterprise is examined by the local government, which has the option of subsidizing it temporarily or of liquidating it.

poses for which intended. In addition, the federal auditing service periodically inspects the books of the enterprise to assure that all legal regulations are being met.

Manipulation of the regulations governing enterprise accounting is a major policy weapon in the hands of the planners. Regulations determine which items are included in costs and which are residual, as we have seen. Other tools are the specification of amortization procedures and the method of valuation of capital goods.

But, in addition to these explicit regulations and controls, there are other forms of social control less explicit and less easy to evaluate. To assess the operation of the enterprise realistically, it is necessary to look at the various forces that influence enterprise decisions. These factors may be divided into two groups, those within and those without the enterprise.

Internal	*External*
Working collective	Organs of local government
Workers' council	Organs of federal and republican
Management board	government
Director	Confederation of Trade Unions
Factory union organization	Economic chambers and associa-
Political party	tions
	Political party

The unique feature of the Yugoslav method of decentralization of economic and political organization is that each of these bodies may exert some influence on the decision of the individual firms.

External sources of influence

The commune, the lowest administrative and legislative unit, is the pillar of decentralized government. Political responsibility in the Yugoslav system is quite decentralized,[45] and the communal government has both legislative and administrative functions.

The enterprise has several specific ties to the commune.

45. Hoffman and Neal, pp. 225-28.

The commune is the body that supervises the enterprise to assure the proper use of social resources. The enterprise must present its annual plans and reports to the council of producers for approval,[46] and the council in turn sends back policy recommendations.[47] The recommendations are advisory and not binding. However, although the enterprise "is under no legal obligation" to follow the commune's recommendations, the "political and moral influence is considerable."[48] A factory director concurred with the above opinion of a political leader: "The workers' council is obliged to consider and discuss the recommendations but it is not bound to accept them. The workers' council's obligation is political rather than legal."[49] Kolaja's study of the minutes of the workers' councils in two factories indicated, however, that communal recommendations were not always accepted.[50]

Throughout the period discussed in this chapter (1954–1960), the commune had a voice in appointing the director of an enterprise located in its territory. The director was appointed by a committee representing the enterprise, the labor union, and the commune. (This procedure was abandoned with the Constitution of 1963, according to which the director is appointed solely by organizations of workers' management.)

Another important influence of the commune stems from the fact that this body was usually the guarantor for bank loans sought by the enterprise. To the extent that the

46. The legislature at all levels was bicameral. One chamber is the council of producers elected by the working people of the given region, representation of different sectors of working people weighted by value added.

47. Jiri Kolaja, *Workers Councils: The Yugoslav Experience* (New York: Frederick A. Praeger, 1966), p. 3. His research was conducted in 1959.

48. Kiro Gligorov, "The Communal Economy," *International Social Science Journal* 13, no. 3 (1961): 413.

49. Kolaja, *Workers Councils*, p. 3, n. 4.

50. Ibid., chap. 2.

enterprise could finance investments from its retained earnings, the influence of the commune would be less. However, few firms were able to do so.

The local political body possibly exercises a stronger influence on the enterprise than does the central government. The Yugoslav press contains frequent reports of alleged "localism." The central government had no direct channels for collecting information or for exercising control over individual enterprises. This did not mean that there was no control. Central influence is exerted through the organs of the federal and the republican government as well as the Confederation of Trade Unions (Savez Sindikata), the economic chambers, and the League of Communists.

Of the federal organs, the greatest direct influences over the firm appear to operate through the banking system, especially that part of it providing investment credits. As noted above, credit policy is centrally determined and effectively controls all investment. However, the criteria for investment allocation used by the Investment Bank are multiple, and hence arbitrary, within any given economic sector. Federal organs also dispense foreign exchange, subsidies, rebates, reduced interest rates, premia, and approval for price increases. These benefits are dispensed through the bureaucracy and can significantly affect the working of the economy. It was dissatisfaction with the kinds of decisions emanating from the center in these circumstances that culminated in the great decentralization debate that gripped Yugoslavia in the years 1961 to 1965.

In addition to governmental bodies, there are other organizations that exert influence over the enterprise. The Confederation of Trade Unions is highly organized and is noted for its political reliability and support of party decisions. The Confederation of Trade Unions possesses, through its hierarchical structure, what the central government administration does not: a clear channel of communication direct from the central organs in Belgrade down to the enterprise level. Such channels facilitated the transmission of policy decisions.[51] The high degree of co-incidence of union and party officials usually insures that their directives will promote central political preferences. The union exerts influence as an organization and through the influence of union members on enterprise decisions. The Confederation of Trade Unions has participated at various times in setting wage guidelines drawn up in association with corresponding economic chambers.

Central political influence can also be exercised through the economic chambers. There are economic chambers for major branches of the economy: mining and manufacturing, service trades, building and construction, agriculture, transportation, and communication. Membership of enterprises in appropriate chambers has been compulsory since 1958. In addition to chambers, there are associations of producers of similar products, more narrow in scope and more professional in function. The associations disseminate technical information, give advice on marketing products, and the like. Chambers and associations have apparently also been responsible for an informal rationing of scarce raw materials among members.

The economic chambers by law cannot limit the autonomy of member enterprises. One of the functions of the economic chambers is to integrate informally the enterprise plans to avoid duplication of facilities arising from ignorance of the plans of other producers in similar or related fields. For this reason, enterprises must submit

51. Unions are organized on an industrial basis and the association of unions is organized on a geographic basis, so that two hierarchies exist. "The so-called horizontal organization is confined to each single industrial union, organized on a national scale. The vertical organization creates the pyramid making up the Federation of Yugoslav Trade Unions, from community organizations composed of representatives of the separate industrial unions functioning within each community, through similar district and republican organizations to the central office in Belgrade." McVicker, pp. 103–04.

their annual economic plans to the appropriate economic chambers or associations of producers. The chambers make recommendations to particular enterprises, and they also formulate broad policy recommendations, such as suggested wage norms drawn up in conjunction with the union. However, any actions of the chambers or associations of producers are in the form of recommendations. The chambers and associations have no explicit powers for controlling their members. In general the role of the economic chambers and their powers have not been clearly defined in Yugoslav writings,[52] and it is possible that they exert a stronger influence than official statements would suggest. Zaninovich concludes that "both the economic associations and trade unions tended to have their top-level bodies dominated by Party members, which in effect 'created an interlocking directorate between the Party and non-Party organizations. The result was to provide the degree of coordination necessary to counter any ill effects that might stem from economic decentralization." [53]

The purely political influence of the League of Communists cannot be neglected. But the League emphasizes the indirect influence of members as individuals on the enterprises, rather than the direct intervention of the party.[54] The party influence through individuals could be significant. In 1958, 27.1 percent of workers' councils members were party members, and 38 percent of the members of management boards were members,[55] a higher proportion than for the working population as a whole.

In general, the extent of political influence through the

52. "Economic Chambers and Cooperative Associations," *Yugoslav Survey* 1, no. 3 (Oct.–Dec. 1960): 325–28.

53. M. George Zaninovich, *The Development of Socialist Yugoslavia* (Baltimore: The Johns Hopkins Press, 1968), p. 81.

54. Hoffman and Neal, p. 244.

55. Ibid., 206. Party membership among the total working population ranged between 10 and 20 per cent, with variations by industry and by geographic region.

party, trade union, economic chambers, and central and local administrative channels is difficult to define. A Yugoslav has stated their functions as those of general supervision.

> This supervision does not entail any formal legal sanction but is confined to social criticism, unobligatory recommendations and similar forms of social assistance aimed at ensuring the appropriate operation of enterprises as organizations that also carry out important work on behalf of society as a whole. . . . They are normally accepted by enterprises . . . although they are not backed up by administrative measures.[56]

Internal sources of influence

Within the limits of the autonomy permitted by these arrangements, management of the enterprise is formally exercised by the workers. The working collective, composed of all the workers in a given enterprise, elects the workers' council (whose membership is about 10 percent of the working collective) which in turn elects the management board. The working collective as a whole meets periodically to discuss the performance of the workers' council. The collective may vote morally binding resolutions recommending specific actions to the workers' council. The collective also has recourse to a legally binding referendum but this has not been used frequently.

The workers' council is the main management body. Its area of jurisdiction is broad: it adopts economic plans, approves statutes about the organization and work of the enterprise, rules about labor relations, sets wages and work norms, distributes enterprise earnings, including net profit to workers' earnings and to various enterprise funds. Its domain is all matters of general policy and all specific questions of labor relations.[57]

56. Rakic, p. 129.
57. "Workers Management," *Yugoslav Survey* 1, no. 2 (Apr.–June 1960): 9–20.

The management board is elected by the workers' council to carry out the more detailed direction of the enterprise activities. It prepares proposals for the consideration of the workers' council and enforces the decisions of that council.

The director manages the current business of the enterprise in accord with the decisions and directives of the workers' council and the management board. The director alone is the legal representative of the enterprise and he alone can make commitments on its behalf. He is also accountable for the legality of enterprise operations.

In principle the division of power among the workers' council, the management board, and the director is clear. The workers' council establishes basic policy; the management board translates policy into specific operational directives; and the director carries them out. In fact, the locus of power within the enterprise no doubt varies with a number of factors.[58] Kolaja in his study of workers' councils in Yugoslavia concluded that the workers' council did have a certain degree of independence from the requests of the commune or council of producers. "There is no doubt, then, that the workers' councils could exercise power, within certain limits. Of course, whether the workers actually had the power within the councils, or whether it was mainly management which acted through the workers' councils, is another issue." [59]

In addition, members of the trade union and the party exert influence within the enterprise. The majority of the labor force belong to the union whose membership includes managerial personnel, as well as production workers. Virtually all members of workers' councils belong to the union. The role of the union within the enterprise is not entirely clear. Many of the functions of labor unions elsewhere such as negotiating work norms, grievance pro-

58. Benjamin Ward, "The Nationalized Firm in Yugoslavia," *American Economic Review* 55, no. 2 (May 1965): 646–52.
59. Kolaja, p. 28.

cedures, vacation scheduling, and so forth, are carried out by the workers' council.[60]

Kolaja distributed a questionnaire to seventy-eight respondents in a factory. (See the accompanying table.) It

Responses to Questionnaire on Influence

	First in influence	Second in influence	Third in influence
Director	27	29	10
Workers' council	45	22	4
Labor Union	2	11	33
League of Communists	4	11	19
Don't know	0	5	12
Total	78	78	78

should be noted that the factory in which he was able to use questionnaires exhibited less party control than the other factory in his sample of two, and these results may not be typical for the economy. One of the questions asked was, "Who has the greatest influence in the enterprise?" [61] "Though the league provided a sort of authorization for the activities of the other organizations, the majority of the respondents in our sample . . . did not consider that it was the most influential authority within the enterprise." [62]

In conclusion, the Yugoslav enterprise appears to be genuinely autonomous in a wide range of economic decisions but this freedom is not absolute. At first glance it resembles the capitalist enterprise subject to government regulation. Overt and explicit interference in the affairs of the enterprise is minimized. However, there are a series

60. Adolf Sturmthal has examined the problem of labor unions and workers' councils in Yugoslavia, Poland, France, and Germany. He found that, when both exist within the enterprise, there usually is not a clear division of function between the two. Adolf Sturmthal, *Workers Councils* (Cambridge: Harvard University Press, 1964).

61. Kolaja, *Workers Councils,* p. 34.

62. Ibid., p. 38.

of checks on enterprise autonomy, and outside political influences further limit the range of choice. Within the enterprise, management is alleged to reside in the organs elected by the workers. The exercise of such rights to manage is difficult to evaluate. This right is not exclusive to the workers, in fact, and it is shared with, or subordinate to, the opinions of the director or the management board. In turn, those individuals are more likely to be union members and party members. Thus the labor union and the party, both of which have clear channels of authority and information from the center in this period, may influence the individuals in positions of greatest authority in the firm. But the implicit nature of the arrangements, the absence of specified channels of command, and the imprecisely delineated relations among the various forces serve to make conclusions hazardous.

Indeed, two major differences distinguish the Soviet-type and the Yugoslav systems of industrial organization and control: (1) the limited explicit controls and the absence of central government channels of authority in Yugoslavia, and (2) the large number of bodies that exert an influence on the affairs of the enterprise. The Yugoslav political system is decentralized and the communal government has considerable authority, although there are also channels for exercising central control over the enterprise. The implicit character of political controls, the reliance on persuasion rather than administrative authority, and the quite real autonomy of the local administrative governmental unit and of the enterprise make it difficult to control the economic system from the center. Benjamin Ward, who has studied the Yugoslav system of industrial organization at length, concluded that "the Yugoslav firm is subject to political pressure from several sources. Because it is often exercised informally, this kind of pressure is very difficult to evaluate, but it is clearly substantial." [63] It is equally

63. Ward, *American Economic Review* 55, no. 2 (May 1965): 646.

difficult to assess whether the political pressures are predominantly central or local.

Although the Yugoslav economic system in the years 1954 to 1960 differed markedly from a Soviet-type system, it would be stretching the point to call it a predominantly market economy of independent enterprises managed by workers. The need to limit market allocation and enterprise independence arose from a number of factors, among them a remaining scepticism about the functioning of the market mechanism, a strong belief that rational development policy required planned allocation of investment funds, and residual doubts about the "social responsibility" of the worker-managed enterprises. The problems that required social control were quite real even if the policy instruments selected did not always promote rational operation.

In a sense, the fifties were the testing ground for the market economy in Yugoslavia. Throughout most of that decade, the Yugoslavs sought to find workable instruments to make the system function. The system did function, despite hindrance, and the scene was set for a new confrontation. The confrontation was between those who were convinced of the ability of the market to make rational decisions, not only within the framework of fixed capacities but also to make investment decisions, and those who were not prepared to entrust the socialist economy to the anarchic market process. In the early sixties a major struggle took place precisely over the limits of the market in a socialist economy.

CHAPTER 6

Plan and Market: The General Issues

Yugoslavs had devoted the first part of the decade after the rejection of the Soviet model to experimentation and pragmatic development. Agreement had apparently been reached on the principles of the economic and political system, and a workable if not totally satisfactory framework for the economy had emerged. The principles of the system were decentralization of production decisions to the enterprises within the limits of existing capacities, central control over the volume and the structure of investment through direct and indirect means, and a certain amount of influence over wage and employment policy of the firms, in part through indirect, political controls.

Radical though these changes had been for a former Soviet-type economy, the need for even this much planning in socialism was soon challenged. The central issue was the role of investment planning and the side issues were the methods of implementing the plans. In contrast to the previous controversy over whether commodity production was consistent with socialism, the level of this debate about plan and market was much higher. Whereas the initial developers of the political and economic system had been primarily political figures, now economists began to turn to analysis of the system.[1] The debate was also significantly

1. "Theoretical research began to develop intensively only when these new relations founded on self-management and commodity production had already developed and become dominant in material production and social relations, which is associated with the appearance of essential political documents in which these new relations were codified." (Jakov Sirotkovic, *Planiranje narodne privrede u jugoslavenskom sistemu samoupravljanja.* Zagreb: Informator, 1966, p. 63.)

more political. The nationality problem, long suppressed under a policy of "Yugoslavianism," began to surface once again.

A brief survey of the sequence of economic events will serve to place the debate over plan and market in context. As one Yugoslav described it, planning from 1952 to 1956 had been on an ad hoc basis, "a complex of different annual political and economic instruments for the current regulation of a free but imperfect market." [2] The principal goals had been to complete certain projects started in the first five-year plan. Once these were completed, it was possible and, indeed, necessary, to turn attention to the longer range planning of Yugoslav development. A five-year plan was completed at the end of 1957 for the years 1957 to 1961. In connection with the drafting of this plan, the economic issues of central planning began to be discussed once again. The Third Congress of the Yugoslav Association of Economists, held in May 1958, was the first large meeting of economists to discuss matters of economic policy.[3]

The second five year plan for 1957 to 1961 was a great success. The Yugoslav economy grew very rapidly. From 1957 to 1961 social product grew at an average annual rate of 12 percent and industrial output at almost 14 percent.[4] In fact, performance was so satisfactory that the plan was declared completed in four years. The Yugoslavs, enthusiastic about the performance of their economic system, prepared a new and ambitious plan for the years 1961 to 1965. Concurrent with the start of the new plan, a number of reforms were introduced at the beginning of 1961, representing an increased emphasis on market forces. That feelings were not unanimous about these reforms was im-

2. Cerne, p. 17.
3. Proceedings of the Conference in *Ekonomist* 11, no. 1–2 (1958): 1–320.
4. *Jugoslavija 1945–1964: statisticki pregled* (Belgrade: Savezni zavod za statistiku, 1965), p. 80. All figures are Yugoslav definition, in constant prices.

mediately apparent. In November 1960, the Federal Institute of Economic Planning presented to economists a paper outlining the five-year plan for 1961 to 1965 and the liberalization measures due to come into effect in January of 1961.[5] The subsequent discussion of the proposals seems to mark the opening of the public debate on the issue of centralization versus decentralization,[6] a debate that gripped Yugoslavia for the next five years.

Starting in 1961, liberalizing reforms were introduced. Changes in the foreign trade system were to bring Yugoslav prices into line with world market prices and to make domestic production more efficient through competition of foreign products on Yugoslav markets. The dinar was devalued; multiple rates of exchange were to be eliminated; and the proportion of imports subject to quantitative restrictions was reduced. Domestically, fiscal reform increased the share of the enterprise earnings that workers could distribute among investment funds, collective consumption, and personal income. Progressive taxes on enterprise incomes were replaced by flat rate taxes to provide greater incentive. In March 1961 the first of a series of changes in the banking and credit system, whose ultimate objective was the transformation of banks from disbursement agents for government agencies into profit-making enterprises, came into effect. All these changes taken together were intended to reduce the scope of arbitrary social control and to expand the role of the market, resulting in greater efficiency, lowered costs, and an increased ability to compete in world markets.

Economic performance in 1961 and 1962 soon brought an end to Yugoslav optimism and fueled the controversy over whether economic liberalization was suitable for

5. *Petogodisnji plan razvoja i privredni sistem* (Belgrade: Savezni zavod za privredno planiranje, 1960).

6. A report of the conference appears in *Ekonomist* 14, no. 1 (1961): 86–128.

Yugoslavia. Social product increased by only 5 percent in 1961 and in 1962; industrial output increased by only 7 percent per year, less than half the rates achieved during the second five-year plan. In addition, prices were rising and the balance of payments situation continued to deteriorate. The economic situation led to extended debates about the causes of the slowdown and the need for economic planning.

During the early sixties, work was also proceeding on a new constitution that represented the stronger position of the liberal factions in Yugoslavia. The constitution ascribed specific functions to political, social, and economic entities and reaffirmed the principles of self-government in each sphere. In other words, economic organizations were to be primarily responsible for decisions about economic matters. Controversy over the principles of the constitution was minimal compared to that aroused by the economic policies that aimed at implementing the constitutional principles. The constitution itself was adopted in 1963, after extensive discussion at all levels in Yugoslavia.

In this connection, the Yugoslav Association of Economists called a conference in December 1962 to discuss the implications of the new constitution.[7] Influenced by the economic difficulties of the years 1961 and 1962, many of the participants pointed to the negative consequences of the "shrinking of social controls." [8] Critics were particularly concerned about the disintegration of national economic unity, the unequal rates of regional development, and about what they regarded as excessive wage distributions by the enterprises. They pointed out that they had predicted precisely these consequences of liberalization at the November 1960 meeting just two years before. The critics concluded that more, not less, planning was needed and more, not less, political guidance.

7. A report of the conference is in *Ekonomist* 15, no. 3–4 (1962): 439–517.
8. Ibid., p. 440.

The December 1962 meeting proved to be a warmup for the more heated session that took place at a conference held in Zagreb, January 17–19, 1963, which was devoted specifically to the problems of the economic system. The conference was sponsored by the Yugoslav Association of Economists and the Federal Planning Bureau. Two studies provided the basis for discussion. One was prepared by Branko Horvat and associates and known because of the color of its cover as the Yellow Book.[9] The other study by a group of Zagreb economists was known as the White Book.[10] The former paper found the immediate causes of the slowdown in economic growth in the defects in the investment structure and in hasty application of new policies (both the liberalization measures of 1961 and the credit restrictions of 1961 to 1962 aimed at curtailing price increases). The latter study argued that the economy functioned poorly precisely because of too much centralization, poor decisions made at the center, inadequate freedom of initiative for the enterprise, and the faulty functioning of the market mechanism due to excessive intervention.

In the discussion that followed, the conflict between the centralizers and the decentralizers was very sharp.[11] The decentralizers argued that economic difficulties were attributable to overcentralization, mismanagement, and

9. B. Colanovic, D. Dimitrijevic, V. Frankovic, B. Horvat, I. Perisin, V. Pertot, V. Stipetic, S. Popovic, V. Trickovic, and F. Vasic, *Uzroci i karakteristike privrednih kretanja u 1961. i 1962. godini* (Belgrade: Savezni zavod za privredno planiranje, Dokumentacioni-analiticki materiali 7, 1962). An extensive summary appeared: Sime Djodan and Uros Dujsin, "Uzroci i karakteristike privrednih kretanja u 1961. i 1962. godini," *Ekonomiski pregled* 14, no. 8 (1963): 657–97.

10. S. Dabcevic-Kucar, D. Gorupic, R. Lang, M. Mesaric, I. Perisin, J. Sirotkovic, and V. Stipetic, *O nekim problemima privrednog sistema*. It subsequently appeared in *Ekonomiski pregled* 14, no. 3–5 (1963): 145–467.

Vladimir Bakaric, secretary of the Croatian communist party, considered himself a "co-initiator" of this study. ("Zakon vrijednosti, planiranje i objektivna odredjenost stope privrednog rasta," *Ekonomist* 16, no. 1 (1963): 224–37.)

11. Presented in full in *Ekonomist* 16, no. 1 (1963): 1–280.

meddling, the "legacies" of a central planning psychology.[12] The solution was to free the enterprises from the morass of regulation and to allow them to make decisions, including investment decisions, on the basis of market forces. In some versions, however, decentralization was used to express an opposition not to planning as such, but to planning done at the national center instead of at the republican or local level.[13] "Polycentric" planning with a possibility of a much enhanced economic role for the republics was suggested. The centralizers were also of two types. Some attributed Yugoslavia's difficulties to too little central planning and the anarchic responses of the uncontrolled enterprises and, accordingly, advocated more central planning and greater control over the enterprises. Others accepted the existing limits of the market economy and believed that central planning of investment continued to be necessary, but they advocated the use of more sound development strategies than had previously been employed.

The debate about plan and market, which continued until the Economic Reform of 1965, had many complex elements. Interpretation of the economic content of this debate is difficult because the participants used economic language to state positions on essentially political issues. There was a serious regional struggle going on in these years concerning the nature and location of political power, a struggle that had many economic aspects. Because of the vast differences among regions in the levels of development and because of the intense national feelings, no

12. Neuberger traces the legacies of central planning, especially the psychological and institutional legacies that leave a residual perfectionist bias, a misunderstanding of the market mechanism, and a penchant for intervention to solve all difficulties. Egon Neuberger, *The Legacies of Central Planning* (Santa Monica, Calif.: The Rand Corporation, RM 5530PR, 1968) especially pp. 32–46.

13. Rudolf Bicanic, "Centralisticko, decentralisticko ili policentricno planiranje," *Ekonomist* 16, no. 2 (1963): 456–69.

fully satisfactory development strategy for the nation as a whole had ever been devised,[14] nor, given the differences, was it likely that such a policy could be devised.

Recognizing the difficulties in interpreting this debate about the roles of plan and market in socialism, a division of labor will be made. The present chapter will examine the general economic issues of plan and market. The Yugoslav debate dealt with two major problems: the changing needs for planning at various levels of economic development and the forms of plan implementation compatible with self-managed enterprises. The next chapter will consider the particular Yugoslav context of the debate.

PLANNING AND THE MARKET FOR
ECONOMIC DEVELOPMENT

The Marxist attitude over the years had been plan *versus* market. The Yugoslavs had slowly freed themselves of the dichotomy of this approach and accepted the principle of plan *and* market. Given the desire to combine plan and market, the Yugoslavs had to ascertain what combination of aggregative and selective controls was most suitable for economic development. Organizational possibilities ranged from complete centralization of all decisions and a continual flow of administrative orders, on the one hand, to a market economy with purely aggregative controls on the other. In addition, the Yugoslavs required a strategy for economic development. Nor was development the sole objective. Yugoslavs have a distinct preference for worker-managed enterprises. They therefore had to establish whether the methods suitable for attaining economic development were compatible with the commitment to independent worker-managed enterprises.

14. Paul Shoup, *Communism and the Yugoslav National Question* (New York: Columbia University Press, 1968), especially chaps. 5 and 6.

No model had existed for the Yugoslav economic system. The discussion in the West in the thirties and forties over the economic possibilities of socialism did not deal with the problems specific to economic development in a backward economy and was not considered highly relevant for the Yugoslav economic problems.[15] Most economists agreed with Samardzija, who stated that "the discussion about the socialist economy among Western European economists, which took place after 1920, did not have, and still does not have, any direct influence on economic practice nor on the leading theoretical conceptions of economists in socialist countries." [16]

Yugoslavs are not sharply divided on the ultimate objectives of their economic system. Some tend to view industrialization and growth almost as ends in themselves,[17] while others see the objectives purely as the better satisfaction of human needs, both social and individual. The majority maintains that the ultimate objective is the satisfaction of human wants and that the means to satisfaction lies only through rapid industrialization and expansion of productive capacities.

Marxist theoreticians were always in agreement about the basic goal of socialist social production. According to them it is the maximal satisfaction of the needs of the entire society relative to the attained level of economic growth; in other words, the uninterrupted increase of satisfaction of human needs is attained by

15. There were a number of studies of the economics of socialism. Among them, see Lange, *Economic Theory of Socialism;* H. D. Dickenson, *The Economics of Socialism* (London: Oxford University Press, 1939); W. C. Roper, Jr., *The Problem of Pricing in a Socialist State* (Cambridge: Harvard University Press, 1931); Abba P. Lerner, *The Economics of Control* (New York: MacMillan Company, 1944).

16. Milos Samardzija, "Problem cena u socijalistickoj privredi," *Nasa stvarnost* 14, no. 12 (Dec. 1960): 488.

17. Radmila Stojanovic, *Teorija privrednog razvoja u socijalizmu,* 2d ed. (Belgrade: Naucna knjiga, 1964), p. 7.

the uninterrupted growth and improvement of socialist production.[18]

Chief responsibility for specifying the major objectives of society fall to the plan. Many Yugoslavs treated the scope of the plan broadly, and there was general agreement with Oskar Lange's postwar interpretation of the minimum requirements of the plan in socialism, according to which the socialist plan must determine not only the rates of investment but also the distribution of investment among major sectors of the economy.[19] Others, disillusioned by the actions of the central planners, doubted that planning could be carried out competently enough to justify its use.

Optimum rate of investment

It does not suffice merely to say that investment is determined by the plan. How are the planners to establish the rate of investment?

There are two possibilities for establishing the rate of investment in a socialist economy. If the objectives of the system include both consumption and growth, and if there is a conflict between consumption and growth, they are competing ends and a political choice must be made. This

18. Ibid., p. 5.

19. In 1936 Lange had maintained that, in the socialist economy, the plan need only determine the rate of investment (*Economic Theory of Socialism*). After some years of experience with the socialist economy in Poland, he altered his views about the minimum requirements of the plan, at least in the initial stages. This shift in plan requirements is presumably associated with a shift in focus to organizing the economy for development.

The requirements of the plan in socialism are, according to Lange: "First, the division of national income between accumulation and consumption. Second, the distribution of investments among different branches of the economy. The first determines the general rates of economic growth, the second determines the direction of development. . . . This is therefore the minimum requirement of the plan." Oskar Lange, *The Political Economy of Socialism* (The Hague: Institute of Social Studies, Publications on Social Change, 1958), pp. 20–21.

seems to correspond to Yugoslav practice, in which the leaders make the basic political and economic decisions about the rate and distribution of investment and the size of collective consumption. In some years planners presented several alternative plans to the political leadership for approval. The alternatives do not specify a complete listing of the marginal rates of transformation among the various types of objectives, but they do consider several combinations of the projected rates of economic growth and the associated levels of per capita consumption.[20] Leaders chose among the alternatives that variant which corresponded to their own preferences or their readings of the political climate. This method of deciding the investment rate appears to work as long as the leaders are able to agree among themselves about this choice. Some Yugoslavs criticized the arbitrariness of this approach that failed to provide any criteria for determining the rates of investment,[21] and the problem was acute in the context of Yugoslav national politics.

The difficulty inherent in political decisions when consensus is lacking made attractive the search for an objectively determined rate of investment that would be free of interpretation, arbitrary decisions, or subjectivism. Among those who sought an objective standard are Branko Horvat and Aleksandar Bajt. Bajt's article appeared in early 1958,[22] and Horvat's article a little later the same year.[23] There were some similarities in approach, in that Bajt pointed both to the positive effects of investment on out-

20. Organisation for Economic Cooperation and Development, *Socialist Federal Republic of Yugoslavia* (Paris, 1964), p. 23.

21. Rudolf Bicanic, for example, criticized Uvalic for his failure to provide any criteria for the determination of the rates of investment or the division of income between consumption and investment. *Ekonomist* 16, no. 2 (1963): 456–69.

22. Aleksandar Bajt, "Optimalna velicina investicija iz nacionalnog dohotka," *Ekonomist* 11, no. 1–2 (1958): 79–91.

23. Branko Horvat, "The Optimum Rate of Investment," *Economic Journal* 68, no. 272 (Dec. 1958): 747–67.

put and to the negative effects operating via consumption to lower the intensity with which labor works. Horvat's article was much more far-reaching.[24]

Horvat's argument about the optimum rate of investment has two parts.[25] The first is to establish the upper limit to investment consistent with maximizing output over some time interval (say one generation). The second is to show that maximizing production over that interval is equivalent to maximizing consumption and, if consumption is taken as an index of welfare, then it is equivalent to maximizing welfare. He ultimately refers to a referendum by consumers on alternative patterns of consumption to establish their preferences. If consumers vote for the high-growth profile of consumption, the rate of investment that maximizes output also maximizes welfare and there is no conflict between growth and the preferred stream of consumption.

In the first part of the argument Horvat proceeds more or less conventionally. Output is a function of the factor supplies, including capital stock. Increase in output depends on the increments to capital, or investment. But the marginal efficiency of investment declines as the rate of investment increases because of the limited absorptive ca-

24. Horvat is one of the most interesting economists in Yugoslavia; his work will be mentioned in various connections. He has a doctorate in economics from the University of Zagreb and one from the University of Manchester. He travels frequently to Western economic gatherings and has lectured at a number of universities in the United States. Horvat considers himself a Marxist but his training gives him a fluency in Western analysis and an ability to express himself in terms familiar to the Western economists that most Yugoslavs do not possess. This sometimes makes it difficult for Yugoslavs to understand him.

25. The article discussed in the text forms a chapter in Horvat's major book, *Towards a Theory of Planned Economy* (Belgrade: Jugoslav Institute of Economic Research, 1964). Benjamin Ward has written a very perceptive review of Horvat's book, in which he appraises Horvat's work as a whole. Benjamin Ward, "Marxism-Horvatism: A Yugoslav Theory of Socialism," *American Economic Review* 57, no. 3 (June 1967): 509–23.

pacity of the economy. First, as the rate of investment increases at any point in time, the amount of product available for consumption decreases. Reductions in absolute consumption usually have a bad effect on the psychological attitudes of the population. If the rate of investment is sufficiently high, decreases in consumption levels also affect the health and the strength of the workers. For both reasons, as the rate of investment increases, the productivity of the workers decreases and with it the additional output obtainable from a given increment of investment declines. Second, organizational strains in the system make it difficult to absorb large increases of investment and to finish various projects. Third, knowledge is scarce. Successive increases in investment have less expert knowledge available with which to carry out the investment and hence are less intelligently applied and less productive. As a result of all these factors, there is a limit on the quantity of effective investment at any one time. "The optimum rate of investment" is that rate at which "social marginal efficiency of investment with respect to the period of twenty to twenty-five years becomes zero." [26] If the rate of investment exceeds this, output would have been greater with a smaller investment. In other words, the investment must pay for itself within twenty to twenty-five years, that is, the marginal productivity of the last project undertaken must be at least 4 to 5 percent.

The second part of his argument is to demonstrate that maximizing production over a generation is identical with maximizing consumption over that same period. With a numerical example he shows that, if the share of investment in total output is increased by only one or two percentage points a year (which amounts to a 12 to 18 percent

26. Horvat, "The Optimum Rate of Investment Reconsidered," *Economic Journal* 75, no. 299 (Sept. 1965): 575. In this note Horvat modified his statement somewhat from the initial version, taking account of certain ambiguities pointed out, among others, by A. K. Sen, "On Optimizing the Rate of Saving," *Economic Journal* 71, no. 283 (Sept. 1961): 479–96.

annual increase in investment itself), and if the capital-output ratio remains constant, several interesting results follow. I shall return to these in a moment. But first it is necessary to examine Horvat's assumption that the marginal capital-output ratio is constant, both as a function of the rate of increase of investment in the range considered (12 to 18 percent per year) and as a function of the ratio of investment to total social product considered (up to 35 percent). Ward notes the following evidence, which fails to support Horvat's assumption: [27] (1) in the NATO countries from 1950 to 1963 rising investment ratios (especially those above 20 percent and rising) had some tendency to be associated with higher marginal capital-output ratios, some of which were above 4.0, and (2) the East European countries (excluding Rumania and Albania) had high investment ratios and high marginal gross capital-output ratios (5.6 average) for the period 1951 to 1964, and the capital-output ratios tended to rise as the investment ratios rose. On the other hand, the Japanese experience in the fifties and sixties with gross investment rates of 30 to 40 percent of GNP suggest that high growth rates can accompany high investment rates. Because it is difficult to reach any firm conclusion on the realism of Horvat's assumptions, I shall follow his assumptions and then note what modifications will be necessary in his conclusions if the marginal capital-output ratio rises rather than remains constant.

Horvat argues that, under his assumptions, the following results occur: (1) after ten years the economy will have attained that investment rate at which further increase in the investment rate is not possible without generating a marginal efficiency of investment less than zero. (2) Consumption at no point declines. (3) For the first ten years, consumption grows more slowly than if there were no increase in investment ratios but the maximum lag is six

27. Ward, *American Economic Review* 57, no. 3 (June 1967): 514–15.

percent, equivalent to about one year's increase; thus the cost of significantly raising the investment rate is for consumption to lag about one year or less behind for a maximum of ten years. (4) After the first ten years, consumption in the economy with higher rates of investment is higher in absolute volume and grows much more rapidly than in the country whose initial investment rate has remained unchanged.

If the marginal capital-output ratio rises, then the increase in output would be slower in forthcoming and the ratio of investment at which mei = zero would be reached at a lower ratio. The first result means that the time period in which consumption lagged behind would be longer (and consumption could even dip downward). The second result would mean that the growth rate after attaining the maximum ratio of investment would be lower and there would be a lesser increase in consumption later on to offset today's reduction. At the same time, a lower maximum rate of investment would mean that the rate of consumption was higher. As a result of these changes, growth could not be obtained as cheaply as Horvat suggests, and the consumers might reject the higher growth pattern of consumption. In this case the conflict between consumption and growth is very real.

The final part of Horvat's argument is that maximizing consumption over a generation maximizes welfare. Horvat argues that the majority of consumers would prefer such a time path: for the sacrifice of one year's increment in consumption, the returns after ten years are enormous—and for those who do not, there is always the possibility of intertemporal transfers among consumers through loans. He believes that consumers given the choice of alternative growth patterns in a referendum (the choice cannot appear as an option if individual decisions govern the rate of investment) would select the higher consumption-production path.

Therefore the socialist society that seeks to maximize consumption should maximize production. Given this co-incidence, there is no "growth versus consumption" con-flict that requires the choice of plan variants by political authorities, but an objectively determined rate of invest-ment that maximizes output and consumption and, if Horvat is correct on the choice which consumers would make, maximizes welfare as well.

Allocation of investment funds

Given a rate of investment, we find that the task is to allocate the investment funds. A brief review of Yugoslav practice in this respect highlights the issues that econo-mists have discussed. Prior to the reforms of 1963 to 1965, investment funds arose from the federally controlled Gen-eral Investment Fund (GIF) consisting of capital tax rev-enues and loan repayments; from the funds of the repub-lics, districts, and communes; and from the funds of enter-prises (both amortization funds and investment from re-tained earnings). The GIF funds were allocated centrally to economic sectors and regions and, exceptionally, to specific investment projects. The allocation was made, after considering forecasts for the use of funds not under direct federal control, to attain overall sectoral and re-gional investment patterns desired. The quantities of capi-tal available to each sector thus expressed the leaders' preferences and their interpretations of the requirements of economic development. Within each sector, GIF funds were distributed among potential users through the bank-ing system, at least partially on the basis of market criteria. The effect of these arrangements, as noted in a previous chapter, was that the center controlled virtually all invest-ment.

Accordingly, criteria were necessary to allocate these in-vestment funds. Here there were important differences of opinion. Part of these differences stemmed from conflicting views on the problems of regional development. Apart from such differences, which will be considered in the next chapter, there were three views on the allocation of investment resources. Some authors held to the priority of Department I (means of production) over Department II (consumer goods) as the basic principle for the socialist society. Others proposed a unitary capital market. The majority advocated central allocation among sectors, based on forecasts of final demand and changes in productivity but without much elaboration of the criteria to be employed. There could be capital markets within each sector.

Priority of Department I

Marx's scheme of reproduction developed in the second volume of *Capital* points out that the size of the producer goods sector determines the economy's capacity for investment. Marx's model can be used to demonstrate the relationship between the structure of the economy and potential rates of growth. In a closed economy the ability of an economy to expand its capital is limited by the size of the investment goods sector.[28] Reliance on market forces to expand the size of the capital goods sector normally means that that sector will expand relatively slowly as a result of derived demand or technological change and not necessarily at the rate desired by planners. It may be more effective to *start* the development process with the expansion of the investment goods sector or the heavy industry base. For these reasons it is possible to argue that the under-

28. If the economy chooses to import capital equipment, then it would want to expand the size of its export goods sector. But foreign trade does not solve the problem of development. It raises further questions about what to export, the elasticity of demand in foreign markets for the export good, etc. In any event, the Yugoslavs made little reference in their theoretical discussions to the possibilities of accomplishing major economic development through foreign trade.

developed economy in the initial stages of economic development may find that to rely heavily on the market mechanism to allocate investment results in supply bottlenecks and fails to attain the desired ends as rapidly as possible. Of course, this does not mean that arbitrary planning of investment allocation is necessarily an improvement.

The standard Marxist development strategy received due attention in Yugoslavia. Nikola Cobeljic is a strong advocate of the priority of heavy industry and the capital goods sector.[29] He takes issue with the Western, static approach to development that accepts factor endowments as given and adjusts to them, rather than try to change the factor endowments themselves. Socialist economies, he argues, develop through a unified strategy involving high rates of investment, high organic content of capital, a high technical level, and the priority of the capital goods sector. In general, heavy industry should be stressed because of important forward (supply) linkages. The machine tool industry must have priority over other sectors in the distribution of investment funds because investments in the machine tool industry have a continuing effect on development, permitting a continual increase in capital goods and hence growth, while investments in the consumer goods sector have only a one-time effect on increasing output. "From this difference in effect on the acceleration of economic growth follows the entire significance of choice of the correct sequence in the development of productive branches." [30] The conclusion that the machine tool industry should be developed first appears relevant if investment rates and hence growth rates are in fact limited by the capacities of the capital goods sector; this is most likely to occur at early stages of development.

29. Nikola Cobeljic, "Kriteriji izbora strukture investicija i mehanizam trzista," *Ekonomist* 16, no. 1 (1963): 215–20.

30. Ibid., p. 217.

Radmila Stojanovic is another staunch defender of the primacy of Department I.[31] She incorporates technical progress into her argument and concludes that the priority of Department I is general and not restricted to the early stages of development. She selects four examples that she believes exhaust the relevant cases. She recognizes that there are other cases that do not require the more rapid growth of Department I, but she considers such cases irrelevant.

In her first example the rate of accumulation, technology, and labor productivity all remain constant. In this instance, there is no change in the relative shares of the two departments, although there is economic growth. She then considers economic development of an extensive type, characterized by an increase in the rate of accumulation without any change in technical equipment or labor productivity. This economy requires that Department I grow more rapidly to sustain the increased rate of accumulation.

The next two cases involve intensive development, in which technology and labor productivity improve, in one case with a constant rate of accumulation and, in the other, a rising rate of accumulation. According to Stojanovic, intensive development involves:

1. Increase in the organic content of capital, which means an increase in the total mass of applied embodied labor relative to the total mass of applied live labor.

2. Increase in the technical equipment of labor (quantity of means of production per worker).

3. Increase in the productivity of labor based on new techniques, hence a decline in the total quantity of labor per unit of product but, regarded as a whole, a

31. Radmila Stojanovic, *Teorija privrednog razvoja u socijalizmu*. See also Slavka Rankovic, "Yugoslavia's Economic Development," *Socialist Thought and Practice*, no. 14 (Apr.–June 1964): 45–63.

more rapid decline of live than embodied labor per unit of output.[32]

Her argument depends on demonstrating that with a constant rate of accumulation Department I must grow relatively more rapidly than Department II because of the nature of technological progress.

> Maintaining the same rate of accumulation, Department I would expand in relation to Department II to the extent necessary to unfold the process of expanded reproduction with the same rate of accumulation while at the same time ensuring a certain technical progress and increase in the organic content of capital.[33]

The logic is not entirely clear. She appears to conclude from the fact that the capital-labor ratios increase (because capital increases more rapidly than labor and because of the labor-saving bias of technology) that Department I (capital goods) must increase more rapidly than Department II (consumer goods). This follows only if personal incomes remain the same.[34] Given technological

32. Stojanovic, p. 187.

33. Ibid., p. 188.

34. This point was made by Horvat in a critique of an earlier article, in which she presented basically the same argument. Branko Horvat, "Jos jednom o zakonu preteznog porasta i odeljka drustvene proizvodnje," *Ekonomist* 14, no. 1 (1961): 32–39.

Actually the requirement is less restrictive than that. If we let C_1 be the capital equipment (means of production); C_2 the materials (objects of production); L the live labor; O the total output; m the consumption per unit of live labor; d the annual rate of depreciation of capital, here equal to one for convenience; and g the rate of net investment, then her argument appears to be as follows:

$$\frac{C_1 + C_2}{L} \quad \text{is rising} \tag{1}$$

$$C_1/L \quad \text{is rising} \tag{2}$$

$$O/L \quad \text{is rising more rapidly than} \quad \frac{O}{C_1 + C_2} \tag{3}$$

progress, we find that it is quite possible to have rising capital-labor ratios along with increasing total output, constant rates (but increasing volume) of investment, and rising personal consumption per unit of labor input. Empirical evidence shows that this is certainly a "relevant" case. It would seem that her attempt to establish the general primacy of Department I over Department II is not convincing.

Sirotkovic attacked the question of the two departments somewhat differently.[35] He did not enter into the debate as to whether a case can be made in a closed economy for the priority of Department I. He argued instead that one cannot neglect the opportunities of foreign trade.[36] He also seemed to refer to changes in the structure of final demand that can cause a shift toward items with different organic content of capital, and hence with different effects on the relations of the two departments.[37] Third, in the

---

From these three propositions she argues that D_I/D_{II} must be increasing. Now, since the output of Department I $= C_1 + C_2 + g \cdot O$, and that of Department II $= L \cdot m$, the question is whether

$$\frac{C_1 + C_2 + g \cdot O}{L \cdot m} \qquad \text{or alternatively} \qquad \frac{1}{m}\left(\frac{C_1 + C_2}{L} + g \frac{O}{L}\right)$$

is increasing. If m were constant, then because $(C_1 + C_2)/L$ and O/L are both rising, we know that D_I/D_{II} would have to rise. The critical question, then, is whether $(C_1 + C_2 + g \cdot O)/L$ is rising more or less rapidly than m, the consumption per unit of live labor. This is an empirical question to be resolved (for market economies) or a policy issue to be decided (for planned economies), but there appears to be no *logical* case to be made for it.

Further, if m rises at the same annual rate as productivity of labor, a not unlikely circumstance, then for Department I to grow relative to Department II, the annual increase in $(C_1 + C_2 + g \cdot O)/L$ must exceed the increase in O/L. Since g (O/L) rises at the same rate as O/L, the annual increase in $(C_1 + C_2)/L$ must exceed the annual increase in O/L. Alternatively, the ratio $[(C_1 + C_2)/L]/(O/L)$ must rise, but this implies that $(C_1 + C_2)/O$ must rise, which contradicts her proposition (3), according to which $(C_1 + C_2)/O$ must fall.

35. Sirotkovic, *Planiranje narodne privrede.*
36. Ibid., p. 63.
37. Ibid., 69–71.

light of the higher degrees of fabrication associated with industrialization, it is necessary to distinguish between the means of labor (capital goods) and the objects of labor (intermediate production goods), and to be clear whether one is talking about the more rapid increase of intermediate goods to final goods in an industrializing, specializing economy, the increase of the capital goods share, or both.[38] As a result of these considerations, Sirotkovic rejected any a priori conclusions about the relative rates of growth of any individual department as the basis for planning.[39]

Unitary capital markets

Two authors departed from the notion of central allocation of funds among sectors and emphasized the merits of a capital market. Both recognized that situations would arise in which there would have to be corrections to decisions taken by individual firms on the basis of market criteria. Horvat, in his study of the planned economy, advocated a single capital market. Enterprises would borrow funds from the state banking system on a competitive basis.[40] Todorovic vaguely suggested the same idea. "All new social means for production . . . must be distributed according to general criteria and competition with the objective of placing them in the most efficient projects within the framework of the planned structure of production." [41] A few pages later he expanded this notion and suggested a uniform market for capital. Speaking of a proposal to permit enterprises to place idle funds in the bank and to receive interest on them, he said that "such a mechanism should also enable the free movement of social 'capital' to

38. Ibid.
39. Milan Mesaric also treats the dominance of Department I with considerable scepticism. (*Problemi privrednog razvoja i planiranja*, Zagreb: Ekonomski institut, 1966.)
40. Horvat, *Towards a Theory of Planned Economy*, pp. 62, 227.
41. Mijalko Todorovic, "O nekim pitanjima naseg privrednog sistema," part IV, *Socijalizam* 6, no. 1 (Jan. 1963): 20.

overcome local borders, to contribute to the formation of a *unitary social capital market* for the entire socialist community, which guarantees the most rational distribution of means of production and labor in the structural sense and in efficiency of utilization." [42]

> The market, and the corresponding form of economic price, is a *sensitive seismograph* which registers each oscillation around the balancing point between production and consumption, i.e., between supply and demand. It is, through a price of this sort, at the same time a *mechanism that automatically guides* new productive forces and accumulation in the right direction.[43]

There were also important differences in the schemes of the two authors. In Horvat's model there is apparently a relatively limited role for investments by enterprises from retained earnings, while such investments play a major role in the Todorovic scheme.

Other authors attacked the concept of a capital market. Lavrac cited the following arguments about the inadequacy of market criteria for investment decisions: [44] present prices are not a sufficient guide to future demand and supply relations; the optimal size of the production unit might exceed that offered by the present size of the market; competitive response to market indicators might result in unnecessary duplication of facilities.[45] These points appear to be based on the reasoning noted in Chapter 2

42. Ibid., p. 22. Emphasis added.

43. Todorovic, "Some Questions of Our Economic System," *Socialist Thought and Practice*, no. 9 (Jan. 1963): 41. This is an abridged translation of parts I–III of his article "O nekim pitanjima naseg privrednog sistema," in six parts; I–III, *Socijalizam* 5, no. 6 (Dec. 1962): 3–69; part IV, *Socijalizam* 6, no. 1 (Jan. 1963): 3–38; part V, *Socijalizam* 6, no. 2–3 (Feb.–Mar. 1963): 3–58; part VI, *Socijalizam* 7, no. 11–12 (Nov.–Dec. 1964): 1387–1444.

44. Ivan Lavrac, "Plan i trziste," *Ekonomist* 16, no. 1, (1963): 203–08.

45. Ibid.

above about the dynamic inefficiency of the market response when the structure of demand is significantly altered.[46]

Planned allocation

The most common position among Yugoslavs was planned allocation of investments according to various criteria. Strasimir Popovic published a volume on the choice of productive structure that tried to establish criteria for determining the optimal productive structure.[47] He ranked industrial activities according to social purposefulness based on several characteristics: total resources required per unit of accumulation; social product per employed person; inventories as a share of output; balance of exports and imports; coefficient of working capital; and share of imported raw materials.[48] He ranked industrial

46. Some Western economists have argued the same point at greater length. Alexander Erlich has argued that, even if the central planners take the "large decisions" about the rate of investment and establish broad sectoral priorities, it may not suffice for the remaining decisions to be taken on the basis of prices that reflect relative scarcities. The process of rapid economic development generates a pervasive but not uniform condition of excess demand. If the elasticity of supply is low, there are bottlenecks; excess capacities appear elsewhere in the system. The more drastic the change in the structure of final demand, the more acute are the sectoral disproportions.

Fiscal policies alone may limit excess demand, but purely aggregative controls cannot eliminate sectoral discrepancies or transfer resources at an optimal rate. Under such circumstances, individualistic decisions may be inefficient and more efficient allocation might be made on the basis of information about the industry or the economy as a whole. This would mean reaching decisions on the basis of other than current market price information; it might also require limiting enterprise autonomy and, certainly, limiting profitability as the sole criterion of investment during the stage of rapid, discontinuous development. "Development Strategy and Planning: The Soviet Experience," in *National Economic Planning*, Max F. Millikan, ed. (New York: National Bureau of Economic Research, 1967), pp. 233–72.

47. Strasimir Popovic, *Izbor proizvodne strukture* (Belgrade: Institut drustvenih nauka, 1966).

48. Ibid., pp. 88, 89.

activities first by giving weights to these characteristics. He then classified activities by giving each activity a mark of good, fair, or poor for each of the several characteristics, then surveying the results for those activities that ranked "good," "fair," or "poor" in most respects. He found both methods produced a similar ranking of the social purposefulness of different industrial activities.

Others sought to derive the structure of investment mainly from the estimate of the composition of future demand. Jelic argued that planning could proceed only in this manner.[49] Market prices and market research must both be used to allocate within sectors and to establish broad distribution among sectors.[50] Planning from demand back to supply was quite different from the a priori principles of investment allocation such as the priority of Department I. Empirical work on demand estimation was proceeding throughout this period.[51]

Todorovic advocated heavy reliance on prices and market indicators, whose influence was represented by a single financial criterion. "Once the purpose of the planned investments has been established and the direction of the investment, then from the viewpoint of the wider community whose needs and tasks are fulfilled by the investment fund, this criterion can only be . . . according to the maximum rate of profit."[52] This appears to contradict his

49. Borivoje Jelic and Albin Orthaber, "Some Characteristic Features of Economic Planning in Yugoslavia," in United Nations, Department of Economic and Social Affairs, *Planning for Economic Development*, vol. 2, part 2, Centrally Planned Economies (New York: United Nations, 1965), p. 246. See also Jelic, "Some Problems of Planning Systems," ibid., 261–66.

50. Borivoje Jelic, *Sistem planiranja u jugoslovenskoj privredi* (Belgrade: Ekonomska biblioteka, 1962), chap. 8.

51. See Vidosav Trickovic, "Strukturne promene u licnoj potrosnji s posebnim osvrtom na rezultate ispitivanja porodicnih budzeta," *Ekonomist* 13, no. 3 (1960): 427–58; Berislav Sefer, "Metodoloske karakteristike planiranja licne potrosnje," *Ekonomist* 14, no. 2 (1961): 253–65; Alica Wertheimer-Baletic, "O nekim aspektima utjecaja ekonomsko-demografskih faktora na formiranje obujma i strukture licne potrosnje," *Ekonomist* 20, no. 1–2 (1967): 246–49.

52. Todorovic, *Socijalizam* 6, no. 1 (Jan. 1963): 7–8.

preferences noted above for a unitary socialist market for capital. But he qualified his views on the sectoral allocation in a manner suggesting an opportunity cost approach, in which social costs and benefits are appraised.

> If the plan, for instance, "says" that additional investments must be made and new jobs created in railway transport . . . without the railways yielding any additional surplus, or yielding less than would be the case if investments were made in some other branch, then the reason for investing that labor in railways must be known, i.e., what does the community get (and where?) as an indirect equivalent. . . . This must be known.[53]

The rate of investment and its allocation are the heart of development policy. Yugoslav practice in allocating investment funds represented the belief that the initial stages of socialist development require planning. The Yugoslavs did not analyze criteria for investment allocation at a high level of economic sophistication but they touched on most of the real problems involved. Despite deficiencies in their logic, they adopted a method of allocation that was potentially consistent with their objectives of rapid economic growth and with the principle of competition among enterprises within sectors. This arrangement permitted political determination of the overall structure and was viable as long as the political leaders could agree on the allocation of investment by sector and by region. When they could not, this arrangement began to break down.[54]

---

53. Todorovic, *Socialist Thought and Practice*, no. 9 (Jan. 1963): 49.

54. In addition, as Bajt has pointed out, the Yugoslavs have been concerned with the problem of distribution in the socialist economy at the expense of giving adequate attention to the problem of stabilization and other macroeconomic problems. Aleksandar Bajt, "Decentralized Decision-making Structure in the Yugoslav Economy," *Economics of Planning* 7, no. 1 (1967): 73–85.

IMPLEMENTATION OF THE PLAN

Yugoslavs had dual objectives, an organizational pattern, on the one hand, and a vision of socialist rational development and equality on the other. The dual nature of the objectives created ambiguities about ends and means. It was not always clear whether the organizational pattern was an end in itself or a means for attaining the socialist objectives. To the extent that the workers' management was an end, this posed limits on the instruments that could be used to attain other social goals. This dilemma, given some attention during the discussion of the economic reforms, assumed greater significance later, when sharp differences in the concepts of socialism began to emerge. It will be considered again in Chapter 10.

Independent worker-managed enterprises

The preference for independent, worker-managed enterprises is based on a number of considerations. Some authors, regardless of their attitudes about the relative merits of planned versus market methods of allocation, accepted the independent enterprises under worker management as desirable in and of themselves. The economic experiment is closely tied to a political philosophy concerning the withering away of the state and alienation. Decentralization of decision making in work and political affairs means the elimination of bureaucracy and provides greater economic and political democracy. These aspects of the system continued to play an important role in the arguments of political leaders. The concept of worker-producers directing their own affairs is equally important to the new Marxist humanists.[55] These philosophers show an

---

55. But see Chap. 10 for some other implications of Marxist humanism for the economic organization.

acute concern for alienation of the individual in contemporary society and some see in workers' management a means to end that alienation.[56]

Additional economic and noneconomic reasons were offered in support of worker-managed enterprises. Horvat argued that workers' control over production is inevitable since it is more efficient than the historically antecedent form of state capitalist bureaucracy.[57] State capitalism (which may be regarded either as the last stage of capitalism or the first stage of socialism) had developed because it was more rational than private capitalist organization. It operates on the bureaucratic principles of hierarchy, subordination, and obedience.

Workers' control over production is inevitable, according to Horvat, for three reasons. First, the bureaucratic method of state capitalism, which involves long lines of control and information, is dysfunctional. Decentralized economic organization offers greater efficiency of information and a better incentive mechanism than bureaucratic command. Further, the basic allocation principle of decentralized market socialism is full cost pricing which, Horvat argues at some length, is an adequate basis for the vast majority of economic decisions.[58]

Second, not only is decentralized organization more efficient. The decentralized units should be managed by

56. Daniel Bell has suggested that there are two paths leading from Marx's concept of alienation, namely exploitation and dehumanization. Most Marxists concentrated on the first concept and sought to remedy it by the elimination of the capitalist ownership of property. The second path was less elaborated and followed a different tradition, often visualizing the solution in some form of workers' councils. The Yugoslavs rejoin the two strands of the problem. Their organizational pattern is designed to eliminate the dehumanized aspect as well as the exploitation of the worker. Daniel Bell, *The End of Ideology* (New York: Collier, 1961), chap. 15.

57. Horvat, *Towards a Theory of Planned Economy*, chap. 3.

58. Ibid., pp. 23–32, for his rejection of the general applicability of marginal cost pricing and for the acceptability, in most cases, of full cost pricing.

workers because workers are more efficient when they participate in management. He supports this view by empirical studies in various countries. He also recognizes entrepreneurship as a critical factor of production necessary to assure efficiency in a world of risk, uncertainty, and dynamic change. Decentralized market socialism without an enterpreneurial agent is impossible and only workers can assume that function. The third part of his argument is historical: worker participation in decision processes has increased in the twentieth century. Thus he concludes that "a federation of self-governing associations—political, economic, and any other . . . is a possible and more efficient alternative to bureaucratic social organization." [59]

As Ward points out, Horvat's argument about the inevitability of this trend is not entirely convincing.[60] He has not demonstrated rigorously the process that brings state capitalism tumbling down nor has he shown that workers' management is necessarily superior. It is relatively easy to make a case that central planning is inefficient at certain stages of development, and rationality may force a reorganization of the central bureaucracy. It is not clear, however, that this reorganization must inevitably move toward workers' management. There is at least the possibility that, with further advance in mathematical, communication, and computer techniques, decentralization will be reversed. Finally, it is not clear that worker-managed enterprises are more efficient. There are two sources of increased efficiency, a better psychological milieu for operation and the fact that workers' incomes depend on the profits of the enterprise. (Horvat emphasizes both types of efficiency but does not commit himself irrevocably to the particular institutional forms.) It may be possible to have participation in the planning process [61]

59. Horvat, ibid., p. 97.

60. Ward, *American Economic Review* 57, no. 3 (June 1967): 521.

61. Adolph Sturmthal, *Workers Councils* (Cambridge: Harvard University Press, 1964).

and to have incomes depend on financial results without making workers entrepreneurs and residual income recipients. Indeed, one problem the Yugoslavs face is the possible inefficiency of worker-managed enterprises that behave like producers' cooperatives.[62] If such difficulties are important, it would pay to consider alternative arrangements.

Other arguments in favor of self-managing enterprises were similar but less systematic. Todorovic concluded that independent enterprises were necessary for a combination of reasons involving both the rejection of the bureaucratic alternatives and the recognition of the requirements of efficient production. "We have become convinced that long years of technocratic-bureaucratic endeavors to put everything into one basket and then to distribute from that central basket according to 'scientifically established uniform norms' leads nowhere but to bureaucracy and all its byproducts! Therefore it is necessary . . . to utilize the market." [63] At the same time he emphasized that "there are not enough means of production for everyone to use them unrestrictedly in his labor according to his own wish and choice. Here, too, the law of value and the market cannot be ignored." [64] For both reasons, Todorovic concluded, "socialist production at the present level of material-productive forces (with present-day means of production) must be organized on the basis of self-governing units: enterprises that are more or less independent in the economic-legal sense." [65]

While a few writers, including Rakic and Uvalic, attached far less significance to the independence of enterprises, most Yugoslav economists and political figures placed a high value on the worker-managed enterprises that were the key feature of the unique Yugoslav system.

62. See Chap. 8 for further discussion of the economics of the firm and of Horvat's treatment of the enterprise.
63. Todorovic, *Socialist Thought and Practice*, no. 9 (Jan. 1963): 34.
64. Ibid.
65. Ibid., pp. 34–35.

Permissible economic instruments

The instruments available to attain the plan may be classified, first, as to whether they are used generally or selectively and, second, as to whether they operate primarily on price variables or primarily on quantitative variables, or affect decisions directly. The Yugoslavs would have preferred to rely on general, price-affecting variables (fiscal and monetary policy, primarily) to attain objectives. These means were entirely compatible with the preferences for independent enterprises in a market environment.

> The new model of social planning in Yugoslavia must take into account, at the very least, the institutional setting of the new association of direct producers . . . and the market mechanism as a special economic form of independent relations between working collectives and consumers within the framework of socially planned norms.[66]

But the Yugoslavs also valued other social objectives. In cases in which production units are independent and managed by workers and when they respond to market forces, it may not be possible to attain desired targets with respect to output, investment, and wage payments by using general fiscal and monetary policies. The question then is, to what extent does the preferred institutional pattern restrict the range of policies acceptable for attaining the plan? Yugoslavs recognized the dilemma.

> The debate has been directed to the more practical problems of how the plan is to fit into the system of enterprise self-management and the self-government of administrative-territorial units. . . . It is particu-

66. Cerne, p. 27.

larly emphasized that we have to distinguish planning
as such from state intervention in the economy.[67]

Obviously, the preferred institutions ruled out direct government production. The form of an independent enterprise was to be maintained. But there was considerable
debate about the use of price-affecting tools selectively by
sector (selective credit allocation, price controls, export
subsidies, differential sales taxes, tax exemptions), even
though these tools were actually employed in the economy.
Finally, the most crucial question was whether the instruments could be applied selectively to individual enterprises, and whether direct intervention in enterprise decisions could be tolerated.

All conceded that state intervention in the market was
occasionally necessary. Lavrac saw such intervention as the
exception rather than the rule.[68] If the social plan established the rate and structure of investment, there would
usually be no need for further intervention. In the short
run the effects of the market are beneficial. If prices rise
above normal, this stimulates production and constricts
consumption. "Short range decisions about production,
that is, decisions about production within the framework
of existing capacities could in principle be left to the commodity producers themselves." [69] This does not mean that
society should never intervene in the market process; indeed, when there are acute shortages, intervention may be
warranted. But state action should not operate primarily
to restrict price movements but to influence the supply
of, or demand for, the commodity.[70]

Jelic argued that the more rapid the rate of change in
the structure of the economy, the greater the need for intervention in the market. Temporary bottlenecks influence

67. Ibid., p. 20.
68. Lavrac, *Ekonomist* 16, no. 1 (1963): 208.
69. Ibid., p. 208.
70. Ibid.

exchange relations and prices become deformed. In such circumstances the market does not provide a stimulus for individual decisions that are rational from the point of view of society as a whole. Therefore, the lower the level of economic development and the more rapid the rate of change envisioned, the greater must be the level and degree of regulation in the economy.[71] Horvat argued similarly about the greater need for regulation at early stages of development.[72]

By and large, Yugoslavs maintained in principle that the right to intervene did not extend to the affairs of the firm. Rakic appears to be an exception. He took a strong view on the obligatory character of the plan.[73] He held that the reason for using economic instruments is merely one of convenience, to reduce the need for direct intervention in the affairs of the firm. The use of general economic instruments, however, "does not exclude the possibility . . . for society to intervene through concrete decisions, irrespective of the specific forms of commodity production and even against their logic. . . . Therefore the market modes of business operation are not inviolable in Yugoslav economic practice." [74]

In general, however, the preference for independent production units and market methods of allocating factors and products restricts the range of methods available for controlling and directing the economy. Samardzija stated it this way.

The initiative of these makers of economic decisions requires relative independence in making decisions . . . and in accomplishing economic tasks. The

71. Jelic, *Sistem planiranja u jugoslovenskoj privredi,* chap. 8.

72. Horvat, *Towards a Theory of Planned Economy,* p. 119.

73. Vojislav Rakic, "Fundamental Characteristics of the Yugoslav Economic System," in Radmila Stojanovic, ed., *Yugoslav Economists on Problems of a Socialist Economy* (New York: International Arts and Sciences Press, 1964), pp. 123–40.

74. Ibid., p. 131.

method of including these decisions into a unified and coordinated system poses not only an economic problem . . . but also a sociopolitical problem. The socialist character of the system excludes administrative centralization as a permanent method of coordination and all forms in which the economic and social initiative of direct producers is limited.[75]

The political, as well as the economic, rationale of the Yugoslav firm precludes direct intervention and requires working through indirect measures. Using a large number of nonfinancial instruments and intervening directly reduces the incentive of the enterprise to maximize its profits. Financial indicators must therefore guide the isolated production units in making the proper responses.[76] Indirect financial pressures are exerted by economic instruments: price policy, wage policy, and tax and credit policy. The actual use of these measures was discussed in the preceding chapter.

Application of economic instruments

Even when they agreed about the desirability of impersonal financial instruments of economic policy, Yugoslav authors did not always agree about how to apply the economic instruments. The instruments may be applied equally to all members of the economic community or they may be applied selectively. In the second case the question is one of the extent of selectivity. If it extends all the way down to the firm level, then each firm would respond to (individually designed) financial indicators. These indicators could be varied by the administrative apparatus as necessary to call forth the desired responses on the part of the firms.

75. Milos Samardzija, *Nasa stvarnost* 14, no. 12 (Dec. 1960): 503.
76. Ibid.

In principle the system of uniform instruments was to prevail. Under social ownership, "everyone has the right, based on social ownership, to use these means of production in his work *under conditions of equality*." [77] As we shall see, Yugoslavs were unable to agree on an interpretation of this high-sounding phrase. Todorovic, among others, took this to mean that all firms should face identical financial regulations. On the other hand, discrimination in tax rates, interest charges, or the availability of credit could be used to induce enterprises to make the decisions desired by planners. This approach prevailed in practice, especially between branches of the economy. Normally, there have been differential rates of tax and interest charges.[78] And, in contrast to Todorovic, Maksimovic and Pjanic asserted that differentiated interest rates [79] provide a "suitable means of fixing the charges of individual branches of the economy and of individual enterprises in connection with the utilization of social resources, thus becoming an important factor of equalization of conditions under which the Yugoslav enterprises are opera-

77. Todorovic, *Socialist Thought and Practice*, no. 9 (Jan. 1963): 33.

78. Rakic, p. 130.

While the standard rate of capital tax was 6 percent of book value of capital equipment, the average rate actually paid was nearer 4 percent. It was systematically lower in many industries: 1 percent for electric power; 2 percent for transportation, food distribution, tourism, catering; and 4 percent generally for heavy industry and mining. Certain agricultural processing plants were exempt. Waterston, p. 101.

In addition to general credit policy, credit availability is influenced by setting the maximum percentage of investment cost of a particular project that the banking system can provide. The remainder must be provided by reinvested earnings of the enterprise. For fuel and power, enterprises are given up to 100 percent loans. In agriculture, enterprises must supply between 10 and 40 percent of the funds; in construction industries, 10 to 30 percent; in transportation, 20 to 50 percent; and in industry generally 20 to 80 percent. Fleming and Sertic, *International Monetary Fund Staff Papers* 9, no. 2 (July 1962): 218.

79. It is not clear whether they are speaking of the capital tax or of interest rates on loans; the statement appears to be true of both.

ting." [80] Obviously, their interpretation of "equal conditions" differed from that of Todorovic.[81]

Todorovic rejected differentiated interest rates and capital taxes not only for doctrinal reasons but also because of
the economic effects. He argued that the capital tax, even
though a source of revenue, "is not basically a tool of fiscal
policy, but is a logical element." [82] Interest charges result
from the "objective fact that . . . the means of production are not unlimited, and that their distribution must be
accomplished directly through the market." [83] Therefore,
"the size of the interest rate is determined on the market.
. . . It cannot be quantified at will." [84] Furthermore, utilization of uniform rates reduces "to the smallest measure
the possibility of subjective treatment and of administra-
tive-bureaucratic appearances." [85] He concluded that the
allocative effect of the tax on capital is more important
than either the tax revenues or the equalizing of business
conditions. On these grounds he emphatically rejected use
of differentiated interest rates which, he said, varied not
only from branch to branch, and from group of enterprises
to group but in practice result in individual interest rates
for each firm.[86]

Economic analysis supports the view that differentiated
signals and incentives usually do not provide a satisfactory solution. If "differentiation" means taking into
account in the interest rate structure of such factors as the

80. Ivan Maksimovic and Zoran Pjanic, *Price Problems in Yugoslav
Theory and Practice* (Sofia: Bulgarian Academy of Sciences, 1964), p. 20.

81. The problem of providing "equal conditions" of work has continued
to plague Yugoslavs. The providing of equitable arrangements was central
to the system of accumulation and funds of 1952 to 1953 that proved
unworkable. The problem of equal access reemerged as one of the critical
issues of the late sixties.

82. Todorovic, *Socijalizam* 6, no. 1 (Jan. 1963): 25.

83. Ibid., p. 26.

84. Ibid., p. 28.

85. Ibid.

86. Ibid., p. 29.

relative riskiness of different ventures, then differentiated interest rates would merely reflect what the market interest rates would have shown. If "differentiation" means different rates of taxation on enterprise residual income, it would alter neither the signals received by the enterprise nor the criterion for making decisions, but it could affect enterprise behavior. Taxes on profits do not cause the enterprise to cease maximizing profits but they do reduce the rewards available and may affect the supply of labor or the energy with which work is carried out.

If "differentiation" means that capital is made arbitrarily cheap in selected sectors (by lower interest rates on loans or through lower capital taxes), the relative costs of different inputs are affected and economic efficiency will diminish. The reason for lowering interest rates selectively is to provide some kind of a subsidy to a sector or activity. Apart from the question of whether the subsidy itself makes any sense, the question remains whether artificially cheapening the price of one of the factors is the best means of providing the subsidy. In general it is not. Only if the cost is the same for all potential and actual users of a given input can there be efficient allocation of resources. When the parameters facing the decision-making units are not identical, there is generally no possibility for maximization and no optimal allocation of resources.[87] If the price of capital varies from sector to sector, so too will the marginal productivity of capital (because the worker-managed enterprise uses the same criterion for employing capital as does the capitalist firm).[88] If the marginal productivity differs among firms, allocation is suboptimal. For example, if authorities set artificially low prices for electric power, the value of the marginal product of capital in power genera-

87. A point argued persuasively by Peter Wiles, "Imperfect Competition and Decentralized Planning," *Economics of Planning* 4, no. 1 (Jan. 1964): 16–28.
88. See Chap. 8 below.

tion will be less than if the market-determined price for power prevailed. Hence if the proper amount of capital is to be employed (or the proper amount of any factor), it could be argued that the factor price must be lower. But clearly this is only a case of two faulty pricing policies that may possibly produce a less inefficient result than if either one were employed alone. If the price of *one* of the factors is held artificially low, the enterprise will use relatively too much capital and too little labor to produce its output. If the authorities believe that a particular economic sector otherwise unprofitable should be encouraged, a system of subsidies to cover losses is more satisfactory. In this way factor prices can still be used for decisions about factor combinations.

We are left, then, with the question of under what circumstances it makes sense to establish different prices for capital. If it is difficult to set up an effective incentive mechanism and an appropriate yardstick of performance with subsidies and grants, then it might conceivably be preferable to set artificial prices for those factors whose prices are easily controlled. It is also possible that, by solving some constrained maximization problem, the planners may know the future optimal capacity and factor mix. Differentiating the interest rates may provide an indirect instrument for achieving the optimal combination. Today's factor prices will not necessarily induce the optimal combination of inputs, so it is necessary to determine tomorrow's prices. Presumably, the shadow price of factors will differ over time as the factor endowments change. If the time span involved for various projects also differs, then there is a case for differentiated factor prices.

In practice it is more important to note that interest rates played virtually no role in the allocation of resources, or when they did, they worked in undesired directions. Interest rates were so low relative to the annual rate of inflation that they amounted to a negative charge (subsidy) on the use of capital, thus not rationing capital but encouraging its maximum use—a point finally recognized by some Yugoslavs.[89]

It is apparent that Yugoslavs disagreed about the economic methods permissible for attaining plan objectives. Behind the different Yugoslav views lie basic differences of opinion about the efficiency of plan and market. Those whose accepted market methods as a basically efficient allocating device, including Todorovic, Pjanic, Maksimovic, Horvat, and Jelic, tended generally (although not agreeing on all points) to recommend minimal intervention in enterprise affairs, uniform application of economic instruments, and maximum reliance upon the market to allocate resources. Those who regarded the plan as the ultimate in rationality (including probably Uvalic, Rakic, Dragosavac, Stojanovic, and Cobeljic) had fewer compunctions about intervention, circumventing the market, or using differentiated signals to guide the enterprises. These divergent views about plan and market in the socialist economy emerge more clearly in the discussion about the more mature economy, when the initial problem of economic development looms less ominously.

PLAN AND MARKET IN A MORE MATURE ECONOMY

The Eighth Congress of the League of Communists of Yugoslavia, held in December 1964, emphasized that with the attaining of a per capita income of approximately $500, Yugoslavia had entered the ranks of the moderately developed countries. It was recognized that a more mature economy required a different organization.[90] For an econ-

89. Milovoje Trklja, *Kamata na investicione kredite u uslovima drustvenog samoupravljanja* (Belgrade: Institut drustvenih nauka, 1966), 144.

90. Todorovic pointed out that the economic policy which had been followed previously had been necessary because of the low level of economic development. "The practice hitherto followed by socialist revolu-

omy engaged in the process of rapid, discontinuous development, the various reasons for circumventing the market had been persuasive. As the period of radical transformation of the Yugoslav economy drew to a close, the Yugoslavs had to reconsider what combination of plan and market was suitable for an economy engaged in smooth and continuous growth. Yugoslavs were not of one mind about what changes in policy were required. The nature of the changes required depended on the assessment of the current situation and of the nature of changes to come, and on the basic initial view about plan and market.

On the one side were those who regarded the market mechanism, appropriately modified, as basically efficient. The chief need for planning arises from discontinuities in the initial, developmental stage. In their view, the plan constituted a corrective to the market to be used only when market decisions failed to produce results conforming with the general objectives of society. In general, with higher levels of development, there were fewer cases requiring intervention in the market. On the other side were those who regard the plan as the basically efficient mechanism. In their view a market exists because of the inability of planners to collect and process all information at present levels of technique. In the future more planning could be expected because of the technological requirement for fewer, larger, and more integrated production units, thus reducing the amount of market exchange among autonomous producers. However, even strong advocates of planning recognized the market as useful to convey the preferences of consumers to producers.

As for the more distant future in which communism

---

tions of beginning socio-economic socialist development with a high degree of centralism, is not the only and inevitable road for all. It is very likely that countries with developed productive forces . . . will, from the very beginning, organize socialist construction, consequently also the planned management of the economy, *on the basis of definite specific forms of self government.*" "Some Observations on Planning," *Socialist Thought and Practice,* no. 17 (Jan.–Mar. 1965): 13–14.

(characterized by the principle "from each according to his ability, to each according to his needs") would be attained, and as for the method of economic organization therein, little was heard.

Plan to correct the market

The philosophy underlying this view is that of the market tradition modified by welfare economics. These authors (including Horvat, Jelic, Bajt, Bicanic, Pjanic, and Maksimovic) considered consumer satisfaction to be the ultimate objective of economic activity and believed the market mechanism to be most suitable for attaining that objective. A rather liberal position on the role of the market was also taken in the White Book.[91] The papers advocated expanding the scope of the market, arguing that the task of socialism is to arrange institutions and policies so as to increase the role of decentralized decisions and to permit consumers' preferences to determine what should be produced. Accordingly, the plan should continue to determine certain long range investment decisions, as well as to specify collective consumption and some aspects of personal consumption. Admitting that decisions about investment could not be left entirely to the market, the authors also argued that, as the differences between the initial system and higher degrees of development diminished, market criteria expressing consumers' preferences could ultimately govern even the allocation of most investments. With few exceptions, decisions about current production could be left to the exclusive domain of the market and of individual firms. For these purposes a more or less competitive market structure is necessary. These arguments were in part directed at the theoretical issues of the optimal functioning of the system. The White Book also had

91. *Ekonomski pregled* 14, no. 8 (1963): 145–567.

a specific political viewpoint and significance as well, representing the view of the more developed regions.

These proposals met with some resistance on the general plane. Maksimovic objected on several grounds, in particular questioning the feasibility of a competitive market structure.[92] He doubted that Yugoslavia could sustain a market structure with sufficient numbers of producing firms. While not disagreeing fundamentally with the White Book proposals, Lavrac emphasized that adequate decisions cannot always be made exclusively on the basis of market criteria and from an individualist vantage point even when the economy has passed the initial stages of discontinuous development. The market cannot allocate investment funds, Lavrac argued, for the reasons noted previously: duplication of facilities, optimum size, and so forth. Therefore the plan would be a permanent feature of socialism, used to achieve results different from those which would have been obtained from the market alone.[93] But the plan is not meant to serve as a substitute for the operation of the market. "The demarcation line between the role of the plan and that of the market mechanism is in principle clear. In commodity production the plan makes sense and is effective only in so far as the objectives laid down in it differ from the effects of the free play of the law of value, and provided the course of spontaneous movement is really changed by it." [94] The plan should not attain major status in making day to day economic decisions. Decisions about production within the framework of existing capacities should be left to the enterprises themselves.[95]

92. Ivan Maksimovic, "Trziste i plan u nasem ekonomskom sistemu," *Ekonomist* 16, no. 1 (1963): 161–68.

93. Lavrac, *Ekonomist* 16, no. 1 (1963): 207–08.

94. Ivan Lavrac, "Competition and Incentive in the Yugoslav Economic System," in Radmila Stojanovic, ed., *Yugoslav Economists on Problems of a Socialist Economy* (New York: International Arts and Sciences Press, 1964), p. 148.

95. Lavrac, *Ekonomist* 16, no. 1 (1963): 208.

Central planners

On the other side were those who remained steadfastly optimistic about the possibilities of nearly total central planning. Uvalic based his view on Marx.

> Marx repeatedly made a comparison between the perfect organization of the divison of labor and the general discipline imposed by technology itself in production within an enterprise, and the anarchy, the unnecessary squandering of the personal and material elements of production characteristic of society as a whole. Therefore he saw in socialist society an extension of the rational division of labor and a scientifically elaborated organization of production in society as a whole.[96]

Complete central planning was not yet possible, however, because of the incomplete and insufficient knowledge of the central planners. At the existing level of science and technique, it was not yet feasible to allocate productive factors through centralized decisions. Presumably, at some future date changes in technology would make central planning more feasible.[97] Yugoslavs did not discuss in detail the prospects of computerized planning.

Both Rakic and Uvalic found the causes for the present

96. Radivoj Uvalic, "The Functions of the Market and the Plan in the Socialist Economy," in Radmila Stojanovic, ed., *Yugoslav Economists on Problems of a Socialist Economy* (New York: International Arts and Sciences Press, 1964), p. 145.

97. This view is close to one expressed by Oskar Lange. Lange outlined the basis for determination of whether decisions should be made centrally or at the periphery. He suggested that decentralized decisions should be reserved to those areas where the benefit of centralized calculations—presumably better because they are taken from the vantage point of society—are outweighed by the loss due to the time lapse in obtaining information, relaying it to the center, processing it, and relaying the decision to the periphery. For completeness, the resources used in the

decentralization in the "complexity" of the economy. Insufficient concentration within economic branches and the
existence of a great number of productive units with varying levels of technical equipment made it impossible to
record satisfactorily the necessary data for the "collective
regulation of the entire social labor." [98] For the interim
period it was necessary to accept, with reservations, the
principle of market relations and of independent enterprises. The market mechanism provided a "more direct
and more reliable means of economizing than the imperfect social recording and control which it would be possible
to achieve under conditions of a still largely fragmented
economy." [99] Market relations, however, were at best transitional features.[100]

Rakic favored increased integration and concentration
of economic enterprises. "The increasing integration and
association of various enterprises show that the specific
market forms and the narrow, particularistic and local interests connected with them, will cease to be the predomi-
nant motive for and form of the realization of the general
interests." [101] Rakic not only embraced concentration but
he basically rejected an individualistic approach to decision
making. Market forms would have an even smaller significance as they were replaced by the conscious planned organization of production.[102] Ultimately there would be direct
organization of economic activity in which "the allocation
of the total mass of social labor to individual groups and

---

information collection and processing system must be included as part of
its cost.

According to Lange, the area of decentralized decision making should
decrease with improvements in electronic techniques and economic fore-
casting. (Lecture at Columbia University, spring 1962.)

98. Uvalic, p. 414.
99. Ibid.
100. Ibid.
101. Rakic, p. 139.
102. Ibid., p. 138.

subgroups of production should be quantitatively established in advance." [103]

Some of the advocates of central planning, nevertheless, saw the market as having a *permanent* supplemental role to correct the plan or to fill in the details. The resulting combination of plan and market did not actually differ greatly from the combination implied by the view that the plan is a corrective to the market. The underlying philosophies were, however, quite different.

According to Dragosavac, the plan is the basic determinant of the allocation of resources. However, he admitted, central planners could not foresee all adjustments.[104] "In our economy the chaotic operation of the law of value is limited because the distribution of the entire social labor is accomplished, or should be accomplished, on a planned basis." [105] A certain degree of flexibility is desirable, however, so that the market can correct the small errors of the planners. "The law of value through supply and demand accomplishes in our system the more precise distribution of social labor and corrects various errors of the planners." [106] Flexibility in the solution of smaller problems facilitates the fulfillment of essential goals, while avoiding the wastes of a tautly planned and therefore centrally administered economy. Administrative orders of minutiae are inefficient and frequently contradictory. The market also has a specific function in determining the composition

103. Ibid., p. 126. Lavrac welcomed concentration, but for different reasons. Technological factors drove him to conclude that, in most areas of production, efficiency was not compatible with a competitive market structure. "It is illusory to aspire to perfect competition where it is . . . irrational because of the advantages of concentration." (*Yugoslav Economists*, p. 152). He advocated adoption of the technologically most efficient methods of production combined with regulation of the enterprise to prevent monopoly practices.

104. Dusan Dragosavac, "Delovanje zakona vrednosti i trzista," *Socijalizam* 6, no. 4 (Apr. 1963): 3–40.

105. Ibid., pp. 18–19.

106. Ibid., p. 19.

of consumer goods. "The market in our case has the function of the corrector of planning. Through it is manifest the influence of the consumer on the structure, quality and quantity of production." [107]

Even Uvalic's view of full socialism allowed for limited market relations to supplement the plan. The consumer goods industries have infinite possibilities in the composition of output and variations of style, assortment, and quality. Planners will never be able to predict what individuals will want in all these respects. The market can convey the preferences of consumers about assortment better than the plan.[108] In his view the market mechanism is suitable for determining the composition of production in the consumer goods sector. The market structure is sufficiently competitive to force socialist firms to minimize their costs. In addition, the ability of the market to convey consumers' preferences to producers convinced Uvalic that the market mechanism in that sector was justified and useful even in "full socialism." [109] Different principles would allocate resources in the producer goods sectors. In areas in which the number of producers was small, production could not be regulated by the market; it would be more efficient to determine production through "the plan." "Hence it follows that the law of value, regardless of its successful applications in certain sectors of the economy, can never assume the character of a general law." [110]

The conflict between plan and market, so long a part of Marxist tradition, is still apparent in Yugoslav economic

107. Ibid., pp. 15–16.
108. Uvalic, p. 144.
109. Ibid., p. 145.
110. Ibid., p. 141. It is not clear whether Uvalic objected to individualistic decisions in an insufficiently competitive framework, or whether he objected to the notion that demands for producers goods were ultimately derived from the demands for final products. He *appeared* to mean the latter.

thought. To some extent these arguments about plan and market were merely the form in which economists—and politicians using the arguments and reasoning of economists—carried on another debate about the form the Yugoslav state was to take. It would be a mistake, however, to regard all this discussion as merely a surrogate for that other, more bitter debate, for the plan-market conflict in Yugoslav thought remains quite real.

CHAPTER 7

Plan and Market: The Specific Issues

The discussion on the roles of plan and market in the socialist economy took place in the early sixties in Yugoslavia in a particular context of political and economic events. As noted, starting in 1961, measures had been taken to liberalize the economy. The immediate economic consequences were an increase in inflation, a decrease in the rate of growth, and a crisis in the balance of payments. The critics of liberalization said self-righteously, "I told you so," [1] and urged a return to centralism.

The economic measures that were followed in the next few years were neither liberal nor central. They were the product of political compromise and, as is often the case with compromise, the results were far from satisfactory. The economic system of the early sixties was neither rational centralization nor rational decentralization but seemed to combine the worst features of each. With justification the decentralizers could criticize the existing state of affairs and blame it on the fetters placed on the initiative of individual enterprises. With equal justification the centralizers could point to the inadequate coordination, the duplication of facilities and the bottlenecks which arose from insufficient coordination.[2] The compromise in economic policy in these years was necessary because of a deep and growing split in the political leadership. The split between the liberalizers and the opposition first emerged openly,

1. Nikola Cobeljic, "Slabljenje plana i drustvene kontrole—glavni uzrocnici usporenog rasta u 1961 i 1962 godini," *Ekonomist* 16, no. 1 (1963): 62–67.

2. A point made by Branko Horvat, "Samoupravljanje, centralizam i planiranje," *Pregled* 16, no. 5 (May 1964): 119–44.

apparently, in March of 1962,[3] although the underlying causes of national tensions were much older.

The first part of this chapter traces the economic events that preceded the 1965 reforms and shows why major changes in the economic system became necessary. If nothing else, economic performance in this period illustrated the disastrous consequences of combining central intervention in an arbitrary manner with an ostensibly market economy. Despite a grave economic situation, changes could not be made until the political conflict was resolved. After several years of maneuvering within the party, the Eighth Congress of the League of Communists took a firm position on liberalization in December 1964. This position was embodied in the economic reform measures passed in the summer of 1965 that continued the policies first started in 1961.

The second part of this chapter examines what was accomplished by the economic reform. The essential feature was the abandonment or sharp restriction of central investment planning in favor of the market. In order for the market mechanism to work, the enterprises had to be motivated to pursue profit and be free to do so. This required not only eliminating the various legal controls and disincentives but also freeing the firms from the clumsy political intervention that had been one form of "social control."

The third part of the chapter considers the regional conflict that lay beneath much of the dispute over economic policy. There was a conflict of interest between the more developed and the less developed regions. Policies beneficial to the poorer areas were considered by the richer regions to be detrimental to their development. The economic policy that the developed regions favored, ultimately embodied in the reform, was regarded by the more backward regions of the country as inimical to their own inter-

3. Shoup, pp. 210, 250.

ests. The battle over economic policy was bitter and has left some wounds unhealed.

ECONOMIC PROBLEMS IN THE SIXTIES

The third five-year plan, for the years 1961 to 1965, had to be discarded in midstream. There were at least three sources of economic difficulty that contributed to the crisis and precipitated the need for economic change: chronic inflation and balance of payments difficulties; misallocations and administrative interventions resulting from the policies to deal with inflation and foreign trade problems; and basic defects in the development strategy itself.

Inflation and the balance of payments

Inflation is common when rates of investment are very high and when the economy is growing rapidly and is scarcely a unique Yugoslav problem. Similarly, developing countries typically have balance of payments difficulties. Continuing trade deficits, however, can exist only as long as creditors are willing to finance them. By the mid-sixties, after twenty years of deficits, Yugoslavia had to give serious attention to the balance of payments and to the related problem of domestic inflation. The trade difficulties and the inflation were aggravated by some specific economic policies. Insufficient control of short term credit volume apparently contributed to the inflation, and the foreign trade situation was certainly exacerbated by the price policies to be discussed below.

There appeared to be several sources of inflationary pressures.[4] Personal consumption expenditures rose significantly, due to an increase in nominal income, an increase

4. The inflationary pressures are explored more fully in my paper on "Reforms in Yugoslav Planning," (mimeo, 1967).

in the number of persons employed, and a large increase in the volume of consumer credit. At the same time, nominal investment expenditures continued to rise more rapidly than did the price levels. The 1961 reform may have facilitated this situation, as the critics of liberalization argued. Greater enterprise autonomy over the distribution of its income made possible the rapidly rising nominal incomes. Yugoslavs claim that rising wages pushed prices up, but it is also likely that the workers were able to obtain wage increases more easily to offset the previous increases in prices. Indiscriminate expansion of credit seems to have been the major source of inflationary pressure. The changes in the banking system in 1961 and 1963 may have affected the ability of the central bank to control the volume of credit.[5] In 1961 short term crediting was transferred from the National Bank to the communal banks. The 1963 reforms transferred the investment funds of the federation, republic, and commune to the capital funds of various banks, making them responsible for loans and also permitting the banks to finance investment from their own long term deposits. In addition to these inflationary factors on the demand side, the relatively poor harvests of the years 1960 through 1962 placed pressure on agricultural prices, and the prices of imported commodities increased following devaluation.

Action to deal with rising prices assumed two major forms: measures to reduce excess demand and measures to suppress the symptoms.[6] Demand was curtailed by various restrictions on the volume of investment and the volume of credit. Other policies coped with the symptoms:

5. On the other hand, credit had been expanding rapidly and inflationary pressures were strong even in 1960 before the banking reforms.

6. The annual OECD surveys of Yugoslavia provide a useful summary of economic performance, along with some analysis and a summary of policy changes. Organization for Economic Cooperation and Development, *Socialist Federal Republic of Yugoslavia* (OECD: Paris), annually, since 1963.

wage guidelines, import restrictions, and price controls. The wage guidelines, initially noncompulsory, became mandatory in 1963. The methods of price control, which had been expanding since the mid-fifties, increased rapidly and, by 1962, 67 percent of the value of manufactured goods was subject to some form of price control.[7]

Misallocation and administrative intervention

The Yugoslavs dealt with their economic problems by suppressing the symptoms of disequilibrium. Every step taken seemed to raise the barriers to rational calculation, to reduce the scope of the market and to increase the substitution of administrative for market allocations. The more inflation developed, the more price controls were applied. Items whose prices were controlled were in short supply and had to be allocated administratively. A similar situation prevailed in foreign trade. Imports of final goods, raw materials, and semifabricates appeared ever more attractive because the goods were frequently unavailable domestically, due to shortages of supply at the controlled prices, because artificially low exchange rates and the low import duties made imports appear cheap, and because the quality of imports was often superior to the domestic products. At the same time exports failed to increase because the domestic prices often exceeded what the firm could obtain at the artificial exchange rate and because the poor quality of Yugoslav goods made it difficult to compete on world markets. To bring pressure on both sides of the balance of payments, more administrative allocation sprang up. There was sharp competition for the limited supplies of foreign currency that were allocated administratively by the bank. Multiple exchange rates for imports and exports and for classes of goods within each category were

7. Kreso Dzeba and Milan Beslac, *Privredna reforma: Sto i zasto se mijenja* (Zagreb: Stvarnost, 1965), p. 71.

introduced. Import quotas were applied and export quotas were often assigned as a condition for receiving foreign currency allotments.

Development strategy

Two aspects of the general development strategy vastly increased the importance of political-administrative influence over economic decisions: the regional policy and the preference given to manufacturing. One objective of national economic policy was to reduce regional income differences. The underdeveloped regions were favored by special credit allocations, subsidies, special interest rates, and tax rebates, all of which further reduced the possibility of rational economic calculation and increased the range of decisions subject to political pressure.

During the late fifties and early sixties much of the economic expansion in Yugoslavia had taken place in the manufacturing sector. This was favored by direct investment allocations and by several price policies that made investment both possible and attractive. The prices of most domestic raw materials were controlled and set at quite low levels. The prices of imported materials and equipment were low as a result of the exchange rate and the low tariffs. The prices of the basic components in the cost of living such as food, rent, power, and passenger transport, were kept low, which permitted wage rates to remain low. Finally, the prices received by the producers of manufactured goods net of turnover tax were quite high. As a result, certain industries, especially the processing industries, often showed high profit margins and were able, under the Yugoslav system of self-finance, to invest and expand capacities. In addition, the existence of high profits seemed to mean that there was little pressure to reduce costs. On the other hand, when prices were kept low by price controls, enterprise income was low and subsidies were necessary for the firm to survive. Under such circumstances the meaninglessness of the prices of the inputs of capital, labor, and the materials made the selection of efficient technology impossible. Finally, plants often operated at only a fraction of capacity because of the shortages of materials or of power.

These defects were not unrecognized in Yugoslavia. To quote the late Boris Krajger, a major architect of the reform:

> The disparity between the prices of raw materials and manufactured products, on the one hand, and between domestic prices and the prices on the foreign market, on the other, led to the irrational use of raw materials and also to a system of distribution which necessitated the administrative transferring of resources. . . .[8]

> We have for years been recording disproportions in the material structure of production, that is to say, the development of the power industry and production of raw materials and semi-manufactures has been lagging behind the development of other industries. While, on the one hand, this production is subsidized, on the other hand, the processing industries are growing and, owing to the low prices of raw materials and semi-manufactures and cheap labor power, are making big profits and also exerting pressure on the import of raw materials at the unrealistically low import rate of exchange of the dinar. . . .[9]

As a result of the disparity in prices, the manufacturing industries developed even though they had no raw material basis of their own. Owing to the restricted scope of the home market, the inadequate

8. Boris Krajger, "New Economic Measures," Report to the Federal Assembly, reprinted in *Economic Reform in Yugoslavia* (Belgrade: Socialist Thought and Practice, 1965), pp. 66–67.

9. Ibid., p. 70.

policy of prices and inadequate import value of the dinar, most of the manufacturing industries have a low productivity and turn out too wide a range of articles.[10]

The need for change

Yugoslav policies of selective intervention were nearly fatal to the entire operation of the market mechanism. There was no possibility of economic calculation or any incentive for it.[11] The profit of the enterprise came to depend less on market variables than on its political connections that determined its access to investment credits, to scarce materials, foreign currency, and import quotas; its receipt of various subsidies and premia such as tax rebates, privileged interest rates, and privileged import and export exchange rates; and its ability to get approval for price increases. Because the taxes on successful enterprises were high, their incentives to maximize profits were low. Enterprises with losses, often due to low price ceilings, had to rely on subsidies and thus had no incentive at all. Individual incentive was weak because personal income depended only slightly on the success of the enterprise and, because of various allowances, subsidized services, and free goods, there was a still lower dependence of personal consumption on earnings. Finally, the more decisions were made by administrators, the greater was the opportunity for political pressure to influence the decisions.

It is against this background that the economic debate about plan and market was going on. There was little doubt of the need for change. Yugoslavs questioned whether their existing system had any rationale at all. At least central planning has a rationale, but in Yugoslavia the composition of output and the methods of production

10. Ibid., p. 71.
11. See the critique of Yugoslav price policy by Dzeba and Beslac, especially part 2.

were not determined by a central plan but by a truly anarchic combination of market and administrative forces.
Under the circumstances, it is not surprising that the discussions revealed considerable support for more, rather
than less, centralization. It was not inefficiency alone, however, that provoked the reform. The administrative arbitrariness and the extension of political considerations into
every sphere of decision making ultimately became in-
tolerable in the context of Yugoslav political problems and
the nationality conflicts.

THE ECONOMIC REFORM OF 1965

Yugoslavs recognized reasonably well the sources of
their economic difficulties. In April of 1964 the Federal
Assembly resolution on "the basic guidelines for the further development of the economic system" proposed that
the liberalization be continued. In November a resolution
on the medium term plan for the years 1964 to 1970 reiterated this position. But it was the Eighth Congress of the
League of Communists, meeting in December 1964, that
resolved the political issue in favor of decentralization and
the constitutional principle of the separation of the political and economic spheres.[12] Economic matters were to be
left to market forces. The 1965 economic reform was a
collection of legislative measures that would make it possible for the market system to function. It was still another
year before the opponents of reform were purged from the
party and the wholehearted commitment to implementing
the reforms was made. Full support for the reform policy
could not be assured until after the purge of Aleksandar
Rankovic, leading political opponent of liberalization, in
July of 1966.

The immediate purposes of the reform were to restore

12. Rudolf Bicanic, "Economics of Socialism in a Developed Country,"
Foreign Affairs 44, no. 4 (July 1966): 633–50.

international equilibrium and to control domestic inflation. But the ultimate objective of the reform was vastly
more far-reaching: to promote greater economic efficiency
by relying on the market. Despite the fact that it was a
socialist country, the role of the plan was to 'be sharply
curtailed in Yugoslavia.

The Yugoslavs had long before abandoned the planning
of production details. They now prepared to abandon investment planning. To do so required a number of changes
in the economic system. When central planners do not
determine investment, initiative to invest rests with the
enterprises. The incentive of the enterprise to invest efficiently depends upon the motivation of the producers and
upon the appropriateness of the price signals received. To
make the system work, relative prices were drastically over-
hauled in a major price reform which had as its ultimate
aim the freeing of prices from controls altogether. In addition, a more realistic, uniform exchange rate was established and quantitative restrictions on imports were reduced. By freeing prices, the complex system of direct and
indirect subsidies could be dropped and, in this way, incentives were significantly sharpened. By reducing the use
of subsidies, enterprise profits depended on the economic
performance of the enterprises. At the same time the incentive to earn profits was greater because, with no central
need to finance investment or provide vast subsidies, the
tax rates could be cut. Indeed, the tax on enterprise profits
was eliminated and total profits were placed at the disposal of the workers council. The reform also cut back the
share of subsidized consumer goods. This meant that personal consumption depended much more closely on earned
income; earned income depended on the success of the
enterprise; and the success of the enterprise, in the long
run, depended on successful investment decisions.

Investments are financed from enterprise profits, the

volume of which was greater because they were untaxed. Those enterprises that have accumulated profits are not necessarily those enterprises in which investments should be taking place in the future. For an efficient use of investment funds, there must be capital mobility in some kind of a socialist capital market. The reform provided such mobility. Enterprises can reinvest in their own firms; they can lend directly to other enterprises or enter into profit-sharing agreements with other enterprises; or they can become shareholders of banks. Banks, previously administrative agencies for government investment funds, became autonomous, profit-sharing enterprises with capital subscribed by shareholders (enterprises and government agencies) who manage the bank.

The first Yugoslav economic reform, which took place between 1950 and 1954, had dismantled the central planning of production details. The second major reform that started in 1961 and was decisively adopted in 1965, dismantled the apparatus for the central planning of investment. The reasons behind this second decision are complex. On the one hand, there are economic arguments that suggest that the need for investment planning may be greatest in the initial stages of development when the adjustments are nonmarginal in character. At higher levels of development the misallocations resulting from use of the market may become less significant relative to the total volume of investment, while the planning system itself may become dysfunctional and produce faulty decisions. It is true that the Yugoslav economy was in a mess from which there seemed to be few exits. But additional noneconomic factors also influenced the Yugoslav decision to abandon investment planning. Centrally planned investment became impossible in Yugoslavia because it was no longer possible to agree politically about such planning. We now turn to the regional aspects of the debate.

PLAN AND MARKET: REGIONAL ASPECTS

The central issue of the debate concerned the process by which investment volume and structure were determined. If there were agreement about the volume of investment and its sectoral and regional allocation, it would be potentially possible to distribute funds within noncompeting capital market according to the profitability of projects. Such a system could attain the desired investment structure, while at the same time providing an incentive and some competition; thus politics and the bureaucracy could be kept out of decisions concerning particular enterprises.

Several features of political and economic life prevented the scheme from working as indicated. The major requirement is agreement on the rate of investment and on the sectoral and regional allocation. Such agreement was lacking. The centralizers, such as Cobeljic and Stojanovic, believed generally in the importance of high rates of capital accumulation for high growth,[13] and they argued against a reduction in the rate of investment. Kiril Miljevski belittled the argument that reduced rates of investment could mean higher increases in personal consumption which would provide a major personal incentive for efficiency.[14] On the other side stood those who believed that the high rates of investment in recent years had left too little for the worker and had blunted the economic incentives. Dzeba and Beslac argued this point in their devastating critique of the Yugoslav economic system,[15] as did the authors of the White Book.

13. Cobeljic, *Ekonomist* 16, no. 1 (1963): 62–67. See also Radmila Stojanovic, "O donosenju investicionih odluka," *Ekonomski pregled* 14, no. 3–5 (1963): 344–49.

14. Kiril Miljevski, "Neprivredna potrosnja," *Ekonomist* 16, no. 1 (1963): 53–58.

15. Dzeba and Beslac, *Privredna reforma*.

The heart of the disagreement was not merely a difference of opinion about the significance of consumption as a stimulus to productivity. It concerned the regional allocation as well as the volume. Yugoslavia has very great regional differences in per capita incomes, and one of the perennial platforms of Yugoslav economic policy is significantly to lessen these differences. Although no specific time table was set for eliminating disparties in income, it was understood that the less developed areas (Montenegro, Macedonia, Bosnia-Herzegovina, and Kosmet in the Serbian republic) should receive large doses of investment in order to catch up to the national average. It was argued that high rates of investment would permit more resources to be devoted to their development efforts and thus permit them to catch up more rapidly.

The dispute also concerned the allocation of investment. It was agreed that the developing republics should have more than a proportionate share of investment, but there was no agreement on what would constitute a proportionate share. The share of the less developed republics in total investment was greater than their corresponding shares of national income generated in each republic. On the other hand, taking per capita additions to capital stock, the investment policy no longer appears so favorable to the developing republics, with the exception of Montenegro which, however, is a very small republic. (See the table on page 180.) The figures given are preliminary and are intended merely to provide a quantitative orientation for the discussion about regional development. I make no attempt to evaluate the claims made by the various sides in the Yugoslav dispute.

By the early sixties, the richer regions appeared to be tiring of the development policy. Despite relatively high investment outlays in relation to the share of the republics in national income, and in Montenegro even on a per capita basis, the less developed regions did not show signs of catching up. (See the table on page 181.) Indeed, the relative position of the less developed republics declined. The advanced regions saw little reason to continue the existing policies of high rates of investment with the attendant high rates of taxes that, in their view, cut incen-

Depreciated per capita additions to total fixed assets, 1947 to 1964, in thousands of dinars, 1962 prices

Montenegro	614.9
Slovenia	610.2
Croatia	408.4
Yugoslav average	390.3
Macedonia	384.0
Bosnia-Herzegovina	341.3
Serbia (including Vojvodina and Kosmet)	330.9

Source: Ivo Vinski, "Rast fiksnih fondova po Jugoslavenskim republikama od 1946 1964 godine," *Ekonomist* 19, no. 1–4 (1966); and *Statisticki godisnjak*, as computed by Sin-ming Shaw, "Regional Investment Policies, Capital Formation and Income Equalization in Yugoslavia: 1947–1964," Master's essay, Department of Economics, Columbia University, 1969, Table A-8.

tives and thus resulted in lower national rates of growth than would have been achieved with lower rates of investment used more efficiently. The representatives of the developed republics complained that the investments in the less developed regions were often wasteful. The method of allocation of investment funds favored the underdeveloped areas in ways that reduced the pressures for efficiency. They received preferential access to certain funds, subsidized interest rates, and tax rebates. They had to put up a smaller share, and sometimes none, of their own funds to receive investment credits, and some funds were received as outright grants. Under this system, economic forces were subordinated to pork barrel politics, and it

Per capita national income, as a percentage of the national average, 1947 and 1964

	1947	1964
Yugoslavia	100.0	100.0
Slovenia	162.7	195.1
Croatia	107.9	118.9
Serbia total	—	90.3
Serbia proper *	96.8	96.4
Kosmet	50.4	37.1
Vojvodina	116.9	115.0
Bosnia-Herzegovina	79.8	71.1
Montenegro	71.1	73.2
Macedonia	68.6	69.4

* Serbia proper excludes the autonomous regions of Kosmet and Vojvodina.

Sources: 1947 figures from *Yugoslav Survey 6,* no. 21 (Apr.–June 1965): 2995; 1964 figures from *Statisticki godisnjak,* 1966.

was not difficult to find "political factories" that had no economic logic whatsoever.

Few denied that the investments in the less developed regions had lower rates of return than elsewhere, but other explanations of this phenomenon were offered. Defenders of the policy of preferential treatment for the less developed regions argued that lower rates of return were to be expected for two reasons: (1) the structure of controlled prices operated against the primary product producers (presumably in the less developed regions) and in favor of the fabricators (presumably in the advanced regions). (2) The poorer educational and skill structure of the labor force and the lower level of social overhead capital in transport, communications, and power made it impossible for the poor regions to compete with the advanced areas without assistance. Both factors made it necessary to allocate resources among regions with reference to other considerations than the rate of return alone. Cobeljic, in particular, emphasized that allocation according to the rate of return alone was a short run, static criterion incompatible with obtaining long run maximum growth rates.[16]

Representatives of the more advanced regions tended to argue that if there is to be investment in the less developed areas from federal funds, the size of those funds should be specified in advance as an explicit policy decision, and then investment from this fund should be allocated as rationally as possible. All other investment was to be allocated according to economic criteria through the banking system, without regard to location. The advanced regions tended to regard federal development funds as a charitable contribution or aid. Needless to say, the developing areas viewed such expenditures quite differently.

Several arguments were offered in opposition to the proposed reliance on the market to distribute investment and a limited volume of federal aid. First, it was argued that such a policy would increase the economic polarization of the nation in two ways. The enterprises and the regions with the funds to invest—the already rich—would become richer by lending out their funds for high interest rates or shares in the profits of other enterprises. Also, if it were true that private calculations would underestimate the true social cost of investment in the developed regions (the higher costs of conglomeration) and would underestimate the true social benefits of investment in the backward areas because not all benefits could be appropriated by the individual investor, there would be systematic underinvest-

16. Nikola Cobeljic, "Kritiriji izbora strukture investicija i mehanizam trzista," *Ekonomist* 16, no. 1 (1963): 215–20.

ment in the poor regions.[17] Horvat stated flatly that "if within a country there are two regions whose levels of economic development are separated by a considerable gap, and the market is left to operate on its own accord, the gap is likely to widen." [18] The view of the market mechanism as a cause of regional disparities was also found in Miljevski [19] and Mihailovic.[20] To the less developed regions, the economic reform appeared to be a device for keeping them permanently underdeveloped. Indeed, when lagging federal revenues caused lags in the disbursements from the fund for the developing areas, those areas revealed their sensitivity.[21]

Second, some argued that the rapid development of the less developed areas was rational from the point of view of the nation as a whole on two grounds. Once certain minimum expenditures for social overhead capital were made in the less developed areas, many activities could be undertaken that had higher rates of return than those available in the more developed areas and which would, therefore, contribute more to the economic growth of the nation as a whole. These activities were presently not profitable merely because of the historical accidents that gave

17. Radmila Stojanovic, *Ekonomski pregled* 14, no. 3–5 (1963): 344–49.

18. Branko Horvat, "Yugoslav System of Self-management and the Import of Foreign Private Capital," in Wolfgang Friedmann, ed., *Joint Business Ventures of Yugoslav Enterprises and Foreign Firms* (New York: Columbia University and Belgrade: Institute of International Politics and Economy, 1967), p. 85.

19. Kiril Miljevski, "Possibilities for the Development of Underdeveloped Areas," in Radmila Stojanovic, ed., *Yugoslav Economists on Problems of a Socialist Economy* (New York: International Arts and Sciences Press, 1964), pp. 7–17.

20. Kosta Mihailovic, "The Regional Aspect of Economic Development," in Radmila Stojanovic, ed., *Yugoslav Economists on Problems of a Socialist Economy* (New York: International Arts and Sciences Press, 1964), pp. 29–45.

21. A revealing discussion followed the visit of a Slovenian official to Macedonia in which he spoke of "aid" to the less developed regions (*Politika,* March 17, 19, and 20, 1968).

the northwestern regions a higher residue of social over-head capital than the south. Mihailovic was a strong pro-ponent of the view that a rational development policy for the nation required the rapid development of the less de-veloped areas,[22] that is, there was no conflict between re-ducing the differences between regions and a policy of overall growth maximization. At the same time, with more equal levels of development, incomes would be more equal; this would expand the domestic market for the manufactured goods of which Yugoslavia had, by this time, an ample supply. In addition, increased volume of demand would permit economies of scale in production.

Third, many saw the fund for the development of the poorer regions not as aid but as compensation that should be paid because of the inequities of the price structure.[23] Macedonian leaders argued that the less developed regions supplied raw materials at relatively low prices to the de-veloped regions, while they paid high, tariff-protected prices for the processed goods they purchased from those areas. Thus compensation, in the form of federal transfers of funds, was only just.[24]

Finally, some saw the transfer of funds as fulfilling the promise of socialism. Citizens in the less developed re-gions had a right, as equal members of the socialist com-munity, to equal conditions in which to work.[25] Yugoslavs

22. Kosta Mihailovic, *Yugoslav Economists,* pp. 29–45.

23. *Politika,* Mar. 17, 1968, p. 9.

24. Many of the arguments used were very similar to those put forth, in a different context, by the members of the United Nations Conference on Trade and Development, more briefly known as UNCTAD. For ex-ample, the terms of trade of the less developed areas are poor (because they sell raw materials at competitive prices but must purchase finished goods at monopoly prices), the terms of trade are deteriorating (because of the relatively slow increase in demand for raw materials relative to the increase in demand for finished manufactured goods), and the richer regions conspire to keep the underdeveloped areas in the position of cheap suppliers of raw materials.

25. Kosta Mihailovic, "Prilog izgradnje koncepcije regionalnog razvoja," *Ekonomist* 18, no. 4 (1964): 561–83.

struggled to define the meaning of equal access to the means of production, which was implied by social ownership. Yugoslavs could not decide what equal access meant when the regions of the country differ significantly in the amount of capital at their disposal. Their dilemma—not yet resolved—is to square equal access to capital with a system in which capital is not distributed equally and in which retained earnings constitute the major source of future investments.

The debate over the relative roles of plan and market in socialism involved both general problems and problems specific to Yugoslavia. The general problem was the same one that troubled Marx: whether planning or the market provides a more efficient allocation of resources. Despite major differences in underlying philosophies, the general conclusion of the Yugoslav discussion seemed to be that, beyond the initial stages of development, the market mechanism would play a larger role, either because the market mechanism performs better at higher levels of development, or because the process of planning becomes increasingly costly, complex, or politically arbitrary.

The remaining doubts were whether Yugoslavia had attained levels of development that made heavy reliance on the market mechanism suitable. The answer to that question seemed to depend on the regional outlook of the viewer for two reasons. First, there were differences of opinion about the rate at which the less developed regions should catch up with the rest of the country. Because few really believed that rapid development of the less developed regions was also a maximum growth policy for the nation, and fewer still believed that their rapid development was economically more beneficial to the already advanced areas than an equivalent amount of investment in the advanced areas would have been, there was bound to be a conflict of interest between the backward and the developed regions. Those from the less developed regions did not believe that capital would flow to those regions on the basis of market criteria alone. It was in their own interest, thus, to advocate a continuation of investment planning that they believed would be more beneficial to them. For the same reason it was natural that those from the developed regions wanted to see investment planning curtailed and market criteria employed to allocate resources, with a specific political decision about the volume of "aid" to the less developed regions.

The second basis of disagreement about plan and market involved the choice of system itself. It is entirely possible that the levels of economic development are sufficiently different in the various regions that, interregional capital transfers aside, what may be a rational system for one area may not be for the other. A more highly planned system than was adopted might better be suited to the needs of the less developed regions today.

CHAPTER 8

The Worker-Managed Enterprise

The 1965 economic reforms proposed to liberate the Yugoslav enterprise from a maze of interventions, and for the first time the question of how a Yugoslav enterprise responds to economic signals and incentives became relevant. The Yugoslavs are beginning to give this problem serious consideration. Previously, plan objectives had been attained by various policies that influenced the enterprises. The principal method of attaining the desired volume and structure was the almost complete control of investments. The economic reform drastically restricted the range of admissible policy instruments. More important, following the reforms the enterprises are expected to make investments in response to market forces. The outcome of reliance on market forces is uncertain and need not be the same as in the capitalist market system because the Yugoslav enterprise differs from the capitalist enterprise in a number of respects. The major analytical difference is that the workers in the Yugoslav enterprises are both managers and profit sharers, as well as workers. It is difficult to know in advance what effect this difference will have on enterprise behavior and how it will alter the enterprise response to a given policy. The Yugoslavs therefore require a theory of the worker-managed enterprise to serve as a basis for predicting the behavior of enterprises and their response to changes in policy instruments. Only then will it be possible to determine how enterprise behavior departs from policy objectives and to select policy instruments to correct the outcome.

Development of an economic theory serves still another

purpose in Yugoslavia. As noted in an earlier chapter, and as will be commented on again in a later chapter, there is some conflict between those Yugoslavs who consider the worker-managed enterprise as a (dispensable) *means* to attaining social objectives and those who see workers' management itself as an *end,* that is, an essential feature of socialism. In order to determine whether the system should be retained and whether there is any cost in terms of other social objectives, modified (and if so, how), or abandoned, the Yugoslavs must understand how this form of economic organization operates. Without such an understanding, the debate is doomed to remain mired in rhetoric and citationism.

In this chapter I shall consider first how the Yugoslavs view the worker-managed enterprise with respect to both its role and its maximizing principles and then I shall turn to the Western analysis of the producers cooperative as it applies to the Yugoslav firm. The last section of the chapter will treat the more complex, longer range questions of economic efficiency and the role of free entry, and the source of investment funds.

YUGOSLAV VIEW OF THE ENTERPRISE

It is not possible to speak of a single Yugoslav theory of the enterprise. There is no generally accepted interpretation of the behavior of the worker-managed firm. In fact, until recently, Yugoslavs had put forward only a few explicit theories of the enterprise. It is possible, however, to cull from the various writings some of the implicit assumptions about enterprise behavior. Many of the earlier writings shared a common tendency to seek parallels between the socialist firm and the capitalist enterprise. The analogy was often carried too far and frequently obscured important differences. It was correctly applied to the *functions* of the socialist firm but it was not necessarily applicable to the *maximizing principles*. Others pursued a more fruitful line of inquiry and focused on the unique features of the Yugoslav enterprise. Although not satisfactorily solved, the economics of the enterprise is now recognized as a vital concern and recently has received greater theoretical and some empirical attention.

Function of the enterprise

Yugoslav authors readily recognized the crucial role of the entrepreneur in the capitalist system. In their view, the capitalist entrepreneur provides the "motive force" that keeps the market economy moving. It is the entrepreneur who searches for maximum profits and who organizes production to this end. In the quest for profits he enters an industry in which supply is inadequate relative to demand. Finding a process for more efficient production or conceiving a new product, he puts it into operation. The capitalist entrepreneur continually scans the economic horizon, seeking to augment his income through perception of new investment and production opportunities. He invests, causing the economy to grow. The capitalist entrepreneur, in short, pursues with a single mind his own self-interest, but in so doing he also furthers the interests of society.

In a centrally planned economy, planners take the initiative in determining the character of the economy and in directing investments into specific activities. In Yugoslavia, however, central planning has been abandoned. The social plan, of an indicative character, is concerned with broad aggregates. It cannot provide a motivating force; it does not undertake to organize production or to direct investment into specific activities. The plan does not exert pressures for cost reduction, innovation, or product improvement. The economic logic of the Yugoslav system requires that the initiative for these tasks originate elsewhere. Decentralized socialism must have an agent to adopt new methods, produce new products, and establish new locations, in short, to select investments and to bear the risks in an uncertain world. In Yugoslav economic thought as well as practice, this function is assigned to the institution of workers' management.[1]

The management of the socialist enterprise legally lies in the hands of the workers. A few authors defined the function of management narrowly, virtually excluding entrepreneurial functions. According to Uvalic, for example, the worker-managers of social property are to be rewarded according to their success in carrying out specific tasks. He stated that "the right of economic organizations to dispose of part of income is exclusively designed to enhance the productivity of labor and to stimulate collectives to exert maximum effort to fulfill their production targets." [2] This attitude toward the enterprise represented a minority opinion, even in the early sixties.

In function the Yugoslav working collective [3] is more than a manager, and most Yugoslav authors have properly recognized that the collective performs the function of the entrepreneur in their socialist system. The working collective of the enterprise establishes basic enterprise policy. The collective in principle makes all decisions about what to produce and how. The collective decides what portion of its earnings to invest, and how to invest them, or whether to lend them to other firms or to become

1. See Ivan Lavrac, "Competition and Incentive in the Yugoslav Economic System," in *Yugoslav Economists*, pp. 147–58; Mijalko Todorovic, *Socialist Thought and Practice*, no. 9 (Jan. 1963): 17–65; Miladin Korac, "Teze za teorije socijalisticke robne proizvodnje," *Socijalizam* 4, no. 1 (Jan.–Feb. 1961): 31–53; Branko Horvat, *Towards a Theory of Planned Economy*, pp. 114–20; Aleksandar Bajt, "Drustvena svojina—kolektivna i individualna," *Gledista* 9, no. 4 (Apr. 1968): 531–44.

2. Uvalic, *Yugoslav Economists*, pp. 140–47.

3. The term "working collective" is used to describe all the bodies of workers' management. For a more detailed discussion of the various management bodies in Yugoslavia, see Chap. 5 above.

shareholders in a bank. The Yugoslav collective makes these decisions from a private vantage point and pursues its own economic interests. Under the accounting system employed, the members of the collective receive residual incomes. From gross receipts, various contractual expenses, excluding wages, are deducted.[4] The remainder, a residual category, is the net income of the enterprise. The collective divides the income into two parts.[5] One part is retained for investment in the enterprise; the other is distributed to the workers as personal income. Most Yugoslav authors recognized the role of the residual part of income: "This higher income realized by the enterprise is the indicator of, and remuneration for, risks successfully taken by the management of the enterprise . . . a remuneration for the working collective as the manager of the enterprise." [6]

Maximizing principle of the enterprise

The role of the enterprise in the Yugoslav economy is understood. It is a self-interested autonomous body that bears risks and receives rewards. What is not clear is the relevant maximizing principle. Extending the analogy of the capitalist enterprise, some Yugoslav authors attributed to the Yugoslav firm the same motives characteristic of the capitalist enterprise. This was particularly true in writings in the early sixties. For example, Rakic stated that "the laws of commodity production and the market mechanism act in the same way as in an economy based on private ownership of the means of production." [7] Like the capitalist enterprise, the Yugoslav enterprise was assumed to

4. Contractual costs include the cost of materials, payment for services, depreciation, interest and principal payment on loans, and the capital tax.
5. Actually, into four parts: income, reinvestment, reserve funds, and enterprise financed collective consumption of the workers. The present discussion ignores the latter two categories.
6. Lavrac, *Yugoslav Economists,* p. 156.
7. Rakic, *Yugoslav Economists,* p. 130.

maximize total profits. Similar conclusions were suggested by Samardzija and Hadzi-Vasilev.[8]

Doubts about the similarity of capitalist and socialist enterprises grew over time and several authors began to distinguish different maximizing principles. Mijalko Todorovic, Miladin Korac, and Strasimir Popovic were among the first to note differences; their analyses, while incomplete, were more fruitful. Somewhat later France Cerne suggested several hypotheses about the objectives of the working collective. Finally, in 1968, Branko Horvat entered the discussion, taking note of the developments in the theory of producers' cooperatives in the West.

The Todorovic analysis of the enterprise is not entirely valid.[9] He stated several times in his long article (appearing in several parts, chiefly in late 1962 and early 1963) that the objective of the socialist as well as the capitalist enterprise is to maximize profits.[10] "In the enterprises in our country which are run by the workers themselves, it is also in the interests of the workers [that] $m/(c + v)$ [profit] be at a maximum."[11] The behavior of the socialist enterprise was presumed identical with that of the capitalist enterprise, and he concluded that the long run supply schedule of the cooperative and the capitalist enterprise were the same.[12] Yet in his exposition he also recognized differences in the motivation of the capitalist and the socialist firm.

> In contrast to the capitalists, the workers find it in their interests . . . that the working collective . . .

8. Samardzija, "Problem cena u socijalistickoj privredi," *Nasa stvarnost* 14, no. 12 (Dec. 1960): 496; Mito Hadji-Vasilev, "Drustveno-ekonomska sustina socijalisticke raspodele prema radu," *Socijalizam* 3, no. 6 (Nov. 1960): 98.

9. Todorovic, *Socijalizam* 5, no. 6 (Dec. 1962); 6, no. 1 (Jan. 1963) and no. 2–3 (Feb.–Mar. 1963); 7, no. 11–12 (Nov.–Dec. 1964).

10. Todorovic, *Socialist Thought and Practice,* no. 9 (Jan. 1963): 46.

11. Ibid.

12. See Chap. 9.

number as few members as possible, because . . . he must share the joint product with them. That is, the individual worker finds it in his interest to have the productivity of labor as high as possible.[13]

Todorovic did not point out that profit maximization will normally be inconsistent with the interests of the workers to keep the number of profit sharers as small as possible. He did recognize, however, that the interests of the workers might mean their refusal to hire additional workers, which could contribute to unemployment. "The desire of the worker to achieve a minimum [number of workers] conceals a contradiction existing among the direct producers themselves and can signify a tendency toward the creation of unemployment." [14] He also recognized that the entire labor force would be less mobile than in a competitive market system. "The links of the worker with his collective and the commune manifest themselves through the *increased inertia of workers,* that is, through lesser mobility on their part." [15] He believed that the effect of the loss of mobility of already employed workers would be offset by the large number of new entrants into the market each year. Interestingly, he appeared to regard the reluctance of the working collective to hire additional workers as a desirable means for raising the average productivity of labor.[16]

In contrast to Todorovic, Korac explicitly rejected the notion that the Yugoslav firm maximizes total profits.[17]

13. Todorovic, *Socialist Thought and Practice,* no. 9 (Jan. 1963): 46.
14. Ibid., p. 47.
15. Ibid., p. 51.
16. Ibid., p. 47.
17. Korac's proposals first appeared in three articles: *Socijalizam* 4, no. 1 (Jan.–Feb. 1961): 31–51; "Teorije socialisticke robne proizvodnje," *Nasa stvarnost* 16, no. 12 (Dec. 1962): 563–613; "Socijalisticki robni proizvodjac u procesu drustvene reprodukcije," *Ekonomski pregled* 14, no. 10–12 (Oct.–Dec. 1963): 1027–1075.
His articles provoked extensive discussion about the normative price

The maximizing principle of the socialist firm is "contrary to the profit rate." [18] Korac constructed a model of the rational Yugoslav enterprise operating under the following conditions: means of production are owned by society and managed by the collective; competitive markets allocate productive factors and final products; enterprise retained earnings are the sole source of capital; and the enterprise can enter any branch of production. Korac also assumed that workers wish to increase their incomes in the future. In his model, since the sole means of increasing future income is through reinvestment of retained earnings, there will be a positive rate of investment from undistributed earnings.

Korac's verbal statement of the enterprise maximizing principle was not clear. He asserted that "the rate of income expresses the profitability of the socialist firm." [19] The collective seeks to maximize its present net income in relation to the capital and labor employed. "The size of the rate of income depends, on the one hand, on the mass of realized income and the mass of engaged factors of production (or the value expression thereof) and, on the other hand, on the organic composition of those factors of production." [20]

In more specific form, however, the principle is either erroneous or unclear. Korac asserted that the rational enterprise would maximize its rate of income. The rate of income, r, was defined by him as [21]

---

and allocation of resources that he and his followers asserted was the corollary of those theses about enterprise behavior. (See Chap. 9 for a discussion of normative price.) Little new was said in later articles about the enterprise itself. His later article, "Zakon vrednosti kao regulator raspodele dohotka u socijalistickom sistemu robne privrede," *Ekonomski pregled* 17, no. 10 (Oct. 1966): 548–579, has virtually the same theory of the firm.

18. Korac, *Socijalizam* 4, no. 1 (Jan.–Feb. 1961): 41–42.
19. Ibid., 42.
20. Ibid.
21. Ibid.

$$r = \frac{\text{realized income}}{\text{engaged means of production} + \text{newly created value}}$$

Realized income here is the net income of the enterprise after taxes and all nonlabor expenses. Engaged means of production includes capital equipment and the materials employed (in Marxian terms, the means of labor and the objects of labor). Newly created value, by the assumption of equilibrium, has the same magnitude as realized income.[22] The rate of income so defined is allegedly the enterprise criterion for making short run decisions about what to produce, as well as decisions involving the investment of capital and possible moves into alternative branches of production.

This analysis of enterprise behavior has been attacked in the Yugoslav literature on several grounds. Strasimir Popovic was among the first to question whether the rational enterprise would behave in the manner Korac postulated.[23] In the form in which Korac presented his criterion, there is no explicit mention of the number of workers in the enterprise. Popovic noted that the *rate* of income would be higher if the number of workers increased relative to a given stock of capital. In that way both realized income per unit of capital and the rate of income would

22. Newly created value is a Marxian category. The total value (Marxian sense) of a commodity at any given stage of processing is composed of the value of the initial raw materials in it, the value added by previous labor, value transferred from the capital equipment that processed it in the present stage, and the newly created value added only by human labor in the present stage.

Realized income, a price and accounting category, could deviate from newly created value primarily for the same reasons—market fluctuations—that price deviates from value in Marxian analysis (see Chap. 2). Deviations could also result from any conscious policies of the state affecting prices directly or indirectly, as well as the existence of monopoly, etc. In simple commodity production, in long run competitive equilibrium, realized income would be identical with newly created value.

23. Strasimir Popovic, "Prilog gradji o ekonomskom sistemu Jugoslavije," *Nasa stvarnost* 17, no. 5 (May 1963): 522–49.

be very high.[24] Income per worker would not. He concluded that the Korac criterion would not be the objective of a rational collective. Todorovic was equally severe in condemning the income rate.[25]

Popovic went on to state the explicit objective of the rational collective. He said openly what had scarcely appeared elsewhere in Yugoslavia: that the rational enterprise would want to *maximize income per worker*. "To achieve larger income per worker . . . is the basic motive." [26] The criterion for decisions in the first instance depends on the effect on "income per worker remaining for free distribution." [27] Popovic also perceived that this behavior might be undesirable for resource allocation but he did not extend his analysis of the problem.

These early discussions about the enterprise took place before 1964. Attention turned again to the theory of the firm after the economic reform of 1965, which made the problem more urgent.

ECONOMICS OF THE PRODUCERS' COOPERATIVE

Yugoslavs had difficulty explaining the behavior of the enterprise. Those who recognized that the maximizing principle of the Yugoslav enterprise might not be the same as that of the capitalist firm found that construction of an adequate model was by no means easy. France Cerne, recognizing the inadequacies of the then-current conceptions, explored several hypotheses about enterprise behavior. He found little reason to support most of the current hypotheses, including the notion that enterprises maximize total

24. See Chap. 9, where it is shown that maximizing the rate of income is probably equivalent to maximizing realized income per unit of capital.
    25. Todorovic, *Socialist Thought and Practice*, no. 17 (Jan.–Mar. 1964): 29.
    26. Strasimir Popovic, *Nasa stvarnost* 17, no. 5 (May 1963): 531.
    27. Ibid.

enterprise income (he suggests that they are interested in personal income, not enterprise income), or total future income (because the worker has no guarantee of permanent association with the enterprise).[28] His article, although inconclusive, raised interesting questions, especially whether efficiency would be enhanced if workers had a more permanent stake in the enterprise.

It is interesting that the Illyrian economy, where worker-managed plants produce for the free market, holds greater fascination for Americans than for the inhabitants of Illyresque Yugoslavia. Branko Horvat finally wrote about the Western literature on the producers' cooperative.[29] In his book *Towards a Theory of Planned Economy*, written in 1958 but published in Yugoslavia only in 1961, he had paid little attention to the maximizing principles of the enterprise (or implicitly assumed it to maximize total profits).[30] Later he was unable to ignore the implications of the work by Benjamin Ward [31] and Evsey Domar.[32] Logically, the Yugoslav firm appears to be a producers' cooperative. A producers' cooperative is characterized by the sharing of profits among members. In the analysis of Ward and Domar, the producers' cooperative would want to maximize income per worker. This maximizing principle differs from that of the capitalist firm. As a result, the producers' cooperative may find it rational to use different input combinations to produce different outputs than would an otherwise identical capitalist enterprise facing an iden-

28. France Cerne, "Pokusaj ekonomsko-logickog testiranje sedam hipoteza iz teorije dohotka," *Gledista* 8, no. 10 (Oct. 1967): 1305–1326.

29. Branko Horvat, "Prilog zasnivanju teorije jugoslavenskog poduzeca," *Ekonomksa analiza* 1, no. 1–2 (1967): 7–28.

30. Horvat, *Towards a Theory of Planned Economy*, chap. 6.

31. Benjamin Ward, "The Firm in Illyria: Market Syndicalism," *American Economic Review* 48, no. 4 (Sept. 1958): 566–89. Ward continued his explanation of the Yugoslav economic system in his book *The Socialist Economy* (New York: Random House, 1968), chaps. 8–10.

32. Evsey Domar, "On Collective Farms and Producer Cooperatives," *American Economic Review* 56, no. 4 (Sept. 1966): 734–57.

tical production function and identical prices of inputs and final product. In general, the response of the producers' cooperative is not identical to that of the capitalist enterprise.

Horvat summarized the results of Ward and Domar and then tried to show that the Yugoslav enterprise did not behave in the manner they assumed and therefore was not subject to the inefficiencies their work suggested.

In the simplest case, with one output and one variable input, labor, Ward showed in 1958 the following results. Let the sole element of cost be a tax on the fixed supply of capital. There are no wages, and workers share equally the entire difference between total revenue and total costs. (The amount available for workers is unaltered if a wage is introduced and included in costs but deducted from the profits. Analytically the introduction of a wage makes no difference.) For simplicity, further assume that the cooperative firm is one of many in a competitive industry and that it faces a horizontal demand schedule.

Output is some function of the given amount of capital stock and of the quantity of labor (x). For a given value of capital stock,

$$O = f(x)$$

Total revenue (TR) is given by the quantity of output times the price.

$$TR = pO$$

Total cost (TC), the tax on capital, is a fixed sum. Total profits (TP) are the difference between total revenue and total cost.

$$TP = TR - TC$$

Since the workers share the profits and receive no wages but a dividend per worker, their objective is to produce that output and employ that number of workers at which dividend per worker is maximized. The collective wishes to maximize

$$\frac{TP}{x} = \frac{TR}{x} - \frac{TC}{x}$$

If TC is fixed without respect to the level of output or number of workers, then TC/x can be expressed graphically by a rectangular hyperbola; TR/x can also be represented with ease. Assume, for example, that output is a function of labor input such that the average product of labor rises to some maximum and then diminishes. The firm faces an elastic demand for its product, so that the price remains constant regardless of the output sold. The expression TR/x is simply the average product of labor multiplied by the price of the product, or the average value product of labor. The two curves are shown in Figure 1.

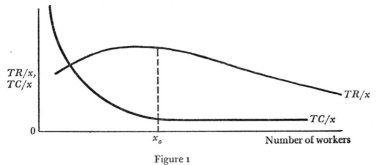

Figure 1

The dividend per worker is the vertical difference between TR/x and TC/x (Figure 2). The dividend per worker is greatest where the vertical distance between TR/x and TC/x is greatest, which occurs where their slopes are equal.[33] To the left of x_0, too few workers are being employed and the dividend is not at a maximum. It pays the firm to employ more workers. Conversely, to the right of x_0, too many workers are employed and the dividend per

33. Maximum dividend per worker occurs when the slopes of the TR/x and TC/x curves are identical, where $[d\,(TR/x)]/dx = [d\,(TC/x)]/dx$.

worker drops. In this case it pays the working collective to reduce its numbers. (There is, of course, a problem in re-

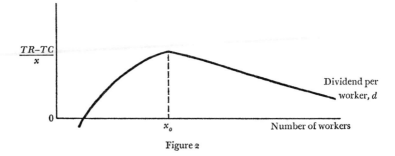

Figure 2

ducing the number of workers, since the workers to be dismissed will probably resist such a move.[34] Let us assume, however, that the number of workers in the enterprise can be freely varied.)

On the basis of this simple model, Ward has drawn attention to some interesting features of the producers' cooperative.

1. *A change in fixed costs will cause the firm to change employment and output in the same direction.* Fixed costs might be raised by increasing the rate of tax on the fixed stock of capital. Increasing the size of fixed costs will produce a new TC/x curve for TC', shifting the hyperbola outward (Figure 3). Graphically, increasing TC will not only raise TC/x; it will alter the curvature in such a manner that the slope is steeper at x_0.[35] Here x_0 is no longer the number of workers that maximizes the dividend per worker. Accordingly, the firm should expand output and

34. This raises the further, intriguing question of the behavior of groups within the working collective who might form voting coalitions in order to reduce the number of workers. However, such complications will not be considered here.

35. The slope of TC/x at x_0 is $d(TC/x)/dx = -TC/x_0^2$. Thus an increase in TC will make the curve TC/x more steeply sloped at x_0 than before. A decrease in TC will make the curve less steeply sloped than before.

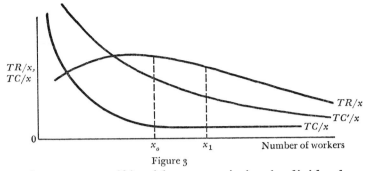

Figure 3

employment to x_1 if it wishes to maximize the dividend per worker (d') under the new fixed cost conditions (Figure 4).

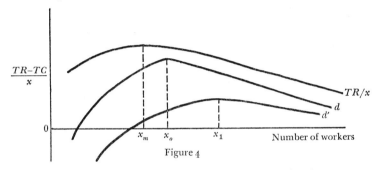

Figure 4

Thus an increase in fixed costs would cause the firm to expand output and employment.[36] When fixed costs are zero, the firms would produce where TR/x is a maximum, that is, where the average product of labor is greatest, at x_m. A lump sum subsidy under these circumstances will induce hiring a number of workers below x_m (and indeed it would pay to decrease the number of workers to nearly zero). Obviously, these responses, as Ward has noted, are quite different from those of the capitalist firm. The criterion of the capitalist firm is to produce at the level at which marginal costs are equal to marginal revenue. And since mar-

36. Provided the fixed costs do not rise so much as to reduce the profit per worker below the statutory minimum wage that society guarantees. In that case it would pay the workers to stop producing and pick up their guaranteed income.

ginal costs are not affected by a change in fixed costs, in the short run the capitalist firm would not find its best output or employment position altered by a change in the level of fixed costs.

2. *A change in the price of the product will cause the firm to change its output and employment in the opposite direction.* If the price of the product increases, then the entire TR/x curve shifts upward, to TR_a/x (Figure 5).

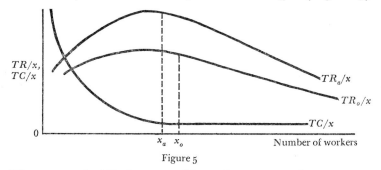

Figure 5

The upward shift is not uniform but proportional to the initial values. Thus a doubling of the price will produce a new curve with not only higher TR/x at any value of x but also with a different curvature. The maximum value of TR/x occurs at the same value of x as before, but the curve rises more steeply and declines more rapidly from that maximum.[37] The rational worker-managed firm would thus seek to reduce output and employment to x_a where $TR/x - TC/x$ is greatest (Figure 6). Thus the producers' cooperative in this highly restrictive case has a negatively sloped supply curve. This has potentially dangerous implications for the stability of the system.

We may now examine the effect on resource utilization by considering employing additional nonlabor inputs. As Ward has shown, the criterion of a producers' cooperative

37. The slope of TR/x is $[d(TR/x)]/dx = [d(pO/x)]/dx = [p(x_0O' - O)]/x_0^2$. An increase in p changes the absolute value of the slope proportionally to the change in p.

for hiring additional nonlabor inputs is the same as that of the capitalist firm. For a given number of workers, anything that increases *total profits* will increase dividend per worker. And total profits will increase if the value of the marginal product of the additional nonlabor input exceeds its cost. This is valid for any hired factor of production.

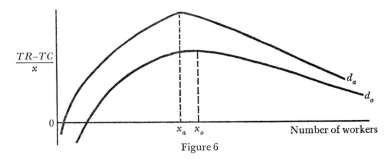

Figure 6

The attitudes of the Yugoslav and the capitalist firm differ toward labor inputs. The capitalist will employ labor as long as the value of the marginal product of an additional laborer is greater than the wage he must be paid. The Yugoslav enterprise will hire an additional worker only if the value of the marginal product is no less than the current dividend paid to currently employed workers. That is, an additional worker will be hired only if the net addition to enterprise income is no less than the current dividend per worker, the amount the new worker must be paid. Thus the marginal product of labor will equal the current dividend.

As Domar has pointed out in this simple model, the differences in resource use between twin capitalist and cooperative enterprises will depend on the differences between the wage rate and the dividend. For otherwise identical conditions concerning production functions and output and input prices, if the dividend rate in the cooperative enterprise is equal to the wage rate in the capitalist enterprise (implying zero profits for the capitalist enterprise), then the capitalist and cooperative use of resources will be identical and allocation of resources in both enterprises is efficient. If the dividend rate is equal for all cooperative enterprises in a socialist economy, then the differences in resource utilization between a socialist and an otherwise identical capitalist society will depend on the size of the uniform dividend rate relative to the wage rate prevailing in the capitalist society. If the dividend rate is larger than the wage rate, then the marginal productivity of employed labor will be greater in the socialist society, although some labor will be unemployed. In addition, there does not appear to be any reason for the dividend per worker to be identical in all cooperative enterprises. Hence the marginal product of labor is not identical in all uses and there is a definite but inestimable misallocation of resources.

Horvat recognized the potential conflict between worker-managed firms and economic efficiency. This conflict hits at the heart of his own theory of the efficiently planned economy, which is in fact a Yugoslav-type economy. His theory rests on two pillars. The first is the high human and economic cost of central planning that produces bureaucratization. The second is that decisions by decentralized, profit-maximizing enterprises are, in the majority of cases, economically efficient. Thus, decentralizing decisions to profit-making enterprises is a feasible and efficient alternative to bureaucratic central planning. But Horvat, in fact, goes further. Bureaucracy must give way not to just *any* type of decentralization but to enterprises under workers' management. The implicit part of his argument—and it is central to his conclusions—is that the Yugoslav-type, worker-managed enterprises, in fact, maximize profits. Only if they do are the efficiency properties of competitive, profit-maximizing systems applicable to the Yugoslav-type economy. For this reason, Horvat must refute the implications of the Ward-Domar model, in order to leave his own theory intact.

Horvat tries to dispose of the Ward-Domar conflict in several ways. First, as Ward and Domar had shown, the differences between the capitalist and the cooperative firms in response to various stimuli diminish with the increasing generality of the model. The responses in the one variable input case were strikingly different (see the accompanying table). However, with two variable inputs, the situation

Responses in One Variable Input Case

Type of change	Response in employment and output	
	Capitalist	*Cooperative*
Increase wages	Negative	No effect
Increase TC	No effect	Positive
Increase product price	Positive	Negative

changes significantly (see Chart 1). As Domar has shown,

Chart 1

Type of change	Capitalist firm	Cooperative firm
Increase in wages		
Effect on:		
Output	Negative	No effect
Employment	Negative	No effect
Input use	Positive for substitutes to labor; negative for complements of labor	No effect
Increase in input price		
Effect on:		
Output	Negative	Indeterminate
Employment	Positive if labor is a substitute; negative if it is a complement	Positive if labor is a substitute; indeterminate if it is a complement
Use of input	Negative	Negative if labor is a substitute for input; indeterminate if it is a complement

Chart 1 (cont.)

Type of change	Capitalist firm	Cooperative firm
Increase in fixed costs		
Effect on:		
Output	No effect	Indeterminate for substitutability between input and labor; positive for complementarity between input and labor
Employment	No effect	Positive
Use of input	No effect	Negative if input is a substitute for labor; positive if it is a complement
Increase in product price		
Effect on:		
Output	Positive	Indeterminate
Employment	Positive	Negative for substitutability between labor and input; indeterminate for complementarity
Use of input	Positive	Positive for substitutability with labor; indeterminate for complements; negative for high complementarity

the enterprise response in terms of output and employment to changes in fixed costs, input prices, product price, and wage levels no longer differs as sharply. Even so, the capitalist and the cooperative responses are still not identical. What is apparent is that, because both capitalist and cooperative firms have the same criterion for the use of nonlabor inputs, an increase in the number of nonlabor inputs makes the response pattern less strikingly different than before with only one variable input, labor.

It may be noted at this point that an increased similarity of response, which decreases the likelihood of negatively sloped supply schedules, is reassuring with respect to the stability properties of the model. It should not, however, be confused with showing efficiency. A monopolist and a perfect competitor both respond in the same way to changes in parameters (changes in fixed costs, input prices, and output prices) but they are not equally efficient.

Second, Horvat followed Domar further, in showing that the responses may be further modified if there is no longer an unlimited supply of labor at the going price.[38] If the supply price of labor is rising, the firm may not be able to employ sufficient labor to maximize income per worker. The supply schedule of labor to the enterprise could intersect the dividend per worker curve from below, before the maximum dividend per worker was attained (Figure 7).

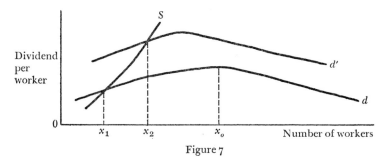

Figure 7

At the initial price level, the dividend per worker curve reaches a maximum at x_0, but because of a rising supply price of labor, the firm is able to employ only x_1 of labor. A higher product price will raise the dividend per worker curve from d to d', and the firm can now expand output and employment from x_1 to x_2. Thus, a change in product price, under these conditions, will cause the firm, even in the one variable-input–one output case, to respond in the *same* direction as the capitalist firm, rather than in the opposite. Similarly, a decrease in fixed costs that would also

38. Part 3 of his article.

shift the dividend per worker schedule upward, as from d to d', would result in an increase in employment and output rather than, as previously, a decrease. (The capitalist makes no response to a change in fixed costs.)

Some comments may be made at this point. If the supplies of labor are limited, it alters the direction of enterprise response to certain stimuli and makes negatively sloped supply schedules and hence potential instability less likely. The efficiency question remains open. Second, it seems unlikely that there is such an extreme inelasticity of supply of labor to each individual firm. Such an enterprise supply schedule presupposes virtually no mobility of the employed labor force and a minimal flow of new entrants to the labor force, as well as an inelastic supply of labor to the economy as a whole. While the last condition might be met in the future (though certainly not in the present, for with substantial unemployment and the continued migration from the countryside, the supply of labor to the nonagricultural sector should be fairly elastic), the other two are more dubious. Ordinarily, the more developed the economy, the more mobile the labor force and the greater the elasticity of supply to any given firm (though not necessarily for the economy as a whole). If the supply to a given firm is elastic, it will hire sufficient workers to attain the maximum dividend per worker. Ultimately, one might expect fewer factories but each one would be maximizing the dividend per worker. Even if already-employed labor is highly immobile, due to some institutional restraint such as living in enterprise-owned housing, the new labor force entering the market annually would be a much more mobile group.

In his final effort to dispose of the Ward-Domar image of cooperative inefficiency, Horvat argues that it is plausible to assume that enterprises decide in advance on the proposed increases in personal incomes. Such decisions are made on the basis of a number of factors such as the disposable income of the enterprise, changes in the cost of living, and personal income increases in other firms. Having done so, he asserts that it is then rational for them to maximize *total enterprise profits* above the specified personal income payments, and not *profit per worker*.[39] Given the compensation scale, to maximize total profits, firms would hire until the value of the marginal product of labor fell to the level of the compensation scale. Since the rate of pay is presumably less than the anticipated total profit per worker (rates higher than that could not be sustained indefinitely) more labor would be hired than if the firms were maximizing the profit per worker, and the total profit of the firm would rise. Indeed, by maximizing total profits the Yugoslav firm would be behaving like a capitalist firm; hence the traditional theory of the firm, with all its efficiency corollaries, would be equally applicable to the Yugoslav firm.

If the firm behaves as Horvat asserts, at the end of the year, the profits available after paying the agreed scale are maximized. These profits are used for investment, and investment is thus maximized. Of course, the investment *per worker* is less than it would have been under the Ward-Domar behavior (with the same rates of compensation). Horvat's proposed behavior requires that workers not only accept this year's compensation schedule but that they not seek to maximize their incomes over time either. To maximize income over time requires high average productivity of labor that, in most technologies, involves high capital-labor ratios. But following his assumption, there is less investment per worker; hence the productivity per worker cannot increase as fast as otherwise, and future income per worker is lower than it might have been.

Horvat, in essence, is asserting that workers do not seek to maximize personal income either in the present or over time; instead, subject to a wage constraint, they seek to

39. Part 4 of his article.

maximize investment, or maximize total profits, which is the same thing if the wage scale is set. He may be correct. It would be more convincing if he could suggest why workers do not want to maximize income per worker and what organizational features might make the Yugoslav corporation, like the Galbraithian corporation, want to maximize growth instead.

The ultimate recourse is to empirical evidence. Two American authors have looked into the matter. Joel Dirlam made a study in 1965 of the principles of enterprise management, based on an examination of the legal regulations, interviews with managers, and perusal of the standard Yugoslav business management texts.[40] He was unable to find clear indication of any maximizing principle. He believed that the situation might alter after the economic reform took effect. Thomas Marschak studied the Yugoslav economy to determine whether the organizational shift from central planning to market socialism had any discernible effect on economic efficiency.[41] In the course of his examination he attempted to find empirical confirmation of some of the kinds of behavior predicted by the Ward-Domar analysis. The Ward-Domar analysis suggests, for example, that labor mobility from firm to firm cannot equalize pay differentials, and that such differentials will be found in a producers' cooperative system. Marschak asked, are there significant interfirm differences in pay for the same specialized occupation? Using data on firms in Belgrade and Zagreb for the years 1963 and 1964, for seven specialty occupations in various industries, Marschak tested the hypothesis that interenterprise wage differentials exceed intraenterprise differentials. For four of the seven specialties, the hypothesis of no wage differential between

40. Joel E. Dirlam, "Yugoslav Pricing Policies and the Public Interest," University of Rhode Island, mimeo (n.d.).

41. Thomas A. Marschak, "Centralized versus Decentralized Resource Allocation: The Yugoslav 'Laboratory,'" *Quarterly Journal of Economics* 82, no. 4 (Nov. 1968): 561–87.

enterprises was rejected at the 5 percent level. He noted, however, that the evidence of income differences, while consistent with the pattern of behavior predicted by the Ward-Domar model, could also be explained by other aspects of Yugoslav institutional arrangements; housing in enterprise-owned apartments could limit mobility and hence permit earnings differentials.

Another prediction of the Ward-Domar model is that enterprises will tend to select capital-intensive investments that in turn will produce higher dividends per worker. Marschak asked whether enterprises with higher than average fixed assets per worker earn higher than average profits per worker. Using a one-third sample of 2,300 enterprise annual reports for the years 1959 and 1960 in 54 different industries, Marschak tested the hypothesis that enterprise profits per man-hour (as a percentage deviation from the industry mean) were positively related to fixed assets per man-hour (expressed as a percentage deviation from the industry mean). For manufacturing as a whole and for Yugoslavia as a whole, the hypothesis that "wealthier" firms have higher profits per man-hour is not supported by the data.[42] Of the selected industries studied in detail only two, hemp and electrical distribution, displayed significant correlation. Since the latter is a regulated monopoly, few conclusions can be drawn.

As the first empirical test of the behavior of the Yugoslav enterprise, it is a path-breaking study. It suffers from a defect that can be remedied when data for later years become available to researchers. In particular, the incentive for, and ability of, enterprises to maximize income per worker was severely limited before 1965, for the reasons stated in Chapter 6. It would be interesting to test the hypotheses for the years after the reform, and hopefully such work is already in progress.

42. Correlation coefficients are .049 for 1959 and .071 for 1960.

LONG RUN PROBLEMS

The analysis thus far has been traditional short run analysis of the enterprise with capital stock fixed, the number of firms constant, no real industry supply schedule, and constant technology. It is now time to modify these assumptions. The principal problems to be explored are the long run efficiency of the system and the crucial role of entry, and the sources of investment funds.

Long run efficiency and free entry

Ward [43] extended his analysis of Illyria to the long run, as did Charles Rockwell.[44] Without reviewing the analysis, some of the results may be stated.

1. In the case of monopoly, long run output in Illyria will never be greater than the output of the capitalist monopolist and is equal only in the case of zero profits.

2. In the case of pure competition, in the long run it is unlikely that there will be a negatively sloped industry supply schedule. However, the industry supply schedule will be highly inelastic.

3. The competitive sector can under certain circumstances be pareto-optimal in the long run. But left to their own devices, the firms will tend to use more capital and less labor than a similarly situated capitalist firm. This would imply either unemployment or firms with vastly differing rates of substitution between labor and capital. Where the marginal rates of substitution differ (including for unemployed workers) the pareto criterion is not met.

43. Ward, *The Socialist Economy*, chaps. 8–10.
44. Charles S. Rockwell, "The Relevance of Illyria for Less Developed Countries," mimeo. Despite the title, the "primary interest is a rigorous analysis of the Marshallian long run."

4. In competition, both increase in demand and neutral technological progress will cause perfectly competitive firms to decrease both labor and output; the monopolist response is similar. The logical extreme of continuing shifts in demand and of changes in technology is the one-man, push-button firm.

The performance, both with and without technological change and shift of demand, shows the key role of entry. Only the rapid entry of new firms can offset the impediments to efficiency. If each competitive firm has a relatively inelastic supply schedule, then industry output can only expand by increasing the number of firms. Increasing the number of firms would lower the product price; it would reduce the dividend per worker, serving to equalize incomes; finally, it would provide employment for the unemployed workers who, unorganized, have no access to capital. If the competitive firms are identical, free entry will drive them all back to the point at which the dividend per worker is just equal to the supply price of labor, which is identical with the zero profit point of the capitalist. If that can be done, the Illyrian competitive firms will be identical to their capitalist counterparts, and the efficiency theorems of competitive free enterprise are valid for Illyria as well. (In firms that are unequal in efficiency, the income per worker, and thus the marginal product of labor, will differ from firm to firm and efficiency will be impaired. If the differences in income are due to some advantage, then a scarcity rent is required; if they are due to superior entrepreneurial skill, it is a factor payment for higher quality entrepreneurship. See Chapter 10.)

The crucial requirement for efficiency in Illyria is free entry. Entry could be promoted by the state or by the localities (they once served such a function, prior to the reform); by private individuals in return for a share of the profit without voice in management, or by specialized socialist enterprises that would specialize in promoting. Such firms would research the field, raise the funds, and set the firm up in return for a share of the profits. If the Ward-Domar-Rockwell analysis is correct, providing for entry should be a major concern. The Yugoslavs have given, as yet, relatively little attention to the problem of instituting effective entry.

Sources of investment funds

Since the early days of decentralization, Yugoslav doctrine has required that the enterprise invest some of its own funds in any project. There are several practical reasons for this provision that may be persuasive. It may reinforce the worker's identification with his factory and thus encourage higher performance and better maintenance of equipment.

Reliance on partial reinvestment also provides an element of risk. In a capitalist system poor judgment in business decisions results in losses for the owner and can ultimately end in bankruptcy. As noted in the earlier discussion of entrepreneurship, the Yugoslavs recognized that a reward for good entrepreneurship was necessary. But there was also concern about the adequacy of penalties for faulty decisions. If proper choices are to be taken in risky situations, there must be not only the prospect of gain but also the possibility of loss. Lavrac, among others, has questioned whether the Yugoslav system provides adequate penalties.[45] If the enterprise makes poor decisions and is unable to meet its obligations, including the payment of the guaranteed minimum income, the state undertakes to pay individuals that guaranteed minimum. This limits the economic penalties suffered by the working collective for poor management and entrepreneurship. In the face of repeated poor performance, of course, the community may

45. Lavrac, *Yugoslav Economists,* pp. 154–56.

disband the enterprise.[46] To increase the econ̶
ties for poor choices, Lavrac advocated (before̶
a compulsory enterprise reserve fund. Part c̶
net income would be set aside in a reserve̶
which the minimum wage would be paid in the event oɪ a
temporary business failure.

> The underlying idea of this fund is, on the one hand,
> to activate the workers as managers of the social means
> of production and, on the other, to help enterprises
> to shape and implement their long-term policy, partic-
> ularly their market policy. Finally, this fund would
> also protect society from having directly to bear the
> expenses caused by any possible failure in business on
> the part of the enterprises.[47]

The economic reform took a different approach to the
problem. It provided that retained earnings (foregone consumption of the workers) be the principal source of investment. If the enterprise decisions are poor ones, the foregone consumption of the workers will not generate future
income; the workers will have lost the income streams that
could have been generated. This change provides stronger
penalties for poor choices.

In earlier years, at least, the provision that enterprises
must provide some portion of their own investment funds
was also designed to keep workers from distributing all
profits to personal income. Loans were contingent upon a
certain volume of enterprise savings. Yugoslavs have long
been concerned about the incentive of the enterprise to
reinvest. Indeed, the entire history of regulation of enterprise income distribution prior to 1965 can be interpreted
as an attempt to find a set of instruments to induce the

46. Actually the guaranteed incomes are quite low, so that workers, in
fact, do suffer a considerable loss.
47. Lavrac, *Yugoslav Economists*, p. 157.

collective to retain a larger share of earnings for investment without totally diminishing incentives.[48]

As time went on, however, Yugoslavs began to question
whether, under Yugoslav institutions, the enterprises had
sufficient incentive to save and invest. Prior to the reforms,
both Popovic and Todorovic recognized a potential unwillingness on the part of the firm to reinvest from its earnings.[49] Their reasoning was not entirely clear but the following economic explanation would be consistent with
their conclusions.

In the simple case with only capital and labor and one
output, let labor be held constant and consider increases
in capital stock. Capital will be invested by the enterprise
only if the marginal productivity of capital is sufficient to
compensate the workers for giving up their present consumption. If the number of workers remains constant
while capital is increased, in the absence of changes in
technology and in demand for the final product, the marginal productivity of capital will decline as capital increases relative to the number of workers. At some point
further reinvestment is no longer worthwhile. The marginal productivity of capital can no longer provide an adequate rate of return as judged by the time preferences of
the workers. However, the returns from the inframarginal
units of capital may be quite high, thus providing considerable income to the enterprise and high profit per
worker.

Of course, as more capital per worker is employed, the
marginal productivity of labor will increase. This need
not induce the collective to hire more workers, however,
because the dividend per worker is also increasing as a
result of the returns to the additional units of capital. It
cannot be specified whether the marginal productivity of

48. See Chap. 5.
49. Strasimir Popovic, *Nasa stvarnost* 17, no. 5 (May 1963): 522–49;
Todorovic, *Socijalizam* 6, no. 1 (Jan. 1963): 3–38.

labor at the initial employment level will rise faster than the dividend per worker. If it does, then the firm would find it rational to employ additional workers, thus further increasing dividends per worker. Expansion in employment would occur even if there was no substitutability between capital and labor only if there were increasing returns to scale. It would not occur with constant returns to scale, for present workers would be unwilling to reinvest from their own earnings, thus sacrificing present income, merely to replicate without adding to their own future income. If there is substitution between capital and labor, then workers would compare the gains per worker from substitution with those available from expansion under conditions of increasing returns. Employment would probably increase only if significant economies of scale were present.

Thus, in the absence of changing technology or changing final demand, the number of workers employed will not increase; shifts in demand and neutral techonological progress do not mitigate the problem, for the competitive firm will respond to them by decreasing output and employment. If that is the case, the marginal productivity of capital will fall to the point at which no further investment takes place. At that point, if the workers have only the choice of investing in their own firm or distributing earnings to personal income, all enterprise earnings would be distributed to the workers.

Strasimir Popovic, writing before the economic reform that made possible alternative investment opportunities for the firm, concluded that because workers have a limited incentive to invest even when profits are high, part of the enterprise funds would have to be returned to the general social funds to be allocated through the banking system. If the funds remained in the enterprise, they would be used for consumption.

Todorovic was troubled by the same problems. Since

beyond some limit the enterprise would have no desire to invest (whether from own funds or borrowed funds) nor to hire additional workers, he envisioned two possibilities. The state might intervene administratively to increase the number of workers in a given firm. Alternatively, the enterprise could "provide its own capital, through the bank, for use by other collectives." [50] Todorovic favored the second solution. In such cases the enterprise would receive interest on the funds placed in the bank.

It is interesting to compare the thrust of this argument about the uses of enterprise profits with other views heard only shortly before the reform. In the early sixties it was frequently maintained that a "capital market" was inconsistent with the principles of socialism. Uvalic rejected it, saying that "it would imply an extension of the right of economic organizations at the expense of society as a whole, a gradual abolition of social ownership and its transformation into group ownership." [51] Korac reached a similar conclusion. "The working collective, unlike the capitalist, is not free to decide whether free funds will be invested in the bank or not; nor does it have any right to earn interest on these funds, since it is not the owner; nor does it have the right to participate in the distribution of social product on the basis of ownership nor to decide who shall be the user of these funds." [52] The changes that Korac regarded as inadmissible in 1963 were precisely those that were adopted in 1965; the doubts that Uvalic expressed were precisely those being uttered in the late sixties.

There are other reasons, only recently recognized by Yugoslavs, which would also reduce the likelihood of a high rate of voluntary reinvestment from enterprise earnings. In addition to institutional instability—the somewhat arbitrary, annual changes in the "rules of the game" that

50. Todorovic, *Socijalizam* 6, no. 1 (Jan. 1963): 14.
51. Uvalic, *Yugoslav Economists*, p. 144.
52. Korac, *Ekonomski pregled* 14, no. 10–12 (Oct.–Dec. 1963): 1067–1068.

decrease certainty about the future—other factors may be mentioned. Even if the workers have low time preferences and are willing to postpone present consumption at rates satisfactory to the policy makers, the investment forthcoming from the enterprise might be low. From the viewpoint of each individual member of the working collective, the "risk" associated with such investment is very high. The investment is immobile, nontransferrable, and illiquid. Loss of job (and there is no guarantee of continuing employment in the enterprise), death, moving, illness, and retirement would all result in loss of income. Thus each individual worker has a considerable risk of not receiving the future income streams arising from his decision to reinvest. Further, there might be differences of opinion within the enterprise, representing the different time preferences of the workers involved. These differences in part are psychological but also reflect such real facts as their age and state of health and their prospects for job mobility.

Cerne was troubled about the incentive of the workers to invest because of the nonpermanence of association with the enterprise.[53] He recognized that a short time horizon would reduce the willingness to reinvest. Cerne concluded that "the collective entrepreneurial system" might function better if certain changes were made. In particular, he saw no objection to the development of "collective share relations" or to a more permanent association of the worker with a particular enterprise.[54] While leaving this proposal somewhat vague, as to just how workers would invest capital and receive interest on it, he suggests that it would promote more rational decisions about saving, investing, and lending to other firms.

While the notion of collective share relations is intriguing, economic analysis suggests that things might move in a different direction. If we assume that private citizens

53. Cerne, Gledista 8, no. 10 (Oct. 1967): 1310.
54. Ibid., p. 1323.

can purchase—as in fact, they can—interest-bearing owned assets, for example, savings accounts at 5 percent, this should have some impact on the reinvestment decision. Investing in the enterprise is equivalent to acquiring a share of an income stream for the duration of employment in that enterprise without acquiring title to the asset. The right to an income stream is acquired by paying the purchase price of the nonowned asset (whether by borrowing and repaying from profits or by purchasing directly out of previously accrued profits is immaterial). The workers can thus generate future income streams in either of two ways, by investing in the firm (from existing profits or from loans to be repaid from future profits), or by distributing all current profits to the workers and letting individuals purchase interest-bearing assets. Under these conditions, it will take a very high rate of return to induce the workers to invest undistributed earnings in the enterprises. The rate of return on such nonowned assets must be significantly higher than on owned assets to make workers indifferent between the two forms of investment. How much higher, as Furubotn and Pejovic have shown, depends on the expected time horizon over which the income streams are received.[55] If the return on owned assets is 5 percent, at the end of a year with an owned asset the individual has the initial value plus the 5 percent. To be in an equivalent position after one year with a nonowned asset, the rate of return would have to be 105 percent! For a time horizon of five years, the equivalent rate of return necessary is 23 percent; for ten years, 13 percent; and for twenty years, 8 percent.

It would seem that, unless the labor force is highly immobile (and if it is immobile, there are other inefficiencies

---

55. Eirik Furubotn and Svetozar Pejovic, "The Firm: Its Behavior and Property Rights in a Planned Economy," paper presented at the annual meeting of the Southern Economic Association, Washington, D.C., Nov. 8, 1968.

and problems), the voluntary incentive to invest through the enterprise would be rather limited. (If reinvestment is not voluntary but compulsory under some formula, then it is equivalent to a tax on realized income, which is returned to the enterprise in the form of a capital grant from the state. In this case the allocation of funds is not rational because the presence of past high income does not assure the existence of future projects with marginal productivity of capital higher than those of the firms with previously low income.)

All of these reasons suggest that the incentives for voluntary investment through the enterprise, even in ventures outside the enterprise, appears to be weak. Yugoslavs tend to minimize the possibility that firms might not reinvest and point instead to the fact that investment by enterprises frequently exceeded planned rates, especially before the reform. The reasons for these high rates of investment were, however, complex. In part, it seems that there was an incentive to borrow whenever funds were available because the rate of interest paid was often less than the annual rate of inflation. In effect, money had a negative price, as Trklja pointed out.[56] If necessary, as part of the deal to obtain subsidized money, the firm would put up a portion of the total investment cost. For a negative price of money, this makes sense. While it may be true that the workers in the Yugoslav enterprises are motivated to invest collectively through their firm under normal, stable circumstances, it is not clear that previous experience is particularly relevant in support of this proposition.

The economic reform, as we have seen, moved to retain voluntary reinvestment. By reducing and ultimately removing taxes on the enterprise, it made enterprise profits the principal source of funds. The voluntary savings of firms may be invested directly in their own enterprise or directly in some other enterprise, or indirectly in other

56. Trklja, p. 144.

ventures, by placing the funds in the bank (from which the depositor-shareholder receives a variable interest rate, depending on the success of the bank). The rejected alternative is a tax on capital, the proceeds of which would be allocated through the banking system. Does this choice make any difference?

Formally, we may analyze two possibilities, one based loosely on Yugoslav experience to date, and the other drawing from Yugoslavia as it is scheduled to be after 1970. In the former version, the chief source of new investment funds is the tax on socially owned capital, which may be regarded as the interest paid to society for the use thereof. The proceeds of this tax are allocated, through the banking system, to the enterprises seeking investment loans. The latter variant has no capital tax and the principal source of investment funds is enterprise profits. The profit-making enterprise invests either in its own firm or makes capital available to other firms through a capital market. We may explore the consequences of the "tax" and the "no tax" version with respect to capital allocation, the effect of the capital tax, the role of the banking system, the rate of savings, and the sources of personal income.

1. I can find no significant difference between the two versions in allocating investment. Under either version, high labor mobility would appear to introduce a bias toward risky investment. If labor is mobile, in the "tax" version, borrowers would tend to engage in risky projects. If the projects succeed, borrowers can remain in the enterprise and capture the higher income streams. If the project fails, they can abandon the enterprise and seek new jobs. There is no penalty for poor choices.

If labor is mobile, the "no tax" results could be quite similar. If labor is mobile, the length of anticipated association with an enterprise is short, the rates of internal return necessary to induce investment in the enterprise relatively high and, due to the limited number of such high return projects, the corresponding rate of investment in nonowned assets would be low. Profits would be distributed to workers. Most of the volume of savings would arise from the personal incomes of workers used to purchase owned assets. Savings would be channeled into investment through the banking system (for savings accounts) or directly by individual purchases of other forms of owned assets such as bonds. The recent authorization of bond sales by enterprises and republics may represent a recognition of the saving (and borrowing) potential that can be realized by providing more forms of owned assets. (From the point of view of the enterprise that is borrowing, the selling of bonds has the added advantage of circumventing the bank.) Thus, with mobile labor, there is little difference of allocation between the "tax" and the "no tax" version; each will resort to loans or indebtedness. In either case, investment funds arise from external sources; there is little penalty to the workers for poor choice and thus a possible bias toward risky investment.[57] The lenders (banks or bondholders) would bear this risk and presumably be compensated by higher interest rates.

On the other hand, if labor is not mobile, as appears to be the case in Yugoslavia, there is a penalty for poor choice, regardless of the source of investment funds. How strong the penalty is depends on the size of the minimum guaranteed wage and the length of time it will be paid. There is still, however, no significant difference in allocation between the "tax" and the "no tax" versions. In the "tax" version, enterprises will borrow from the bank. The workers expect to be associated for a long time with the enterprise. The workers both expect to repay the loan and

57. If there is no tax but an upper limit on the share of profits that can be distributed to personal earnings, this is equivalent to a profit tax, which cuts incentives, and an offsetting capital grant. With mobile labor, there would be all the difficulties associated with the versions considered in the text, as well as reduced incentive to maximize profits because of the tax.

to receive the net after-tax income generated by the investment. It is in their interest to make the best possible investment, since poor choices will mean lower incomes over
the lifetime of their association with the firm. In the "no
tax" version with immobile labor, the time horizon of association with the enterprise extends, and the differences between owned and nonowned assets diminish. With a
twenty-year horizon, an 8 percent internal return is required to make the worker as well off as with a five percent
owned asset. There are probably many investment opportunities within the enterprise yielding above 8 percent, and one would expect that some profits would be retained. In any case, with a long time horizon, reinvesting
and borrowing are equivalent ways of generating an income stream within the enterprise. Under either version
the right to an income stream is acquired by paying, from
enterprise profits, the purchase price of a nonowned asset.
This payment cannot be avoided by changing jobs, since
labor is immobile. Thus whether investment funds rise
from a tax or from retained earnings seems to make no
significant difference in the uses to which funds will be
put, provided that the banks are appropriately organized
as business enterprises which lend funds to maximize their
own profits.

2. The "tax" version involves a capital tax but the effect
is not necessarily detrimental. For a given capital stock, the
capital tax is a lump sum that reduces the total amount of
enterprise profit but does not take any portion of additional profits. Such a lump sum reduction could even increase the quantities of labor and of entrepreneurship
forthcoming.[58] With respect to additions to capital stock,

58. The effect on the supply of labor and entrepreneurship will depend
on the nature of leisure and risk aversion as goods. If leisure and risk
aversion are superior goods (if more leisure and risk aversion are con-
sumed at higher incomes), a reduction in income will decrease the consumption of leisure and risk aversion and increase the supply of labor
and entrepreneurship.

the tax on capital should make no substantive difference. With a tax, the supply of investment funds in any given year is determined by the existing stock of capital and the tax rate, and thus fixed. The quantity of investment funds demanded at each price depends on the productivity of potential investments. The capital tax is a tax on capital. As with any tax imposed when the supply is fixed, neither the quantity demanded nor the price paid (inclusive of tax) is altered by imposing the tax.

3. Finally, there is the possibility that making retained earnings the source of investment is somehow more efficient. As Samuelson has said in another context, "profits go to those who have been efficient in the past—efficient in making things, in selling things, in foreseeing things. Through profits, society is giving command over new ventures to those who have piled up a record of success." [59] While this is true, it is also true that past success is not a foolproof predictor of future success. Nor need banks making investment loans ignore the quality of management. A record of past success will mean easier loans on better terms at the bank. Society can give command over new ventures to the successful without having the funds for new ventures arise solely from enterprise profits.

4. There is, however, one major difference between the two versions of supplying investment funds. In the "tax" version, the tax rates (given the volume of enterprise capital) determine the volume of saving. In the "no tax" version, savings decisions are voluntary. This change has two effects, each significant for the socialist economy. First, it means that the rates of savings and investment depend on the decisions of many individuals and may be expected to be lower than was previously the case. Second, it means that there will be a significant volume of interest income. Interest income may appear either as explicit interest pay-

59. Paul A. Samuelson, *Economics,* 7th ed. (New York: McGraw-Hill, 1967), p. 602.

ments for owned assets or as higher personal incomes for workers in plants where investments have been made. The choice of the "no tax" option sanctions interest income.

In conclusion, there seems to be no compelling economic reason to select the no-tax, interest-paying version. As will be seen in a later chapter, this choice has a number of other implications regarding personal incomes and the concept of social property. The ostensible reason for doing away with the tax and relying on retained earnings in Yugoslavia is to avoid the bureaucracy involved in allocating funds through the bank. Yugoslav fear that the banking system will necessarily become another central planning, administrative bureaucracy, while not altogether unfounded in view of past experience, does seem a weak pillar upon which to base a policy choice that has such significant implications.

Jaroslav Vanek has recently completed an important book, *The General Theory of Labor-Managed Market Economies*. On the basis of closely reasoned arguments about both microeconomic and macroeconomic aspects of the labor-managed economy, his "general conclusion then is that the labor-managed economy is not only highly efficient in absolute terms, but also more efficient than other existing economic systems. This holds from the point of view of both allocational and distributional efficiency." [60] Unfortunately, considerations of time made it impossible to evaluate his reasoning and to incorporate his findings into the present work.

60. Jaroslav Vanek, *The General Theory of Labor-Managed Market Economies* (Ithaca: Cornell University Press, 1970), p. 403.

CHAPTER 9

Price Theory and Price Policy

The concepts of value and price have generally given Marxist economists difficulty. Although Marx recognized that principles of valuation would be necessary in the socialist economy, he did not provide his followers an adequate guide to the analysis of value or of price. The quest for the proper principles of valuation has produced a lengthy Marxist literature. The Yugoslav discussion has assumed a form somewhat different from that in other socialist states because of the differences between a market and a planned economy and the corresponding implications for price.

This chapter discusses the role of price in the Yugoslav market economy and how this affected thinking about price theory. It then examines the state of price theory in Yugoslavia, considering the reaction to Western price theories, as well as the development of Marxist price theory in Yugoslavia. It concludes by considering the causes of the failure of the quest for a "normative price" and the shift of attention from product pricing to factor pricing in an effort to resolve fundamental questions of market socialism.

THE ROLE OF PRICE

An earlier chapter discussed Soviet views on price determination in socialism. Yugoslavs likewise sought the principles of socialist price formation. There is, however, a major difference between the Yugoslav and the Soviet approaches. In the Soviet Union actual prices are established administratively, and what is required are principles according to which to set the prices. In the Soviet case, neither the allocation of resources nor the distribution of incomes depend significantly on price policy. In a market economy, by contrast, prices directly affect profits, resource allocation, rates of investment, and income distribution. Thus price assumes an importance in a market economy that it lacks in the planned economy.

There are two specific factors to consider in the Yugoslav discussion of prices. One is that, prior to the economic reform of 1965, price policy was an active instrument of overall policy. The principles of pricing, as well as the results of specific policies, were the subject of discussion. The other is that, because of particular institutional features, the function of prices may be different in Yugoslavia from that in other market economies.

Active price policy

From the early days of decentralization in Yugoslavia it had been accepted that socialism required the intervention of the planners to correct the otherwise anarchic outcome of the market mechanism. At the same time, the independence of the workers' collective required that there be a minimum of direct intervention. Social planners were to operate indirectly, through prices, to achieve their objectives. Thus the allocation of investment, while decentralized in form, was affected by a series of policy instruments. In addition to the availability of credit, investment structure in a market economy also depends on the profitability of the various industries. Profits provide a source of investment funds and an incentive to invest. Profits, in turn, depend on the direct pricing policies and on tax policies, as well as on market phenomena. By controlling the size of profits in different industries through price and tax policy, the government could and did influence the flow of investments funds. The size of personal incomes in different branches was also affected.

Dispute over the use of price policy reached crisis proportions just before the 1965 reforms for two reasons. First, the various interventions in the market process, in the form of price controls, subsidies, rebates, quantitative restrictions, and the like, had reached an all-time high for decentralized Yugoslavia. Not only were those policies numerous and cumbersome but they were highly controversial because of their effect on profits and, thus, on income and investment patterns. The second reason for the crisis was the breakdown in consensus about social goals, especially about the allocation of investment and the distribution of income. Both the structure of investment and the distribution of income became sensitive topics. Because of the pervasive use of price policy to accomplish social objectives, the controversy over the principles of pricing was in reality as much a dispute about the structure of investment and income as about the inefficiency of the pricing policies.

The function of prices

The economic reform of 1965, which accepted the principle of freely determined prices and of the market mechanism as the allocator of investments, altered the perspective on prices but did not make socialist price policy any less difficult. In an ordinary, competitive market economy, prices allocate resources in conformity with the desires of the consumers (typically, but not necessarily, individual households). To achieve this allocation, producers seeking profits hire factors of production. Labor and capital move into the activities where compensation is highest. Factor mobility is essential to the functioning of the market economy as we understand it. Prices are signals for the resource allocation. At the same time, factor incomes are equalized by competition and investment takes place in those areas in which prospective profits are the greatest, and not necessarily in areas in which past profits were reaped.

If the Yugoslav economy functioned this way, one suspects that the problem of price would be much simpler. But, in fact, there appear to be substantial impediments to the mobility of both capital and labor. This means that prices affect not only the quantities of goods produced (and, as we have seen in the last chapter, they may not affect the quantity greatly) but also the personal income levels and the amount of investment in each branch. In the event of extreme supply inelasticity with no effective entry and no mobility, prices would affect primarily the income levels of workers. They would do so through the effect of price on total revenue and because profits enable additional investments that will normally be used to increase the average product of labor. Product price in Yugoslavia may have a limited effect on output but it has a significant effect on the income of workers and on investment in the various branches. In this way the role of price differs in Yugoslavia from that in a normal market economy. It is in this framework, where price affects income and investment patterns and where income and investment patterns are precisely the matters on which agreement is lacking, that the quest for normative pricing principles took place.

THE STATE OF PRICE THEORY IN YUGOSLAVIA

There were two major strands of price theory which tackled the problems of socialist pricing, that following the Western, neoclassical analysis and that emanating from Marxian analysis. In addition, there were attempts to bridge the gap between the two, apparently contradictory price theories.

Neoclassical price theory

By the mid-sixties, judging by the Western books on economics translated into Serbo-Croatian, by the number of scholars who had visited centers of Western economics, and by the number and quality of Yugoslav books on bourgeois economics, Yugoslavs were generally familiar with the essential elements of neoclassical price theory. Critical studies of the major Western writings on the economics of socialism and on the important propositions of welfare economics showed that a number of authors had a fairly high level understanding of that body of theory.

The following list of works, by no means complete, gives some idea of the development. In 1956 a collection of articles on bourgeois economic thought appeared.[1] In 1958, Ivan Maksimovic reviewed for Yugoslavs the Western literature on the theory of socialism and also provided a general introduction to welfare economics.[2] In the same year Ivan Lavrac published a study on the role of demand in the analysis of Alfred Marshall.[3] In 1959, a collection of works on the welfare state appeared,[4] as did a text on bourgeois political economy.[5] In 1960, France Cerne published in Slovenian a text on prices and markets, presenting much of the material found in standard Western introductory texts.[6] It appeared in 1966 in a Serbo-Croatian edition. In 1961, Branko Horvat's *Towards a Theory of Planned Economy*,[7] appeared in Serbo-Croatian. In 1962, Zoran

1. Branislav Soskic et al., *Iz istorije gradjanske ekonomske misli* (Belgrade: 1956).
2. Ivan Maksimovic, *Teorija socijalizma u gradjanskoj ekonomskoj nauci* (Belgrade: Nolit, 1958).
3. Ivan Lavrac, *Traznja u ekonomskoj analizi Alfreda Marshalla* (Belgrade: Nolit, 1958).
4. *Drzavni kapitalizam* (Belgrade: Kultura, 1959).
5. D. Sabolovic, *Suvremena burzoaska politicka ekonomija* (Zagreb: 1959).
6. France Cerne, *Trziste i cijene* (Zagreb: Informator, 1966).
7. Belgrade: Jugoslav Institute of Economic Research.

Pjanic's study of the theory of demand appeared.[8] His principal topic was the theory of consumer behavior, and his discussion of that theory and of the problem of measurable utility was quite sophisticated. In 1965, Soskic published a study of the development of economic thought including pre-Marxian, Marxian, and bourgeois variants.[9] While his analysis of the reasons for the development of economic thought is based on class interest, he was careful to show that Western economic theory could usefully be applied in socialist economies.

Most Yugoslav economists viewed Western economics from the Marxist position. The Marxist sees a number of inadequacies in neoclassical price theory that may be briefly mentioned.

1. The principal objection is the nature of the value theory itself. From the Marxist viewpoint, Western value theory has its origin in subjective factors, that is, it depends on the intensity of human satisfaction from consuming a given object or the intensity of dissatisfaction of providing a factor of production. These subjective feelings can neither be compared among individuals nor aggregated in any meaningful way. In contrast, it is alleged that Marxian value theory is objective, in that value depends on the quantity of measurable labor inputs necessary to produce a given item.

2. In contrast to the Marxian approach to political economy, which focuses on the relations among men to determine whether there is exploitation, Western economic theory looks at the relations among commodities or among factors of production. Such an approach is not only superficial; it obscures the real concern of political economy, the relations among men. Bourgeois theory, by justifying payment for nonlabor factors of production, is rationalizing the exploitation of man by man.

8. Zoran Pjanic, *Savremene burzoaske teorije vrednosti i cena* (Belgrade: Institut drustvenih nauka, 1965).

9. Branislav Soskic, *Razvoj ekonomske misli* (Belgrade: Rad, 1965).

3. In its usual form, Western price theory focuses on the relation between quantity and price to the virtual exclusion of other components that determine demand, for example, population change, technology, tastes, advertising, and income distribution. The latter group of factors are probably the more important determinants.

4. Western economic theory devotes excessive attention to building models of a nonreal, usually static world, the results of which have little applicability to problems of a growing, complex world.

Despite these general criticisms of bourgeois economics, there was a certain openness of mind and receptiveness to Western economic theory. Even Yugoslavs highly critical of bourgeois theory recognized that neoclassical economics had devoted much more attention to modern market phenomena than had Marxists and that some features of this theory were relevant for Yugoslavia. Pjanic and Lavrac were both enthusiastic about the analysis of imperfect competition and the need for Yugoslavs to apply it to their own market socialism.[10] In their views, such theoretical constructs could easily be integrated into the Marxist framework. Cerne advocated more application of market research.

Bridge-building theories

Two writers, Aleksandar Bajt in 1953 [11] and Branko Horvat in 1961 [12] attempted to build bridges between Marxian and neoclassical economics. Instead of the customary view that the two approaches were irreconcilable, Bajt and Horvat found them compatible. The Yugoslav

10. See especially Zoran Pjanic, "Problem formiranja cena," *Nasa stvarnost* 17, no. 3 (Mar. 1963): 274–97; Ivan Lavrac, *Yugoslav Economists*, pp. 147–58.

11. Aleksandar Bajt, *Marksov zakon vrednosti* (Ljubljana: Pravna fakulteta, 1953) and "Labor in Marx's Value Theory (An Alternative Interpretation)," forthcoming.

12. Horvat, *Towards a Theory of Planned Economy.*

response to their efforts was quite hostile, a striking contrast to the Yugoslav willingness to accept direct transplants from Western economic theory.

Bajt wrote his doctoral dissertation on Marx's law of value. According to Bajt, the standard interpretation of the law of value is that the value of a commodity, which in some manner determines the price of the commodity, depends solely on the quantity of labor embodied therein. Demand affects the relative quantities of goods provided but does not affect their values, that is, their relative quantities of labor. To introduce demand as a determinant of value would be to introduce subjective factors. Bajt proposed, alternatively, first to define the restrictive conditions under which this interpretation is valid (in the long run in constant cost industries in which labor is the only input), and then to examine how the law of value would have to be modified if the restrictive assumptions were abandoned. Bajt argues that Marx recognized that value was not independent of demand in the case of increasing cost industries. Finally, he argues that even in the case of industries with constant technical inputs, demand cannot be dispensed with in determining value. Demand (jointly with supply conditions) determines the relative wage rates of different types of labor, which are the basis for "reducing" all different types of labor into the homogeneous simple labor that is the measure of "value." By showing that the standard interpretation of Marx was too restrictive and that a broader interpretation leads to a theory not incompatible with neoclassical analysis, Bajt challenged a central Marxist doctrine, and his work provoked a series of attacks, principally by Pjanic,[13] Samardzija,[14] and Mlakar.[15]

13. Zoran Pjanic, *Ekonomist* (1956).

14. Milos Samardzija, *Ekonomski anali*, 1955; *Cena proizvodnje* (Belgrade: Nolit, 1957); "Odnos vrednosti i cene," *Ekonomist* 12, no. 1–2 (1959): 1–24.

15. Cveta Mlakar, "Drustveno potreban rad u Marksovoj teoriji vrijednosti," *Ekonomist* 15, no. 1 (1962): 111–29.

Branko Horvat attempted to reconcile Marxian and Western value theory in a different and imaginative way. Although he wrote his book in 1958 (portions of it had appeared earlier in articles in Yugoslav and Western journals), he was only able to publish it in its entirety in Yugoslavia in 1961. It was received with hostility in the party press.[16] The principal criticism was his rejection of the labor theory of value, traceable to his acceptance, however obscured, of subjective principles of valuation. As Horvat pointed out in his reply to the critics, his theory of the pricing of productive factors is distinctively different from that of traditional bourgeois theory.[17] (This part of his analysis will be treated in the next chapter.) Both he and his critics were correct. On the one hand, he did repudiate the labor theory of value and developed value theory in a direction not commonly interpreted as Marxist. On the other hand, he regarded all factor payments except payment to labor as economic rent. Thus labor, if not the sole factor of production, is the sole variable factor of production for the economy as a whole and it alone should receive factor payments. This certainly differs from the standard neoclassical view.

Marxian value theory

Most Yugoslavs have approached the problem of price from the Marxian viewpoint. In contrast to the Western tradition in economics, in Marxist economic thought value and price are not synonymous. Value is that point around which the actual market price oscillates in a market economy. In a market economy of the simple commodity production type, Marx identified "labor value" as the gravity

16. Adolf Dragicevic and S. Stampar, *Nase teme* 6, no. 6 (June 1962): 872–94; Pirec, *Nasa stvarnost* 16, no. 5 (May 1962): 600–07.
17. Branko Horvat, "Lekcija iz ekonomske teorije A. Dragicevica i S. Stampara," *Nase teme* 6, no. 9 (Sept. 1962): 1318–1333.

point; in capitalist commodity production it was the "price of production" around which actual prices oscillated. He arrived at these conclusions by examining the institutional features and the motives of decision makers and deduced the prices that would, in the long run, prevail in such systems. Marx also noted that resources would be allocated differently in simple and in capitalist commodity production because of the differences in ownership of factors and in the motivations of decision makers but he did not evaluate the efficiency of resource allocation in either system. Since Marx did not discuss socialism in detail Marxist economists must develop their own interpretations of the corresponding motivations, institutions, and the point around which prices oscillate in the socialist market economy. In socialist commodity production of the Yugoslav type, the means of production are owned by society but they are managed by independent enterprises, guided by their own self-interest; these groups determine what to produce and how to produce it. Yugoslav authors sought to identify the prevailing price in socialist commodity production. There were three major answers to this question: labor value price, the price of production, and the income price.

Labor value price

Davidovic [18] and Zarkovic,[19] among others, maintained that the labor value price is the correct form of value in socialist commodity production. In precapitalist commodity production, where labor is the only remunerated factor of production, competition causes the return to homogeneous units of labor to be uniform. In equilibrium, equal

18. Radivoj Davidovic, "Distribution in the Socialist Economy—Some Principles and Methods," in Radmila Stojanovic, ed., *Yugoslav Economists on Problems of a Socialist Economy* (New York: International Arts and Sciences Press, 1964), pp. 158–65.

19. Dragoje Zarkovic, "Nacela politike cena," *Ekonomist* 16, no. 3–4 (1963): 646–52.

values exchange for equal values, that is, items with equal labor inputs exchange on an equal basis. In socialism, where labor is the only factor of production that is remunerated, the labor value price is the normal and proper form of price.

Price of production

The majority of Yugoslavs came down on the side of the price of production as the normative price. Two types of reasons were offered: (1) it was presented as the prevailing long run price in a Yugoslav-type system and (2) as an efficient price. If the Yugoslav enterprise is considered basically similar to the capitalist enterprise, with identical maximizing principles, then prices would tend in socialism, as well as in capitalism toward the price of production. Hadzi-Vasilev concluded that

> In socialism, the same mechanism that forms "average profit" forms the "price of production," although this mechanism does not restore the typical capitalist categories, because private ownership, profit, and spontaneous adjustment of the social division of labor do not exist.[20]

Mijalko Todorovic also tended to assume that socialist enterprises maximize profits and that, as a result, the price of production would prevail in socialism as well as in capitalism.

> In all forms of commodity production where the means of production play an iota of a significant role . . . and also in socialist commodity production, therefore, the natural, normal price . . . that is, the price around which market prices oscillate, must be in form the price of production.[21]

20. M. Hadzi-Vasilev, *Socijalizam* 3, no. 6 (Nov. 1960): 3–99.
21. Todorovic, *Socialist Thought and Practice*, no. 9 (Jan. 1963): 36.

Todorovic went further in saying that the price of production is not only the prevailing price but also the correct price. Todorovic emphasized that scarce capital can be allocated efficiently only if the rate of profit is the criterion. For this purpose he proposed a unitary socialist capital market. If the rate of profit is everywhere equal, then the prevailing price must be the price of production.[22]

> From the standpoint of the economy of labor time, the form of the price of production is also the most suitable and the most objective for this phase of socialism. The law of competition on the socialist market, too, inexorably drives each enterprise to economize, i.e., to economize on the means of production and on the labor force that is directly involved.[23]

As long as commodity production exists and as long as capital is scarce (the two conditions are identical, says Todorovic),[24] the price of production is both the prevailing tendency and the correct price.

> The price of production is a form which, in principle, applies to all developed commodity production where the means of production play an important role. The value price is a typical form only in the initial phases of commodity production when these means, as previously produced and amassed as material wealth (produced) are practically nil, or small in quantity. It follows that when the amassed produced material conditions of production reach a level where they are infinite in number, meaning sufficient for the unlimited wants of all the subjects and all the branches of production, it is only then, in the final

22. The price of production requires that the average rate of profit on *all* capital be equal. A unitary socialist capital market would only assure that the marginal productivity of capital in all uses is equal.
23. Todorovic, *Socialist Thought and Practice,* no. 9 (Jan. 1963): 43.
24. Ibid., p. 38.

analysis, that the law of value and commodity production cease to operate.[25]

Income price

The most provocative normal price is the proposal of Miladin Korac. It is an original Yugoslav contribution to the Marxist theory of value and price. Korac sought to identify the prevailing price in socialism. He started from the property relations and the motivations of decision makers and deduced the long run equilibrium prices under conditions of mobility of labor and capital. In socialist commodity production, Korac argued, the working collective pursues its own self-interest. The enterprise seeks to maximize its "rate of income." [26]

$$r = \frac{\text{realized income}}{\text{engaged means of production} + \text{newly created value}}$$

He argued that competition among socialist enterprises and the freedom of entry of existing enterprises into different fields of production would mean that the rate would become equal throughout the economy. This process is analogous to the equalization of the rate of profit in the capitalist economy. The long run equilibrium price in such a system is the "income price," the socialist analog of the price of production. The allocation of resources in socialist commodity production would differ from that in capitalist commodity production.[27]

Korac did not state the explicit form of the income price in the standard Marxian terms. He indicates that newly created value is equal to realized income in the aggregate and, in equilibrium, in the firm as well. Assuming this to

25. Ibid. Original in italics.

26. Miladin Korac, *Socijalizam* 4, no. 1 (Jan.–Feb. 1961): 31–51.

27. However, because Korac's analysis of the enterprise is both unclear and implausible, as noted in Chap. 8, it is impossible to deduce the resulting allocation of resources.

be the case, it is possible to write the enterprise maximizing principle in the form

$$r = \frac{R}{K + R}$$

where R stands for newly created value or realized income and K for the engaged means of production. Dividing numerator and denominator by R, we get

$$r = \frac{1}{(K/R) + 1}$$

The enterprise objective could therefore also be stated as minimizing K/R or maximizing R/K. Korac appears to assert that enterprises will want to maximize realized income per unit of capital. In Marxian terms, this is equivalent to maximizing $(v + m)/k$, where v is the labor value added, m is the surplus, and k the engaged means of production. The income price can be expressed in these Marxian terms and then compared to the labor value price and the price of production.[28]

$$\text{income price} = c + k \cdot \frac{V + M}{K}$$

$$\text{labor value price} = c + v + v \cdot \frac{M}{V} = c + v \cdot \frac{V + M}{V}$$

$$\text{price of production} = c + v + k \cdot \frac{M}{K}$$

where c is the materials cost plus depreciation, per unit of output; k the capital per unit of output; V the aggregate wage bill; M the aggregate surplus; K the aggregate engaged capital; and v the wage cost per unit of output.

The labor value price is the price that prevails if the producers' objective is to maximize surplus per unit of live

28. Horvat also concluded that this is the form of the income price. Branko Horvat, "O nekim pitanjima formiranja cene," *Borba*, Jan. 16, 17, and 18, 1963.

labor and if this rate is equal throughout the economy. The price of production is the prevailing price if the objective is to maximize surplus relative to capital engaged and if this rate is equal throughout the entire economy. The income price corresponds to a situation in which wages are zero and producers maximize net value added per unit of capital if this rate is equal throughout the economy.

It has already been indicated that there is little reason for the rational worker-managed enterprise to behave as Korac postulates. But one may further question whether his criterion is rational under any circumstances. As Horvat has pointed out, it would only be rational if capital is the only scarce resource and the marginal productivity of labor is zero.[29] In such a situation, with only one scarce factor of production, the principle of maximizing net value added per unit of scarce resource is rational. (The labor value price implies maximization of net value added per unit of scarce labor and is rational only if labor is the only scarce resource.) Obviously, the Korac criterion is not a rational basis for decisions in an economy in which there is more than one scarce factor. The supporters of the income price were not really concerned with the productive efficiency in maximizing output. They merely asserted that their research had described the behavior that would occur in a Yugoslav-type economy. The policy implications of their work will be considered below.

NORMATIVE PRICE AND ITS USES

The Yugoslavs sought a "normative price" for socialism, usually the socialist analog of the value price of simple commodity production or of the price of production in capitalism. In the two latter cases, the normative price is

29. Ibid.

normative in a dual sense. It is the long run equilibrium price that tends to emerge through the normal operation of the system. As such it is neutral and not the result of some arbitrary policy. At the same time it is an efficient price (because the associated resource allocation is efficient) and can therefore serve as a basis for price policy. The Yugoslavs sought a price for the socialist market economy that would similarly be normative in this dual sense. It proved impossible to find such a price.

Among the normative standards proposed were value prices, the price of production, the income price, world market prices, marginal cost prices, and average total cost prices, to mention only a few. One study of pricing in Yugoslavia concluded, somewhat aptly, that "the fact that such a broad spectrum of prices are proposed as 'normatives' . . . is the best proof that a central dilemma exists among Yugoslav (and not only Yugoslav) economists which still waits for a unique solution." [30] The Yugoslav difficulty in developing adequate concepts of price seems to have several roots: (1) the lack of a maximizing concept in most Marxian analysis and the associated failure to perceive the relationship between resource allocation and relative valuation, whether in a market or a nonmarket system, (2) the problems posed by factor immobility in conjunction with a desire for equity to be attained in a market economy, and (3) the confusion over what the normative price was and about its policy applications.

Objectives, resource allocation, and prices

A normative price exists only with respect to a particular resource allocation. Part of the Yugoslav problem was the result of confusion about resource allocation. For neoclassical economists, as well as for Soviet linear program-

30. Ivan Maksimovic and Zoran Pjanic, *Price Problems in Yugoslav Theory and Practice* (Sofia: Bulgarian Academy of Sciences, 1964), p. 17.

mers, price represents the alternatives foregone in attaining the objective. Except for Horvat, this approach to price was not prevalent in Yugoslavia.

Horvat was concerned with maximizing the value of output. The normal conclusion of neoclassical theory is that, to attain this goal, price must reflect the marginal cost. Horvat examined the literature on marginal cost pricing at some length, agreeing that in principle it is quite acceptable and that the socialist society would apply certain marginal cost concepts, for example, the classic example of (noncongested) toll-free bridges. After an extensive discussion, he concluded that marginal cost pricing is not fully satisfactory in practical terms for the socialist economy. He advocated pricing on the basis of average total costs.

> The analysis has shown that [the full cost principle] is logically an imperfect principle but that, when applied, it is likely to lead to a better approximation to ideal output than the rival [marginal cost] principle. This contention is based on the findings that, in the short run, the full cost principle leads to approximately the same results as the marginal cost principle; with regard to investment it is open to check and so immensely less arbitrary.[31]

Horvat's reasons for accepting the average total cost principle were several. First, there are conceptual difficulties in marginal cost pricing that make another rule necessary in some cases. For example, in the case of decreasing cost industries, it is necessary to determine whether the investment should be undertaken at all. Second, he argued that, practically speaking, short run marginal costs are incalculable and hence an unsatisfactory guide. Third, marginal cost pricing rules are generally inadequate outside the framework of fixed capacities. Thus Horvat concluded that since marginal cost pricing is not suitable in all cases,

31. Horvat, *Towards a Theory of Planned Economy,* pp. 27–28.

an alternative must be employed. He proposed that long run average total costs are the least undesirable practical method of pricing. Finally, since this is the result which tends to be attained when the individual enterprises maximize profit in a competitive environment, it is also desirable, because it means that the majority of microeconomic decisions can be left to the enterprise.[32] In this manner Horvat (and Todorovic, less rigorously) advocate the pricing practices of the competitive market as being both efficient and consistent with Yugoslav economic organization.

Others adopted a more active approach to pricing. Starting with some vision of the desired resource allocaton, it remained merely to find pricing policies to accomplish the desired allocation. Samardzija emphasized that prices have many objectives. Prices not only reflect the current structure of productive relations but are also a device for changing that structure.[33] "For an economy which is socially rational . . . price cannot be solely the resultant of the action of economic processes and a neutral instrument. . . . It becomes a factor to be utilized consciously for the purposes of influencing the formation of economic processes."[34] Cerne also subscribed to the view that prices serve many purposes and thus he tends to reject a single normative price.[35] Such prices are difficult to establish, as Maksimovic and Pjanic note, because they must satisfy multiple requirements "concerning optimal allocation of production factors, maximization of productive activities, and the exclusive orientation of the enterprise towards

32. Horvat considered socialist enterprises to be profit maximizers. His model of the enterprise does not include the particular features of producers' cooperatives and, within his model, it is an accurate and adequate statement of enterprise objectives.

33. Milos Samardzija, "Problem cena u socijalistickoj privredi," *Nasa stvarnost* 14, no. 12 (Dec. 1960) 488–515.

34. Ibid., p. 491.

35. Cerne, *Trzista i cijene.*

earning maximum income." [36] In these approaches, determination of the allocation is separated from the pricing process and the price is merely a financial tool to attain the desired allocation.

Still others, lacking confidence in any vision of socialist resource allocation, because such visions are essentially arbitrary, sought instead an "objective" or neutral resource allocation. The Korac group, especially, through examining the functioning of an economy with Yugoslav institutions, sought both the normal price and the normal, neutral distribution of resources.

Factor immobility and the function of prices

The difficulty in the Yugoslav quest for normative prices is compounded by the factor immobility that seems to exist and that certainly underlies much of the thinking on price. With limited mobility of both capital and labor, the price of the product determines both income distribution and the relative rates of expansion of different branches of production. Thus a particular feature of the Yugoslav quest for pricing principles is to seek price norms that would not only determine the quantities of goods demanded and supplied but also the rates of investment and the distribution of income among branches. There were, accordingly, efforts to find the set of prices under which incomes would be equal in various branches, or the set of prices under which profits would permit equal rates of expansion of all branches.[37] In either case there was tacit acceptance of the immobility of factors and the equalization was to be achieved by altering the price of the final product and not by the movement of factors in response to different rates of compensation.

36. Maksimovic and Pjanic, p. 17.

37. Radivoj Davidovic, "Cena kao faktor drustvene reprodukcij
Ekonomist 17, no. 4 (1964): 509–20.

Uses of normative prices

In no area was the confusion greater than concerning the use to be made of the normative price, once found. There seem to be three possibilities:

1. Set prices according to the norm and let investment, personal income, and quantities demanded and supplied adjust to the price. Presumably, there will be disequilibrium on the product market. (For example, assume that there is initially equilibrium on the product market but that the price of the good is low, relative to some norm. By applying the normative price, profits may be greater; hence investment may be higher and the industry may expand, despite the fact that demand is lower than before the imposition of the normative price. Conversely, there will be excess demand in industries whose prices are found to be higher than the normative price and are consequently adjusted downward.)

2. Retain equilibrium prices on product markets but allocate investment, so that the market prices move toward the normative prices. By shifting the supply schedule, through control of investment, the equilibrium price can be brought to virtually any desired level.

3. Take no direct action on either price or supply but intervene through taxes to reduce the income discrepancies among branches. If it were possible to identify a norma-
- price, then one could observe the differences between
 rmative price and the actual price, or between the
   income and the actual income. Having com-
     me that would have accrued to a given sector
       price prevailed, through taxes and sub-
        could be brought to the normative

              suggested in conjunction with
             e prices. The discussion generated

in connection with the income price, the most controversial of the Yugoslav proposals, will illustrate the confusion about application of normative prices.

The authors of the income price, after working out their theoretical model, undertook an analysis of the "economic position of groupings" in the economy, the groups being various census classifications of industrial activity. By computing first the national "rate of income" and then the actual rate of income for each branch, it could be seen how far each branch deviated from the national average. It will be recalled that maximizing the rate of income is equivalent to maximizing realized income (net value added) per unit of capital. Thus the higher the net value added per unit of capital stock, the higher will be the rate of income. Thus the rate of income will be higher than the national average for groupings with less than average amounts of capital relative to output or to labor and will be lower than the average for groupings with high amounts of capital relative to output or to labor. It was also possible to compute what income would have to have been earned in each branch for it to realize the national average rate of income, or, alternatively, at what prices it would have to have sold its product to attain that income. If prices were everywhere on the level of the "income price," then the rates of income would have been equal for all economic groupings and branches. The authors compared the actual distribution of realized income with that which would have occurred if the income prices had prevailed. It was then vaguely suggested that economic policy should redress these differences but the policy recommendations were extremely (and purposefully?) vague.

The entire income price proposal was highly controversial in Yugoslavia. It was supported by respected economists who hold important academic and administrative positions: Miladin Korac, the principal author, is professor of economics in Belgrade, as is Tihomir Vlaskalic; Savka

Dabcevic-Kucar and Jakov Sirotkovic are both professors of economics in Zagreb, and have both held high governmental positions; Milos Samardzija, professor of political economy at the law faculty, Belgrade; and Rikard Stajner, general director, Federal Institute for Social Planning, Belgrade. In view of what appear to be the numerous inadequacies of the income price proposal, it is somewhat surprising that such important individuals support it and that funds continue to be spent, apparently in considerable volume, on empirical research on the income price.[38]

The income price was the subject of a meeting of the Yugoslav Association of Economists held in Sarajevo on December 17 to 19, 1964.[39] Most of the shortcomings of the income price were noted in the various papers and comments. What was most interesting, however, was the

38. The list of works is long and continues to grow. *Problemi teorije i prakse socijalisticke robne proizvodnje u Jugoslaviji* (Zagreb: Informator, 1965), edited by Korac, reprinted his earlier articles on the income price, along with several comments by colleagues. Tihomir Vlaskalic, closely associated with Korac's line of thought, published "Proizvodni proces u socijalistickom preduzecu," *Ekonomski pregled* 17, no. 8–9 (1966): 445–63. Korac has published a number of additional articles: *Ekonomiski pregled* 17, no. 10 (Oct. 1966): 548–579; "Raspodela prema radu u sistemu socijalisticke robne privrede," *Gledista* 7, no. 8–9 (1966): 1021–1036; "Kreditiranje prosirene reprodukcije u sistemu socijalisticke robne privrede," *Socijalizam* 10, no. 3 (Mar. 1967): 302–24 and no. 4 (Apr. 1967): 471–89.

In addition, Korac directed what appeared to be a major research project, *Analiza ekonomskog polozaja privrednih grupacija na bazi zakona vrednosti (1962–1966)* (Zagreb: Ekonomski institut, 1968). In his introduction to the book, the director of the Economic Institute, Rikard Lang, noted that about forty persons had assisted in the preparation of the empirical analysis. This was a more extensive study, following the methodology employed first in Korac et al., *Analiza ekonomskog polozaja privrednih grupacija* (Belgrade: Savezni zavod za privredno planiranje, Study No. 7, 1964), which was prepared for private circulation. Some of the principal findings of the original study appeared in Tihomir Vlaskalic, "Teoretske osnove i neki rezultati analize ekonomskog polozaja robnih proizvodjaca u nasem privrednim sistemu," *Socijalizam* 7, no. 5 (May 1964): 598–614.

39. Proceedings of the Conference were published in *Ekonomist* 17, no. 4 (1964).

discussion about policy implications. Nor surprisingly, in view of the work presented on the income price, many of the papers attacked the proposal on the grounds that it reverted to administrative pricing. They concluded this because it was evident that the income price would never exist under any other circumstances.[40] The supporters could only reply somewhat weakly that they did not intend their proposal to be applied administratively but they failed to show what policy uses it could conceivably have.[41]

The Yugoslav quest for a "normative price" was doomed to fail. No single pricing principle exists that would meet all the conditions, often contradictory, imposed on the normative price. In this sense the pragmatists were more realistic, recognizing that, if one is merely using prices as tools, then one must fashion the tool to fit the specific purpose. But the failure to agree on a normative price did not really matter because the economic reform lessened the acuteness of the pricing problem in two ways. First, price policy was no longer to be used as a major tool for attaining planned objectives. Second, by deciding to let the market determine the flow of investment, the need for an investment policy was eliminated, and no longer had to be achieved by pricing policies.

What remained controversial was the distribution of income. In a market economy, the distribution of income depends on the prices of productive factors and the distribution of the productive factors among the population. The Yugoslavs needed a theory of factor pricing and a theory of factor distribution. Because of the particular institutional arrangements, neither factor pricing nor factor distribution were the same as in other countries. To these matters, we turn in the next chapter.

40. Stevan Kukoleca, "Osvrt na dohodna cena," *Ekonomist* 17, no. 4 (1964): 770–77.

41. Jakov Sirotkovic, "Ekonomski polozaj privrednih grupacija i drustveno planiranje," *Ekonomist* 17, no. 4 (1964): 727–37.

CHAPTER 10

Ownership and Distribution

Over the years Yugoslavia has moved closer and closer to a real market economy. Several reasons account for this trend, among which are the presumed greater efficiency of the market at the Yugoslav level of economic development, the ability of the market to function without a massive planning organization, and the fact that the market requires a lower level of political consensus than is necessary in political choices. As we saw in the last chapter, an important stage in the process of adopting a market economy was the decision to let product prices be determined freely on the market. As a result, price policy could no longer be used to affect income distribution and investment decisions. Yugoslav thinking about investment in a socialist economy has been discussed in a previous chapter. This chapter treats the thorny problem of income distribution that has proved to be inextricable from the concept of ownership in socialism.

In a market economy in which product prices are determined on the market, the distribution of income among individuals depends on the prices of the factors of production and on the distribution of the factors of production among the population. The prices paid for the factors of production are determined largely on the market (market pricing having been accepted as necessary for efficient allocation), while the distribution of factors among the population is determined largely by institutional and legal arrangements. The problem of income distribution is really

This chapter is a revised verison of an article that appeared in *East Europe* 18, no. 7 (July 1969): 13–19.

a problem of determining which factors of production can be owned by individuals and groups and which are owned by society at large. The effective owner is the one who receives the income accruing to the factor of production.

Any decision about claims to factor incomes must be made in the context of the deep socialist commitment to a just distribution of income. The traditional principle of distribution in communism, as is well known, is "from each according to his ability, to each according to his needs." Marx recognized this as a goal to be reached and not a prescription for immediate implementation.[1] According to Marx, until full communism is attained, goods and services must be distributed in proportion to the labor supplied. The traditional socialist principle of distribution is "to each according to his work."

On the one hand, this means that labor is the only legitimate source of income. In Marxian economic analysis, only labor is productive. All nonlabor sources of income must represent income appropriated from the workers. Although sometimes tolerated, rent, interest and profit incomes are not sanctioned as socialist.

On the other hand, the socialist principle limits the income differences between individuals. Marx did not maintain that his principle was egalitarian. He recognized that "one man is superior to another physically or mentally" and would, therefore, receive a greater share of social goods.[2] He emphasized that the only equality was the right of individuals to receive income in proportion to the labor supplied. There is a serious problem in measuring the quantity of labor, and Marxists have debated such standards as labor time, labor intensity, or the quantity of output. Regardless of the measure used, if earnings are proportional to the labor supplied, the differences in earnings

1. Karl Marx, *Critique of the Gotha Program* (New York: International Publishers, 1933), p. 14.
2. Ibid., 13–14.

between individuals will probably be smaller than those which would arise if earnings were proportional to the total amount of factors supplied by private owners.

The socialist principles are clear—payment only for labor supplied—but it remains to secure them in a decentralized economic system. In areas in which there are private owners of nonhuman resources, the owners seek the maximum return to the factor and thus assure an efficient allocation of those resources. In a decentralized system in which the nonhuman factors have no owners, that is, no persons responsible for their use and receiving the income therefrom, it is no easy matter to assure the proper placement of these resources. The direct interest in efficient factor use that ownership provides has proved difficult to simulate in socialism without, in fact, simulating ownership. For this reason, the attempt to produce efficiently in a decentralized market economy seems to generate pressures for establishing private claims over the socially owned resources.

The troublesome question for market socialists, thus, is whether the market mechanism, operating through the use of financial incentives, is compatible with socialist notions about a just distribution of income. Yugoslav experience seems to suggest a conflict between the goals of efficiency and equality. The system of accumulation and funds introduced in 1952 was the first of many Yugoslav efforts to be just, while relying on financial incentives to promote efficiency. It attempted to make workers equally well off, regardless of the branch of the economy in which they worked. It proved inadequate to the task of attaining either efficiency or equality, and was followed by virtually annual changes in the economic system as Yugoslavs sought to achieve both objectives simultaneously.

In the face of the apparent conflict between equality and efficiency, official emphasis has shifted to efficiency. The Yugoslav leadership, as revealed more fully in its policy than in its theoretical statements, has taken the position that the collective is entitled to the income produced by the factors of production placed at its disposal by society. By its application of labor, the collective has produced a certain real income. The distribution of income "according to work performed" is interpreted as the distribution that follows from the actual earnings of the enterprise. This interpretation is held to be necessary to stimulate the efficient use of the socially owned resources and to avoid the stultifying effects of bureaucratic solutions. It is recognized that equality is sacrificed to the interests of efficiency, but, in the eyes of the leadership, equality without efficiency is merely equality in poverty.[3] In contrast, both Bajt and Horvat argue that the conflict between equality and efficiency is overstated, that all factor payments need not accrue to individuals, or collectives, but only a portion thereof. Furthermore, they argue, their proposals achieve greater equality without any sacrifice of efficiency. The Marxist humanists, more philosophers than economists, have argued that, if there is a conflict in the market system between equality and efficiency, perhaps it is the market system, and not equality, that may have to be abandoned.

OWNERSHIP AND DISTRIBUTION IN YUGOSLAVIA

Traditional socialist doctrine posed obstacles to tapping individual initiative and to providing an adequate structure of reward and penalty to stimulate efficient investment decisions. The economic reforms of 1958, 1961, and 1965, which reduced enterprise taxes and expanded enterprise freedom to distribute profits among personal incomes and reinvestments, probably increased the efficiency of opera-

3. Edvard Kardelj, "What Is the 'Authentic' Revolutionary Nature of the Working Class," *Socialist Thought and Practice*, no. 30 (Apr.–June 1968): 22.

tion and certainly increased income inequality over the initial, rather egalitarian, levels. The reforms constituted an assault on the entire concept of social ownership. The traditional socialist doctrines on private property are being reinterpreted, and distribution "according to work performed" is becoming synonymous with appropriating all income from the resources placed at the disposal of the collective.

Private property in socialism

The resistance to private property runs deep in socialist doctrine. Many arguments have been used against it. (1) Private property has been identified with capitalism and regarded with distrust because capitalism is exploitative. (2) Private property has been identified with simple commodity production, a technologically backward remnant of the past that can be tolerated but certainly not encouraged because it is outmoded and inefficient. (3) Working with self-owned means of production means that factor payments of rent, interest, and profit are received. Private enterprise cannot be sanctioned because it contradicts the socialist principle of payment for labor alone.

In Yugoslavia, although the private sector encompasses the vast majority of agricultural producers and an important segment of the service sector, it was hoped that the private sector would wither away as people transferred to the more modern and more productive social sector. As a consequence of the attitudes toward private enterprise, the size of the private sector was restricted by laws governing the number of employees who could be hired, the size of plots, and the activities in which private persons could engage. Agriculture illustrates the application of this policy. Traditionally, the prices of agricultural products were kept low, the sizes of plots and the amount of labor employed was restricted, and the use of machinery and fertilizers made difficult and expensive. Similarly onerous restrictions, high taxes, and local harassment prevailed in the private service sector. These policies did not produce satisfactory results. While the quality of service and the quantity of goods remained low, the private entrepreneurs did not flock to the socialist sector.

Gradually, the official attitude toward private enterprise changed. Although domestic consumers were the chief sufferers, the foreign trade crisis of the early 1960's was apparently instrumental in bringing about policy changes. To reduce imports of foodstuffs, agricultural prices were raised and restrictions eased somewhat, making modern agriculture more accessible than before. The decision to increase foreign tourism led to the realization that socialist hotels and restaurants could not satisfy the entire demand. Individuals were encouraged to augment the supply, and loans were provided to modernize private tourist accommodations. There was also a new attitude toward foreign capital. While Yugoslav enterprises had been operating under foreign licenses for some years and had received loans from foreign firms, now, to make Yugoslav goods more competitive on world markets, foreign capital was invited to invest in Yugoslavia and to share the profits.[4] Domestic consumers benefited, of course, from the new attitude toward private enterprise in the wake of the economic reform. In 1967 retail trade was opened to individuals on a very limited basis. Private persons could obtain licenses to run small shops in certain limited areas, where no socialist firms existed.

Since private activity was no longer ruled out a priori, the Yugoslavs had to determine the limits of private activity. There seem to be no firm guidelines for policy toward the private sector. There was an intense discussion in 1967

4. Although the legal form is a joint venture, rather than direct equity investment, the contract provides for sharing the profits of the Yugoslav enterprises.

and 1968 about the nature of social property and the role of the private sector in a socialist economy,[5] and a number of arguments were offered in defense of private enterprise. While conservatives clung to the traditional view that private activity was not compatible with socialism, Bajt, Horvat, Lavrac and others used several lines of argument to demonstrate that it was.[6] One line of attack questioned the view of private property as an undesirable remnant of the past. Lavrac argued that a private sector could be necessary even in socialism.[7] The technology of production is such that the social sector cannot provide all services adequately and some spheres remain suitable for individual activity. It was also argued that socialist firms have been reluctant to engage in some types of activity [8] and have been reluctant to bear risk.[9] With reference to a temporary problem, it was argued that the private sector could absorb part of the surplus unemployed labor.[10]

Another approach to the question of private property suggested that the essence of socialism does not lie in the legal forms of property relations but in the absence of exploitation. Using suitable definitions of exploitation, Bajt and Horvat show that private ownership need not imply

5. Mito Hadzi-Vasilev, "Fenomen privatne svojine u socijalizmu," *Komunist* (May 5, 1966); *Privatni rad: Za ili protiv* (Beograd: Komunist, 1967); Miodrag Orlic, "Licni rad—integralni deo socijalizma ili saputnik," *Gledista* 9, no. 3 (Mar. 1968): 445–52; France Cerne, "Otvorena pitanja privatnog sektora," *Gledista* 9, no. 4 (Apr. 1968): 559–66.

6. Aleksander Bajt, *Gledista* 9, no. 4 (Apr. 1968): 531–44. Ivan Lavrac, "Licni rad i privatna svojina u socijalizmu," *Gledista* 8, no. 6–7 (June–July 1967): 897–907; Branko Horvat, "Individualno i drustveno vlasnistvo u socijalizmu," *Gledista* 8, no. 3 (Mar. 1967): 335–48; V. Raskovic, "Eticka granica privatnog sektora u samoupravnom sistemu," *Politika*, Jan. 16, 1968.

7. Lavrac, *Gledista* 8, no. 6–7 (June–July 1967): 897–907.

8. A. Dragojevic and N. Papic, *Borba*, Nov. 26, 1967 (cited by Orlic, *Gledista* 9, no. 3 (Mar. 1968): 447).

9. H. Furlan, *Politika*, Jan. 23, 1968 (cited by Orlic, ibid.).

10. Cede Grbic, "Mjesto i uloga licnog rada na licnim sredstvima za proizvodnju i usluge u SFRJ," *Vjesnik*, Jan. 1968 (cited by Orlic, ibid., p. 445).

exploitation and that exploitation can exist even with the legal forms of social ownership.[11] The problem is to specify the conditions under which the private sector can be allowed to operate in socialism. Horvat made these points. (1) From the viewpoint of Marxist doctrine, the critical question is not the number of employees but the point at which the individual owner ceases to be primarily a worker and becomes primarily an organizer of others. As long as the owner's principal activity is his own work, individual activity is acceptable in socialism. (2) Exploitation can arise not only from employing labor but also from the ownership of a great amount of capital; thus there must be limits on the total amount of capital an individual may use privately. (3) Some activities will thrive and grow. Society must make possible their transformation, at a critical point, from individual into social property. The workers in the private enterprise should develop the same rights as workers in the social sector, as the basis for transformation. They may transform the enterprise, through compensation of the owner, into a socialist enterprise in which the owner will remain as the manager. (4) Certain areas such as health and education have been excluded altogether from commercial activity, social or private, in Yugoslavia. These are the considerations, Horvat argues, for individual activity to be compatible with socialism.[12]

The leadership of the Socialist Alliance of Working People of Yugoslavia, the mass political organization, plunged into the discussion in October of 1967 with a controversial set of theses on "Personal Labor with Means of Production in Personal Ownership." [13] In January 1968, it passed a

11. Bajt, *Gledista* 9, no. 4 (Apr. 1968): 531–44; Horvat, *Gledista* 8, no. 3 (Mar. 1967): 335–48.

12. Horvat, *Gledista* 8, no. 3 (Mar. 1967): 335–45. By the end of his article Horvat has modified these conclusions.

13. "Teza o licnom radu sa sredstvima za rad u licnoj svojini," adopted by the Presidium of the Federal Conference of the Socialist Alliance of

similar resolution.[14] The resolution conceded that previous policies toward the private sector had caused too few persons to enter certain activities, that private activity was necessary in socialism, and that new laws should be drawn to clarify the role of private activity and to encourage it in specific areas. Despite the tactical retreat by the Yugoslav leadership from any expansion of private activity after the outcry raised by Yugoslav students in the summer of 1968, it is clear that Yugoslav thinking about private enterprise has moved a long way from the traditional socialist views.

Distribution of income

In the social sector, encompassing the vast majority of nonagricultural activity, the means of production are owned by society and the declared principle of income distribution is "according to work performed." Unfortunately, there is no unambiguous way of interpreting how work is to be measured. At one extreme, labor time can be adopted as the measure of work performed. This approach fails to recognize the psychic differences between desirable and undesirable types of labor, the intensity or the laziness with which an individual works, the fact that skilled labor is more productive, or the fact that labor may be used on useless and undesired products. The application of this principle would most likely lead to the highly inefficient use of resources. At the other extreme, the market results can be adopted as the measure of work performed. That an enterprise has profits and is thus able to pay high personal incomes can be taken as an indication that the work of its members was very productive and that

Working People in Yugoslavia, Oct. 26, 1967. Appeared in *Borba,* Nov. 23, 1967.

14. "Tasks of the Socialist Alliance in the Development of Private Work," resolution passed by the Federal Conference of the Socialist Alliance of the Working People of Yugoslavia, Jan. 30, 1968. Printed in *Yugoslav Survey* 11, no. 2 (May 1968): 11–18.

they are entitled to such rewards as the market gives them. A number of other proposals for determining the measure of work performed fall between these two extremes.

The Yugoslav leadership has adopted the market principle of income distribution. Factor prices have come to reflect more closely the marginal productivity of the factors of production than was hitherto the case. Yugoslav practice has also apparently sanctioned the distribution to individuals of income from nonlabor factors of production. The incomes generated by capital and land and socially owned means of production, in fact, accrue to specific working collectives. This in turn also affects the equality of income distribution.

Individual income differences

There are several sources of differences in the incomes of individuals; these differences increased as a result of the economic reform.[15]

Occupational differentials. The spread in pay for various types of labor grew after the reform, and persons with certain technical skills markedly improved their positions. Earning differentials are often closely related to training and in part represent a return to the capital invested in humans by the socialist state. Thus the returns to social capital in this case accrue to individuals.

Personal interest income. Although citizens have long received interest on their savings accounts, personal interest income became more important after the reform. The reform increased individuals' monetary income, and part of that income was used to purchase bonds or was put into interest-bearing savings accounts. If those with high incomes saved more than those with low incomes and if they purchased interest-bearing assets, the difference between rich and poor could be sustained or even increased.

15. "Differentiation of Personal Incomes," *Yugoslav Survey* 10, no. 1 (Feb. 1969): 81–90.

Private sector. The private sector is a highly visible source of extremely high incomes for a few. Long years of restrictive policies meant that too few people entered certain lines of activity and that prices for their services were accordingly high. The risk was very high in private activity because of local harassment and because laws frequently changed. The new attitude toward the private sector should in time reduce the risk and increase the supply of services forthcoming, but in the short run it seemed to increase the number of persons earning exorbitant incomes.

Different pay for the same job. While it may be possible to tolerate large differentials between different skill groups, unequal pay for the same work is a particularly difficult problem. The trade unions have been especially concerned about this point.

Differences in pay for the same job arise for several reasons. There are vast differences in income levels between northwest and southern Yugoslavia. Per capita incomes are several times higher in the richest republic than in the poorest. Very often, those in the south receive less pay for the same job. If the factors of production are mobile, these differences will eventually diminish. The abundant labor of the south will seek higher wages in the north and the capital of the north will try to utilize cheap southern labor. Labor mobility, in fact, seems closely correlated with such economic factors as job availability and rates of pay.[16] Still, language barriers and nationality differences limit interregional labor mobility in Yugoslavia. In addition, the high levels of unemployment since the reform (domestic unemployment near 10 percent and up to 20 percent if the several hundred thousand Yugoslavs working abroad were included in the ranks of the "unemployed") further limit mobility because it is difficult to find jobs. The eco-

16. "Internal Population Migrations in Yugoslavia," *Yugoslav Survey* 9, no. 2 (May 1968): 1–10.

nomic reforms of 1961 to 1965 attempted to stimulate capital movement by providing for interenterprise flows of funds and by revoking previous restrictions on such flows. Capital is not as mobile as had been hoped, however, whether for economic, nationalistic, or political reasons. Despite cheap labor, investment in the south may be less profitable because of the low skill levels and limited supplies of transportation, power, and other forms of social overhead capital.[17]

Different pay for the same job can also occur within the same region. The Yugoslav system of economic organization does not appear to provide an equalizing mechanism. In a competitive, private enterprise economy, pay differentials for similar work would tend to be eliminated (within a given geographic region) as employers sought to hire at the lowest possible wage and workers to obtain the highest possible wage. The Yugoslav enterprise functions differently. It appears to be a producers' cooperative in which workers share the total enterprise profit. Since some enterprises have greater profit than others, the profit per worker differs among firms. Such differences will not tend to be eliminated over time. Workers in prosperous firms can continue to receive higher personal incomes for the same work as those in less successful enterprises. In the short run, with fixed plant and equipment, although the low income workers from the unprofitable enterprises are willing to move to the high profit enterprises, the highly paid workers have no reason to let them in. To do so would only mean that the high profits would have to be shared among a larger number of workers. In the long run, although some additional labor will be employed in the high profit firm as it expands, the choice of technical

17. The reform also requires each region to finance most of its own expenditures. Poor regions will have limited tax revenues from which to construct social overhead capital. The bonds issued by the Republic of Bosnia-Herzegovina to build roads is an interesting experiment.

equipment that uses relatively little labor will tend to perpetuate the income gap.

Enterprise profit differences

The most troublesome inequalities in personal income arise from differences in enterprise profits. Differences in profits, in turn, can be attributed to monopoly position or privilege, interest income, rental income, or quality of entrepreneurship.

Monopoly and privilege. The market for some goods is not large enough to support many suppliers. Some producers have a monopoly situation and can profit accordingly. In other cases, for various reasons, subsidies and other privileges had been granted. Monopoly position, protection, or other privileges could be the source of differences in enterprise profits. A major purpose of the economic reform of 1965, both for equity and efficiency, was to eliminate privileged positions protected by subsidies and by high tariffs.

Enterprise interest income. The old doctrine that socialist enterprises should not earn interest incomes crumbled in Yugoslavia in 1963 when enterprises were enabled to purchase nonnegotiable interest-bearing bank bonds. The economic reforms of 1965 that abolished taxes on profit simultaneously made capital mobility essential. In addition to changes in the banking system to provide mobility of capital, enterprises were also allowed to lend directly to other enterprises. The interest income resulting from such transactions cannot be distributed to the workers but must be reinvested in the enterprise. This does not prevent workers from receiving gains, whether immediately (by shifting funds originally scheduled for investment into personal income and replacing these funds by the interest income) or ultimately (by receiving the income generated ⸱⸱ ⸱ ⸱ional investment). It should, however, prevent enterprises other than banks from deriving a major portion of income from money-lending.

Such explicit interest income is highly visible, but the more important interest income is implicit. Although the means of production are supposed to belong to society, society makes no charge for their use. The interest rate on social capital (the capital tax), always far below the equilibrium price, was scheduled to be abolished in 1970. If there is no charge to the enterprise for the use of social capital, then the enterprise itself receives the return to the factor capital. That is, part of enterprise profit is really an implicit interest return on the social capital society has placed at the firm's disposal.

The difficulty is that the socially owned means of production are not distributed equally among enterprises. Firms have different capital endowments. If firms paid a market-clearing price for the use of social capital, this would present no problem. Capital would be just another factor of production, in this case purchased from society. This is true whether one thinks of financial capital for which the firm pays an interest charge or of capital equipment for which the firm pays a rental fee. The enterprise would receive only the inframarginal returns as profits. These inframarginal returns could be attributed to the entrepreneurial skill with which capital was utilized by the firm. However, this is not the case. No fee is charged. Since enterprise profits include implicit interest income on social capital, and since firms differ in the amounts of capital at their disposal, profit differs from firm to firm.

Rental income. In a similar manner, one portion of enterprise profits represents unpaid rental charges for the use of scarce resources. Society fails to collect the appropriate rental fees from firms using social property. Socialist rents are low on urban land sites and nonexistent in mining since 1964. The absence of rent leads to the inefficient use of such properties. It also means that enterprise profits contain implicit rental incomes. These rental incomes arising from exclusive access to scarce resources are distributed unequally among firms.

Entrepreneurial income. The concept of profit as used by economists is crucial to the understanding of entrepreneurial income. Economists mean profit exclusive of the implicit return to other factors of production (exclusive of interest or rent). Apart from a monopoly advantage, profits so defined can arise for several reasons. The innovative acts of entrepreneurs continually create temporary profits until the adoption of these innovations on a wide scale eliminates the initial advantage and the profits. Thus profit is the reward to creative innovation. Yet by its very nature innovation involves risk. If people prefer to avoid risky situations, then on the average a price must be paid to induce risk-bearing. This will also appear as part of profit.

The Yugoslav collective is an entrepreneur. It innovates and it bears risk. Profits are the return to its managerial activities, innovations, and risk-bearing. This has long been recognized in Yugoslavia, and references to socialist payments for entrepreneurship appeared as early as 1953.[18] Bajt, among others, has argued more recently that, just as some labor is more productive and will be paid a higher price, some collectives are better entrepreneurs than others and will receive higher entrepreneurial incomes.[19] According to this line of reasoning, differences in entrepreneurship are still another source of differences in profits among firms. The economic reform created more incentive for entrepreneurs and increased the rewards.

Thus we see that there are three sources of profit differences among firms: differing degrees of monopoly protection, differing amounts of implicit factor income, and different levels of entrepreneurial skill. If there were no

18. Serjige Krajger, *Nasa stvarnost* 7, no. 2 (Feb. 1953): 47–67.
19. Bajt, *Gledista* 9, no. 4 (Apr. 1968): 531–44.

monopolies and if society charged market-clearing rental and interest fees for the use of social property, the differences in profits and in personal income could be attributable to the superior entrepreneurship of the firm. Profits would still vary widely from enterprise to enterprise in a given year and over time, but such differences are inevitable in a world of innovation and change. But, clearly, actual Yugoslav enterprise profits also include monopoly profit, rent, and interest. Firms with large profits will pay higher personal incomes for the same type of work. There are no economic pressures to equalize personal incomes between firms. Therefore personal incomes differ for the same work in part as a result of monopoly advantage and implicit rental and interest income.

The traditional socialist principle of distribution is "to each according to his work." Yugoslavia has departed from the traditional interpretation in several ways: (1) by extending the concept of returns to include all factors supplied by the human agent, including entrepreneurship and the capital invested in the human agent; (2) by sustaining a situation in which equal work does not receive equal pay; (3) in sanctioning nonlabor factor incomes, both explicit and implicit, in both the private and the social sector. The Yugoslav principle of distribution becomes "to each according to the factors of production supplied by the human agent or to which the human agent has access, as valued on the (imperfect) market." This principle is scarcely distinguishable from that of private enterprise.

A change in property rights

Ownership is a bundle of property rights. In Yugoslavia, the rights over productive property were divided between the state (as representative of society) and the enterprise. As a result of changes over time in the system of economic organization, the property rights of the enterprise and the worker-managers increased vis-à-vis the state. On the basis of these changes I have previously spoken of a "privatization" of property or an "individualization" of property rights, and even asked whether there was a "transition from socialism to capitalism?" [20] None of these terms seems entirely satisfactory to describe what took place. I shall provisionally refer to "a change in property rights."

The concept of "social ownership" of productive factors, always vague,[21] in fact proved vacuous. Gradually, certain members of society increased their effective rights over social property. The erosion of state property rights started with the first economic reform of 1950 to 1954. That reform decentralized the management of existing capacities and gave each enterprise exclusive access to the social property at its disposal. In a reaction against the days of central planning and administration, no state organ could remove social property from the enterprise. Access to social property initially meant the right to work with that property. How the social property was to be used was to be decided by the workers in a given enterprise.

Although it seemed apparent that in socialism all should have equal access to social property, the meaning of equal access had never been made clear. It was used variously to mean identical productivity of labor, equal personal income, or equal opportunity to bid for social capital under identical conditions. In fact, of course, social property is distributed unequally among the population because identical capital-labor ratios are neither necessary nor desirable.

The unequal distribution of social property per employed person initially had no major significance for in-

20. Deborah Milenkovitch, "Yugoslavia: The Transition from Socialism to Capitalism?" paper presented at the Northeastern Conference of the American Association for the Advancement of Slavic Studies, Boston, Mar. 1969.

21. See, for example, the effort of Djordjevic to give it content. Jovan Djordjevic, "A Contribution to the Theory of Social Property," *Socialist Thought and Practice*, no. 24 (Oct.–Dec. 1966): 73–110.

come distribution for two reasons. Earnings generated by the socially owned factors were taxed away and did not accrue to individuals or groups; and in any event they were a minor source of influence on enterprise profits compared with the subsidies, price controls, and other devices. The economic reforms starting in 1961 brought a number of changes. First, subsidies and other discriminatory devices were reduced. Second, charges for the use of social resources were virtually abolished, so that the enterprise acquired exclusive right not only of access to social property but also to the income streams generated by the social property at their disposal. Third, enterprise members gained the exclusive right to make decisions regarding the firm's activities and the use of profits, and influences from outside the firm were curtailed. Finally, the enterprise acquired the right to lend funds and to receive interest for money lent (even at variable interests rates, depending on the profitability of the enterprise to which funds were lent) and to transfer, for limited time periods, the right to shares in the enterprise income to other firms.

Exclusive group property rights

As a result of the economic reforms of the sixties, the property rights of the enterprise expanded vis-à-vis the state. The enterprise was still restrained from using up or liquidating the stock of social capital and was still restricted in the terms under which, and to whom, it could temporarily transfer shares of income or lend money. But it had gained significant rights in the course of the economic reform, rights that have important implications for the economic system as a whole.

For one thing, free entry becomes crucial in a way that it had not previously been. Earlier, if imbalances of any kind existed, the centrally determined investment policy could alleviate them (if it chose to do so). Now this option was significantly restricted. It was recognized that the new rights granted the enterprise required a capital market to permit capital to flow from the firms which earned profits to those firms with the best investment opportunities. A mechanism was established to make capital flows possible, either directly by enterprises or through the banks. What was not adequately recognized was the need for greater attention to the provisions for entry and the establishment of new firms.

In principle, in a market economy, new firms should emerge spontaneously as profitable opportunities arise. This is the function of private entrepreneurs in a capitalist system, but socialist entrepreneurs could presumably do the job also. New firms might be developed by existing firms, although under Yugoslav arrangements, the existing firm might be reluctant to reinvest its funds in ventures that could subsequently demand to become independent, self-managing units. If that were to happen, the founding enterprise would lose any income stream from its invested earnings. Alternatively, groups of workers might band together in a new enterprise and borrow funds. If the workers were previously unemployed, they would be willing to pay a relatively high price to borrow funds to start a business, especially if their alternative earnings are zero. Similarly, if a particularly profitable opportunity arises, even employed workers would find it worthwhile to form an enterprise and borrow funds to start the new business. One can even, I suppose, conceive of socialist firms specializing in researching investment opportunities or constructing turnkey projects.

To the extent that the operation of market forces, including capital flows and free entry, make social capital available to all members of society on equal terms for equal risk where this had not been the case before, it reduces the differences in factor payments and factor marginal productivities and increases efficiency. The more interesting question is whether, (perfect) markets for nonlabor factors having been established, the existence of a capital market in a producers' cooperative system serves to equalize factor endowments. The functioning of a producers' cooperative economy, in terms of both efficiency and equality, depends on the factor endowments.

As noted in Chapter 8, the producers' cooperative which is maximizing income per worker will hire nonlabor marketed factors of production according to the same criterion as the capitalist firm, that is, up to the point at which the marginal revenue product of the hired factor is equal to the price of the factor. The producers' cooperative criterion for hiring labor is up to the point at which the marginal revenue product of labor is equal to the dividend per worker. As noted, the size of the dividend, and thus the marginal product of labor, may vary from firm to firm. There is no equalizing tendency possible through the voluntary movement of labor. If neither labor nor capital are mobile, neither equality nor efficiency will necessarily occur.

The question is whether introducing the flow of capital and free entry solves these problems. Provision for entry and capital flows should result in a more efficient distribution of capital than in their absence. But the economy will not become fully efficient unless the operation of the market mechanism serves to reduce inequalities of factor endowments. It is true that poorly endowed firms and the unemployed will improve their position by borrowing money. It is also true that rich firms get richer by lending money to poor firms and to the unemployed. Thus a voluntary exchange beneficial to both parties will take place, signifying an improvement in efficiency. The question is what happens to the relative positions of poor and rich firms in terms of dividends per capita. The one tendency—more efficient distribution of capital stock among the labor force, raising the marginal productivity of labor of the poorly endowed—may be offset by the increased nonearned income going to the lenders, which in turn raises the dividend per worker if the distributon of nonearned income is not proscribed. (If the distribution of nonearned income is proscribed and such income can only be reinvested, it would only make sense for a firm to lend money if it had profitable but not immediate internal investment opportunities.) If the dividend per worker rises, the enterprise will prefer a small number of workers, so that the marginal product of labor would be equal to the new, higher dividend. Capital flows in a producers' cooperative system could lead, in the extreme, to a greater inequality of factor endowments, dividend per worker, and marginal product of labor and therefore to a decrease in equality and to negative effects on efficiency. In any event, due to the offsetting tendencies, efficiency and equality need not improve rapidly merely as the result of instituting capital flows and free entry. If they do not improve rapidly, then the question of the distribution of social assets among the population remains an important problem.

If (1) social assets (social productive property, location advantages, and protected monopolies) are unequally distributed among the population, if (2) the taxes that would capture the returns to social assets have been abolished, and if (3) the enterprises are free to maximize their objective free of constraints, the income streams from these social assets will also be unequally distributed.

Further, because firms with such advantages cannot be forced to hire workers, workers in these firms will presumably follow their self-interest by restricting access to those assets to a small number, if not by firing from their own ranks, then by failing to replace all the retired and departed workers. Alternatively, one can imagine a situation arising, not unlike that in certain American craft unions, where access to a favored position could command a price or be an inherited right. Despite the fact that the individual worker's claim to the income stream generated by social assets is a temporary, nontransferable right, the situation has the possibility of creating continuing, exclusive access to unequal endowments of social, income-generating assets.

Individual property rights

Independently of the possibility of establishing exclusive, continuing group property rights described above, another important change may occur as a result of changes following the economic reform. Because the worker-managers are now free to choose between investment in nonowned assets or investments in individually owned assets, a shift toward owned assets should occur for two reasons:

1. Even if the worker-managers in a given enterprise have identical time horizons of employment, time preferences, and risk preferences, the rate of return required internally on nonowned assets, in order to be equally attractive, must be greater than that on owned assets, as was shown in Chapter 8. The shorter the time horizon of expected employment within the given enterprise, the higher must be the rate of return on nonowned assets.

2. Because time horizons, time preferences and risk preferences are *not* identical among the members of an enterprise, the reaching of an agreement binding on all members has significant costs in terms of the time required for negotiations and the losses of freedom involved in accepting binding, collective decisions.[22] Because few clear benefits arise from acting collectively that could offset these costs of reaching collective agreement, one would expect collective action to be the exception rather than the rule.

Certainly, if a major portion of investment were to be supplied by individuals in the form of owned assets, one could hardly speak with any confidence of "social owner-

22. James Buchanan and Gordon Tullock, *The Calculus of Consent* (Ann Arbor: University of Michigan, 1962).

ship." This remains true, even if individuals can purchase only fixed-debt assets and not equity shares. As Peter Wiles points out,[23] the purchase and sale of equity shares is the real core of capitalism, so a system without private, individually owned equity shares would not really be capitalism. But what remains of socialism in a society in which fixed-debt owned assets are not only permissible (savings accounts bearing interest exist in virtually all socialist countries) but where it becomes the *primary* source of saving and thus a very important source of income? The next logical step, proposing that individuals could own not only fixed-interest assets but that the interest rates might be variable, depending on the profitability of the enterprise, has already been proposed.[24] This would come even closer to personal ownership of equity shares, although they would be, apparently, nonvoting shares because actual management remains vested in the workers in the enterprise.

Shift toward capitalism?

As indicated at the outset of this section, I have not found a term that satisfactorily describes what happened to social ownership as a result of the changes in property rights which were the corollary of the economic reforms. If private, individual ownership of equity shares is the essence of capitalism, Yugoslavia has not reverted to capitalism. However, we are left semantically and ideologically on a very uncomfortable middle ground. Two changes follow from the economic reforms: (1) the right to income streams from social assets, albeit in group form and in principle only temporarily, is made available exclusively

23. Peter Wiles, "Convergence: Possibility and Probability," in Alexander Balinky, *et al., Planning and the Market in the U.S.S.R.: The 1960's* (New Brunswick: Rutgers University Press, 1967), pp. 112–13.

24. A report on a study published by Lazo Rupnik and Janez Bubovec, members of the Slovene economic council, as reported in *The Economist,* Dec. 14, 1968, pp. 20–21.

to a limited group of persons, and (2) the possibility arises that individually owned assets could become a major source of savings and of income.

Either of these changes separately would mark a departure from any historically recognized definition of socialism. Even less can we speak of socialism if both of these changes are taking place simultaneously, as they appear to be in the newly defined Yugoslav property rights. Looked at from a "class" point of view, if a group of persons working in favored locations have a disproportionate share of the income generated by social capital, if they can restrict access to favored positions, and if they can also use this income to invest in owned, transferable, income-generating assets, the possibility exists of self-perpetuating income strata on the basis of wealth. Such a state of affairs is surely neither socialism nor capitalism. But on the continuum between socialism and capitalism, relative to the prereform position, Yugoslavia would seem to have moved in the direction of capitalism. I shall leave it to the reader to supply a name for this state of affairs.

EQUALITY AND EFFICIENCY IN A
SOCIALIST MARKET ECONOMY

Economic efficiency requires that factors and products be transferred (in competitive markets) at market-clearing prices, whether in socialism or in capitalism. Although it has taken some socialists a long time to grasp this principle, most Yugoslavs now accept it. A price paid for a factor need not, however, constitute a personal income. The question is whether the factor payment serves any useful function in socialism. There have been several serious efforts to produce an explanation of factor payments and to answer this question. As we have seen, the present system in Yugoslavia has virtually abolished any payment by the socialist firm for the socially owned factors of production that it employs. Both Bajt and Horvat reject such an approach because it generates income inequality without improving economic efficiency.

The factors of production are land, labor, capital, and entrepreneurship. Bajt argues that payments to labor are necessary because they affect the quantity and the quality of labor supplied. In the case of land rental, the supply of land remains the same regardless of whether the rental fees constitute an income, and thus payments by the users are necessary but payments to the owners as incomes would serve no function. The crucial questions for socialism revolve around the return to capital and to entrepreneurship. Bajt has argued that all firms should pay the same, market-clearing rate of interest on financial capital.[25] In his view, the essence of the entrepreneurial act is translating formless monetary capital into a specific structure of plant and equipment. If the entrepreneur makes good choices, he will by innovation create temporary scarcities or take advantage of them, and profits, the reward to entrepreneurship, will result. The firm is entitled to these profits in the same manner that labor which works harder or more skillfully is entitled to higher compensation. Just as with labor, these profits induce a supply of entrepreneurship, rewarding those whose acts are valued by society, while penalizing those with faulty judgment. The reward and penalty structure of profit is necessary in decentralized socialism to induce the appropriate attitudes toward risky ventures and to give birth to innovations.

In his book *Towards a Theory of Planned Economy*, Horvat uses a similar approach but reaches different conclusions.[26] Horvat distinguishes four factors of production and four types of factor incomes: monopoly (including

25. Bajt, *Gledista* 9, no. 4 (Apr. 1968): 544.
26. Branko Horvat, *Towards a Theory of Planned Economy*, chaps. 2 and 3.

land) receives rent; capital receives interest; labor receives wages; and entrepreneurship receives profits. Horvat seeks the maximum equality of income consistent with maximizing output. Accordingly, he approaches the question of allocation of factors of production from the standpoint of marginal productivity analysis. Resources should be allocated where the marginal productivity is greatest; in a competitive market economy, the prices paid in equilibrium reflect the marginal productivity of the factors in their best uses. On the other hand, he approaches distribution from the point of view of equality. He would not pay the suppliers according to the marginal productivity (gross factor payments) but would exclude any portion of the factor payment that was an economic "rent." An economic rent payment has the property that the quantity of factor supplied will not be reduced by excluding the rent payment from the factor's income. In other words, Horvat argues that beyond some point the supply schedule of the factor of production rises vertically, and payment of prices higher than the minimum price at which the supply schedule rises vertically will not increase the supply of the factor. Paying out only the nonrent portion of the factor price cannot reduce the factor supplies or output but it will increase the equality of income distribution. In this way Horvat seeks to minimize the conflict between equality and efficiency, just as he earlier placed the conflict between consumption and growth in a new perspective.

Horvat then seeks to determine what portion of each factor payment is a supply price and what portion constitutes a rent. The return to monopoly is, by his definition, a rent. In his analysis, interest is also a rent. This is because the supply of capital is determined independently of any interest rate. The optimum rate of savings and investment, it will be recalled, is that rate which maximizes output (and, in his view, consumption and consumers' satisfaction as well) over a time horizon of about twenty-five years. In other words, the social marginal productivity of investment with respect to a twenty-five-year time horizon is zero and any further investment would diminish output over this time interval. Accordingly, the opportunity cost or supply price of capital is zero to society. Capital, however, has positive marginal productivity for each socialist firm individually, and it is necessary to allocate the capital among users. For efficient utilization, capital must be distributed among the firms according to the highest marginal productivity. The interest paid for capital remains a rent from the viewpoint of society, and should not accrue to any person as a factor income. (Horvat argues that the time preferences of individual consumers have nothing to do with the interest rate on productive investment. In the analysis employed by the neoclassical welfare economists, the optimum rate of savings and investment depend on the time preferences of the members of society that determine the supply of capital forthcoming, and on the marginal productivity of capital, which determines the demand. In the neoclassical analysis, interest is a supply price that induces savers to save. In Horvat's analysis, it is not. The time preferences of consumers do not determine the supply of productive investment. The consumers' time preferences will, however, be reflected on another market, the market for consumer credit. Consumers with different time preferences may reasonably want to alter their income streams over time by borrowing or lending. There can be interconsumer transactions and the rate of interest, which could be zero or possibly negative as well as positive, depends on whether there are more savers or more lenders.) Financial capital borrowed by the enterprise is converted into concrete form, that is, plant and equipment. Money will be borrowed only if the enterprise can produce a rate of return at least as great as the interest rate by converting capital into specific form. The enterprise can pay interest only when there are uses for capital that have a positive rate of return. Because these uses will be eroded away in the stationary economy, interest can exist as a continuing factor price only in a growing and dynamic economy.

Horvat then turns to the income to be paid to labor. The gross factor price (wage) reflects the marginal productivity of labor. If it contains an element of rent, arising from the temporary or permanent scarcity of certain types of labor reflected in vertical supply schedules, this rent should be taxed away. The worker receives a net wage that represents the minimum price at which the maximum quantity of labor will be supplied. He rejects, on two grounds, the view that any surplus over the minimum supply price of each *individual* worker is rent and should be taxed away: one is the administrative impossibility of collecting such a rent; the other is that paying different wages for the same work has an adverse effect on the supply of, and the effectiveness of, labor. An attempt to collect psychic "rent" from workers would reduce labor effectiveness and would be incompatible with maximizing output.

Horvat argues that the supply of labor depends not so much on the absolute level of wages as on the relative levels in proportion to social expectations. Society should determine relative wage scales that are consistent with social expectations and that will maximize the supply and the effectiveness of labor. These relative wage scales will reflect social estimates of the differences in psychic satisfaction among occupations, risk, disagreeableness, and other forms of positive or negative costs of specific types of occupation.

These wage scales constitute the net wages to be paid to workers. The actual transfer price is the gross wage. The difference between the gross transfer price (paid by the users of the factors and reflecting the marginal productivity) and the net wage will be taxed away. For efficient resource allocation, it is necessary that the workers seek to maximize the gross wage, despite the fact that they receive only the net wage. This assumption, as we shall see, is crucial to his analysis.

Horvat then turns to the other human factor of production, to entrepreneurship and to the interpretation of profit as its factor payment. He considers the two principal theories of profit, the return to uninsurable risk and to temporary scarcity resulting from innovative activity. Horvat (along with Schumpeter and Marx) argues that the actual innovator does not fully bear the uncertainty. In capitalism it is the supplier of finance capital, and in socialism it is society, who bear the brunt of the risk. In socialism, the uncertainty facing the socialist entreprenuer is further reduced because the state maintains macroeconomic stability and provides the information necessary to coordinate investment decisions with a minimum of risk. Accordingly, in socialism, the profits are the results of the innovative activities that constitute the essence of entrepreneurship. It is thus entrepreneurship that accounts for the productivity of capital equipment over and above the interest rate which is paid to society for the use of capital funds. In this reasoning, Horvat's position is similar to that taken by Bajt. Both agree that the enterprise should pay society the market-clearing interest rate for the use of social property.

But where Bajt would ascribe the profit remaining to entrepreneurship and distribute it to the entrepreneur, Horvat argues that not all of profit need be distributed to entrepreneurs. Only that portion of profits need be paid as factor income which is necessary to ensure the maximum supply of entrepreneurship. (Horvat admits it would be difficult to determine the price that would induce the maximum quantity of entrepreneurship, and here he has recourse only to a socially determined "fair scale." [27]) Beyond some level, higher profits do not draw forth any additional entrepreneurship. Such superprofits also constitute a rent and should be taxed away. Conversely, the failure of the

27. Ibid., p. 119.

enterprise to attain the socially approved scale of compensation signals a below-average supply of entrepreneurship.

In order to allocate the scarce factor of entrepreneurship among productive activities, Horvat must assume that enterprises maximize gross before-tax profits. Here we come to one of Horvat's most important assumptions. Just as the nonhuman factors of production are allocated according to the marginal productivity in various uses, it is necessary that both entrepreneurship and labor allocate themselves according to the gross rate of return to the factor, despite the fact that they receive as income only the net return. In Horvat's version, firms, the entrepreneurial unit, maximize gross profits, and thus "allocate" the scarce factor of entrepreneurship efficiently among alternative uses. What is still missing from Horvat's exposition is a convincing explanation that will show *why* the collective entrepreneur wishes to maximize total gross profits rather than net profits per worker, as was explored in Chapter 8. It would not be difficult to construct a theory of total gross profit maximization and perhaps it is not improbable that firms actually do behave that way. If he could provide this missing link, Horvat's exposition of the planned economy would be considerably strengthened.

There are some other troublesome spots in his imaginative and highly lucid theory of the socialist economy. Nowhere does he explain how entrepreneurship is supplied or how it is paid. Horvat identifies the working collective as the collective entrepreneur. If entrepreneurship is supplied collectively, how does the collective supply "entrepreneurship," and how does the collective as a whole receive factor payments? What is the effect of the payments to entrepreneurship on the allocation of labor, the distribution of income, and on the enterprise maximizing principle? Despite these areas in his analysis that have not been fully clarified, Horvat has provided a new way and a challenging way of looking at the traditional conflicts that

trouble the Western welfare economist, the conflicts between growth and consumption and between equality and
efficiency.

The effective set of property rights and the resultant income distribution that followed from the Yugoslav economic reforms is at the center of the Yugoslav debate
about whether the Titoist system is socialist. To this debate we turn in the next chapter.

CHAPTER 11

Is This Socialism? The Yugoslav Debate

The three traditional doctrines of socialism are production planning, investment planning, and social ownership of property with the distribution of income according to labor supplied. Yugoslavia has, one by one, abandoned these traditional doctrines. The most recent departure is the effective redistribution of rights over social property, which make the income from socially owned assets available to an exclusive group of people. The intriguing question is, "why?" Was it necessary to achieve efficient economic growth? As we have seen, both Bajt and Horvat answer "no" to this question on economic grounds. Are the new property rights merely a sign of still another class defending its interests? Or are they an essential component of self-management? The Yugoslav Establishment, not surprisingly, maintains that the system it has constructed is socialist. Two other groups, the conservative socialists and the humanists, find very little they can call socialist in today's Yugoslavia.

THE ESTABLISHMENT VIEW

The ruling Establishment is essentially a coalition of party liberals, socialist technocrats and managers, and party leaders in the developed republics, against the various conservative factions. According to the chief spokesmen of the Establishment, including Edvard Kardelj,[1] Milentije Pop-

1. Some of Kardelj's principal articles have appeared in English in *Socialist Thought and Practice:* "The Principal Dilemma: Self-Manage-

ovic,[2] Mijalko Todorovic,[3] and Najdan Pasic,[4] true socialism requires three conditions: direct democracy, the absence of exploitation, and the rapid development of productive forces. In their view, only a system based on self-
governing associations and a market economy can fulfill
these conditions. Let us examine the argument in more
detail.

According to the Establishment, socialism requires direct democracy. Direct democracy means that citizens participate in the decisions concerning their lives, both in the
work place and in the community. Direct democracy in
the work place requires independent and self-managing
production units, that is, enterprises in which workers
make decisions. Direct democracy in the community requires decentralization of authority to the community
level, these matters to be decided by members of the community. Direct democracy in any form requires that self-
governing units be free from arbitrary administrative interference (by party officials, higher organs of state, etc.).
Intervention destroys initiative, cuts incentives, and prevents the full development of social responsibility by the
community.

The chief obstacle to direct democracy is the central,
statist bureaucracy. Bureaucracy, by its very nature, cannot avoid intervention in the affairs of self-governing units.
Bureaucracy arises wherever functions are centralized.

ment or Statism," no. 24 (Oct.–Dec. 1966): 3–29; "The Working Class,
Bureaucracy and the League of Communists," no. 29 (Jan.–Mar. 1968):
3–28; "What Is the 'Authentic' Revolutionary Nature of the Working
Class," no. 30 (Apr.–June 1968): 10–31.

2. "For the Re-evaluation of Marx's Teaching on Production and Relations of Production," *Socialist Thought and Practice*, no. 19 (July–Sept.
1965): 64–117; no. 20 (Oct.–Dec. 1965): 62–98.

3. "The Working Man, Capital Formation and Investments," *Socialist
Thought and Practice*, no. 22 (Apr.–June 1966): 29–44; "A Revolutionary
Vanguard—The Abiding Need of Our Self-Managing Community," *Social-
ist Thought and Practice*, no. 31 (July–Sept. 1968): 7–20.

4. "Critical Survey of Different Conceptions of Self-Management," *Socialist Thought and Practice*, no. 31 (July–Sept. 1968): 32–49.

Thus, to avoid bureaucracy, socialism must minimize the need for centralization. Because central planning inevitably implies a central, statist bureaucracy,[5] central planning is incompatible with direct democracy. The economy must be composed of independent enterprises making their own production and investment decisions. Enterprises therefore must retain sufficient funds from profits to carry out their investments.

Direct democracy is seen to require independent enterprises, market relations, and the abolition of investment planning. The Establishment analysis of alienation reinforces these conclusions. Capitalism is characterized by the alienation of the worker from his product. Alienation is interpreted as the presence of an intermediary between the worker and his product. The state bureaucracy in socialism is just such an intermediary.[6] Central planning of investment, which takes from some firms in order to give to others, prevents the workers from disposing of the product of their labor. Only when independent, worker-managed enterprises dispose of their income is alienation brought to an end.

The third requirement is efficiency. Socialism must make possible the rapid and efficient development of productive forces. According to the Establishment interpretation, the central planning of investment in the past had led to poor decisions, had prevented a rational use of resources, had reduced incentives, and had held the economy back. At the present level of economic development, only market forces can produce the types and qualities of goods required at minimum cost. There is a price to be paid for economic development, in the form of inequality.[7] Labor with desirable skills and workers in efficient enterprises

5. Milentije Popovic, *Socialist Thought and Practice*, no. 19 (July–Sept. 1965): 64–117.

6. Todorovic, *Socialist Thought and Practice*, no. 22 (Apr.–June 1966): 29–44.

7. Adolf Dragicevic, "Income Distribution According to Work Performed," *Socialist Thought and Practice*, no. 26 (Apr.–June 1967): 76.

will receive higher pay. At the same time, capital must flow where it will be of greatest use as determined by the market and not according to administrative fiat.

Socialism requires direct democracy, the absense of exploitation, and rapid and efficient development. In the Establishment view, only a society based on self-government, market relations, and a minimum of central functions can fulfill these conditions.

CONSERVATIVE SOCIALISTS

The conservatives, sometimes called the centralists in Yugoslavia, have remained true to many of the traditional doctrines of socialism. One suspects that some have been a little uneasy ever since Yugoslavia dismantled the central planning apparatus and introduced independent enterprises. Many influential economists, including Kosta Mihailovic, Radmila Stojanovic, and Nikola Cobeljic [8] were opposed to the economic reform on several grounds. In particular, the conservatives questioned the conclusion that investment planning had been inefficient.[9] Investment planning in their view is necessary for rapid economic development. Planned allocation results in a better use of investment funds than would be possible through reliance on the market mechanism. The market mechanism can coordinate decisions only after the fact, adjusting to failures, whereas the plan can coordinate decisions from the start and thus avoid waste. The conservative socialists also believed planning was necessary because of the different levels of development. Socialism could be fully realized in

8. See their articles in *Yugoslav Economists on Problems of a Socialist Economy*, Radmila Stojanovic, ed. (New York: International Arts and Sciences Press, 1964).

9. See the report of the papers and discussion at the annual meeting of the Yugoslav Association of Economists, Zagreb, January 17–19, 1963. (Reprinted in *Ekonomist* 16, no. 1, 1963.)

Yugoslavia only when the economic differences between regions were significantly reduced. The market would exaggerate these differences, while to reduce them would require specific, planned economic policies.

Finally, the traditional socialists saw a fundamental conflict between the private self-interest of the enterprises and the welfare of society.[10] They rejected the notion of a socialist invisible hand, assuring that the pursuit of self-interest by the individual, profit-seeking firms would inevitably attain the highest level of social well-being. To the contrary, they maintained that enterprises make decisions that could be harmful to the community at large. Therefore, the social authority must intervene in the affairs of the firm when necessary to protect the interests of society as a whole. For all these reasons, the conservatives conclude that there must be central planning. They reject as erroneous the Establishment interpretation that emphasizes the independence of the enterprise and its freedom from intervention. Socialism is not equivalent to local autonomy.

Many older party members are more comfortable with these centralist views. In addition, many in Yugoslavia seem to agree that less planning favors the developed regions, while a return to centralism would be more favorable to the less developed areas. Political representatives of the less developed republics are usually centralist-traditional in outlook.

SOCIALIST HUMANISTS

Among the humanist authors concerned with the organization of society are Ljubomir Tadic,[11] Svetozar Stojan-

10. See the discussion in Najdan Pasic, "Critical Survey of Different Conceptions of Self-Management," *Socialist Thought and Practice*, no. 31 (July–Sept. 1968): 32–49.

11. Ljubomir Tadic, *Poredak i sloboda* (Belgrade: Kultura, 1967).

ovic,[12] Veljko Korac,[13] and Stevan Vracar.[14] In the view of
the humanists, the present social system of Yugoslavia is a
travesty of socialism. It not only restores an anarchic and
inefficient market mechanism and prevents the establishment of humane relations among men; the present system
represents the class interests of a privileged group, the
technostructure of the technical elite in industry and the
party bureaucracy. This group is vigorously protecting its
interests. It has transformed social ownership into group
or personal ownership by establishing effective property
rights for those employed in an enterprise. It dispenses
various forms of monopoly protection and other favors
over which it, the governing elite, has exclusive control.[15]
Decentralization or self-government in the community is
no improvement; it only brings a brand of local bureauc-
ratism that is even more stifling than the central bureauc-
ratism.[16] The Establishment attempt to justify these measures in the name of efficiency and direct democracy is
mere rhetoric to conceal their own class interest.

The humanists also believe that socialism requires democracy, efficiency, and the end of alienation. But their
interpretation of these, and of the social institutions that
make them possible, is quite different from that of the
Establishment.

Like the conservatives, the humanists tend to view the
market as anarchic and inefficient. They disagree as to how
much central planning is necessary. Some have a romantic
vision, reminiscent of Marxism before the Russian revolution, of the totally planned society, while others are more

12. Svetozar Stojanovic, "Social Self-government and Socialist Community," *Praxis* (International ed.) 4, no. 1–2 (1968): 104–16.

13. Veljko Korac, "The Possibilities and Prospects of Freedom in the
Modern World," *Praxis* (International ed.) 4, no. 1–2 (1968): 73–82.

14. Stevan Vracar, "Dilema oko drzavne vlasti," *Gledista* 8, no. 5 (May
1967): 771–84; "Partijski monopolizam i politicka moc drustvenih grupa,"
Gledista 8, no. 8–9 (Aug. 1967): 1053–1066.

15. Vracar, *Gledista* 8, no. 8–9 (Aug. 1967): 1054.

16. Vracar, *Gledista* 8, no. 5 (May 1967): 783–84.

realistic about the limitations of planning. Whatever the degree of planning, the enterprise would lose much of its present independence with the exercise of more social control. This would be desirable, in their view, on the grounds of efficiency alone, but there are other reasons favoring it as well.

The humanists view alienation as the failure of man to realize his full potential. Social relations among men are dehumanized in a market economy. The reliance on financial incentives gives everything a monetary value. A pecuniary reward system makes the definition of property rights crucial. Relations among men become dehumanized because they are secondary to man's legal relation to income-producing things. When men are dehumanized, they cannot realize their full human potential. Therefore, a market economy is not compatible with a humane society.[17]

Distribution of income according to work performed would continue, but the humanists are wary about "effectiveness" of work as the measure. In an underdeveloped country, payment according to effectiveness of output results in artificial handicaps for the untrained or those with old and poor equipment, and artificial advantages for the others. A highly qualified worker has no claim to higher pay on the basis of his qualifications because the training costs were borne by society. The humanists believe that ideally individuals should give equally of what they have, even though being unequal, and unequally trained and equipped, their labor will be of unequal effectiveness. Ultimately, more and more goods will be provided free of charge until both parts of the communist goal, "from each according to his abilities, to each according to his needs," prevail.[18]

17. Korac, *Praxis* (International ed.) 4, no. 1–2 (1968): 79.
18. Donald Hodges has two sympathetic articles on the views of the humanists, "Yugoslav Philosophers in the Struggle against Bureaucracy," *Florida State University Slavic Papers* 1 (1967): 77–94; "Yugoslav Marxism and Methods of Social Accounting," ibid., 2 (1968): 40–49.

The humanists emphasize the need for democracy and for representative social institutions. They have proposed a society considerably more planned than is presently the case. The humanists do not propose to entrust the task of planning to the party or to the present government structure. (A major difference between the conservative socialists and the humanists is that the former are inclined to accept the guiding role of the existing party.) Although vague about how to establish them, the humanists want genuinely democratic bodies to legislate the politically established norms. "The development of social self-government as an integrated system assumes, of course, an essential change of the sociopolitical structure up to the top; i.e., constituting vertical association of self-governing and self-managing groups, developing truly representative bodies from below upwards, placing under their control not only all state organs but also social life." [19]

POLITICAL ASPECTS

The conservative socialists and humanists are at odds with the Establishment. These differences of opinion are not merely a doctrinal dispute. They are intimately connected with the political tensions in Yugoslavia. Dissenters who question the existing Yugoslav social and economic measures pose a potential threat to the Yugoslav leadership, as became apparent in the student demonstrations of June 1968.

The threat arises because the Establishment doctrine, translated into policy, has established a definable group of beneficiaries and a group of disadvantaged. The beneficiaries of the Establishment policy are the skilled workers and technicians, the technically proficient bureaucrats, the employed, and those in the developed regions. The dis-

19. Svetozar Stojanovic, *Praxis* 4, no. 1–2 (1968): 108.

advantaged are the unskilled workers, party hack bureaucrats, the unemployed (especially those with skills such as
students), and those in the less developed regions. The
division between the haves and the have-nots is serious and
is compounded by nationality tension in Yugoslavia. The
have-nots, if brought together, could form a politically
powerful alliance against the Establishment. The humanists have great appeal among the student population and
the intellectuals; the conservatives represent the interests
of the traditional party bureaucracy and of the underdeveloped regions; and the trade union position has begun to shift in the last few years away from being an Establishment mouthpiece toward becoming a representative of
workers' interests. It is conceivable that the anti-Establish-
ment groups might join forces to mobilize a dissatisfied
public opinion. Indeed, both Kardelj and Todorovic have
commented on the possibilities of dangerous alliances.[20]
The humanists and the conservatives, in fact, have much
common ground. In comparison to the Establishment,
their view of socialism is more centralist,[21] more political
(although perhaps more democratic in the case of the humanists), and less trusting of the market because of its ir-
rationality and inefficiency or because of its competition
and inequality. The trade unions, potential defectors from
the Establishment because of unemployment, differential
earnings, and low pay for the unskilled, might easily find
common cause. All three advocate policies that are similar
in many respects and appeal to the large numbers of Yugoslavs who feel disadvantaged under a market regime.

The Belgrade student uprising of June 1968 may have
been a harbinger of such a coalition. The student political

20. Kardelj, *Socialist Thought and Practice*, no. 30 (Apr.–June 1968):
22; Todorovic, ibid., no. 31 (July–Sept. 1968): 13–14.
21. From the Establishment point of view, the conservatives and the
humanists are both unreformed centralists at heart. And the Establishment analysis of socialism shows resurgent centralism to be *the* greatest
danger to attaining true socialism.

action program of June 4 made the following principal
demands: [22] (1) elimination of social inequality by providing clear principles for determining personal incomes and
by taking action against monopoly, privilege, and illegal
operations; (2) resolution of the unemployment problem
by establishing the right to employment and an expansion-
ary investment policy; (3) curtailing of the bureaucracy
and democratization of the party and the news media;
(4) reversal of attempts to convert social ownership into
group ownership; (5) provision of a new system of the gov-
ernance and the finance of higher education.

The students attempted to mobilize the workers in support of these demands. The Establishment directed vast
attention to preventing (successfully) such a worker-stu-
dent alliance. The principal tools were the Establishment
control of the principal press organs, which printed versions of the student uprising that were considered to be
very biased, and the party organization at the enterprise
level that prevented students from establishing direct contact with the workers.

Interestingly, there was some evidence of worker support for the students. In many cases workers renounced the
telegrams sent by the factory party organizations. The paper of the Confederation of Trade Unions, *Rad,* gave a
carefully reasoned endorsement of the student demands
and even approved the student methods of protest.[23] Finally, the resolutions passed by the Sixth Congress of the
Confederation of Trade Unions a little later in June are
essentially quite similar to the demands of the students

22. For a sensitive and detailed account of the student uprising, see
Dennison I. Rusinow, "Anatomy of a Student Revolt," parts 1 and 2,
Fieldstaff Reports, American Universities Field Staff, Southeast Europe
Series 15, no. 4, 5 (Aug., Nov. 1968). The appendix to part 1 of his report
contains the student demands.

23. *Rad,* June 7, June 14, 1968, as cited by Rusinow, *Fieldstaff Reports*
15, no. 5 (1968): 12.

if somewhat less strident.[24] The resolutions, while sup-
porting the reform, called attention to the low rates of
growth, the inadmissible differences in personal incomes
and the problems of unemployment. They called for
higher rates of investment, full employment, a minimum
guaranteed income, progressive income taxation, and en-
forcement of laws against illegal income-producing activities. The congress also emphasized the need for genuine
self-management to assure that the workers really manage
the enterprises and are not mere rubber stamps for the
management.

The events of 1968 make it clear that there are deep and
intensely felt political consequences of the controversial
economic policies adopted in 1965.

24. "Sixth Congress of the Yugoslav Trade Union Federation," *Yugoslav
Survey* 9, no. 4 (Nov. 1968): 69–84.

CHAPTER 12

Lessons of the Yugoslav Experience

We have explored the evolution of Yugoslav thinking about the economic organization of a socialist society, starting from the intellectual heritage of Marx and from the Soviet interpretations. Gradually, and under the pressure of political and economic events, the Yugoslavs liberated themselves from Soviet tutelage and developed a new system based on market relations in the area of current production decisions. In the process the Yugoslavs defined a new Marxist relation between plan and market. Yet investment planning within the market framework proved unsatisfactory and centrally planned investment came under attack. The choice to abandon central planning had important consequences. Entrepreneurship, both existing and potential, proved necessary to organize the factors of production, and capital had to be allocated among users. Decentralizing the supply of capital and its allocation expanded effective group and individual property rights over social property and raises doubts about whether socialism still exists in Yugoslavia.

A brief outline of the Yugoslav experience might then read: Soviet-type planning—decentralization of current production decisions—decentralization of investment decisions—redistribution of property rights. We may now review this sequence of events and hazard some remarks about what factors accounted for it and whether and how much it is possible to generalize the Yugoslav experience. There are three separate questions to be explored.

1. Why did the Yugoslavs decentralize production decisions? A general thesis has been outlined that appears to

explain reasonably well the economic reforms in Eastern Europe. According to this reasoning, a central planning model is very possibly well suited for an underdeveloped country whose goals include modernization and rapid rates of growth and which is faced with a low level of technology, small markets, and inelastic supplies of productive factors. Especially where there are crucial bottleneck sectors that limit the expansion of the rest of the economy, Soviet-type planning and incentive systems may be effective initially in raising output, at the expense of cost and quality. Once bottlenecks are broken, however, there are good economic reasons to modify the system of physical planning and output targets that characterize the Soviet-type model. That system provides insufficient incentive to produce what is required or to minimize costs. The centralization of all decisions requires an enormous expenditure on information collection and processing. The reforms in the Soviet-type economies in the sixties seek to remedy these defects in the plan and implementation system.

The first Yugoslav reform, which took place between 1950 and 1954, dismantled the centralized system of administrative planning, eliminated price controls, and made costs more rational by introducing interest payments and repayable investment loans. Within the limits of existing plant and equipment, enterprises could determine what to produce, how to produce it, and at what prices to sell it. At first glance, this appears to be a classic case of central planning giving way to decentralization; in many respects it closely resembles the reforms of the sixties in Eastern Europe. We must look further, however, to explain the Yugoslav decision. Yugoslavia in the early fifties certainly had not eliminated production bottlenecks and it was far less developed than the innovating countries in Eastern Europe today. While a case for the Yugoslav economic reform can be made on economic grounds, an equally good if not better case can be made for continuing the old methods, judging by the growth rates of the economies that did not decentralize in 1950. That the Yugoslav decision to decentralize is fully understandable only in conjunction with the political repercussions of the Cominform Resolution, is supported by the form and the content of decentralization. The form of decentralization, based on independent enterprises managed by workers, served as a key feature in emphasizing the distinctness of the Yugoslav model from the Soviet system. The economic content of decentralization was delayed for some two to four years, following the establishment of workers councils in the enterprises.

In general, then, the notion that administrative central planning must give way to decentralization of production decisions is limited in value as an explanation of Yugoslav events for three reasons. First, central planning of the Soviet type probably does grow stale but this does not prove that the solution of the defects lies solely in adopting the market mechanism. Second, when Yugoslavia decentralized, few of the economic forces that make decentralization of production decisions attractive were present, while there were considerable factors which would make administrative allocation suitable. Finally, the Yugoslavs not only decentralized but adopted a particular form of decentralization based on workers management which was central to their total political-ideological realignment.

2. Why did the Yugoslavs decentralize investment decisions? Standard economic reasoning tells us that, in a typical underdeveloped country, the market mechanism can produce inferior investment decisions. With few buyers and sellers, the consequences of enterprise decisions are less predictable and coordination of investment decisions can result in significant improvement. As development proceeds, and with it an increase in the size of the market, the need for coordination diminishes, while simultaneously

the cost of planning increases. In addition, the systematic rigidities of the planning apparatus appear to become more important, and planners frequently continue to allocate investment as they had in the past, thus producing the wrong products with the wrong technology. Just as tautly planned production may be effective in the beginning but later leads to the wrong assortment of goods produced at high cost, planned investment may initially have great advantages but may later produce an inappropriate structure of the economy at excessive costs and must similarly be abandoned. The Czechoslovaks have been especially vocal about the defects of the classic Soviet-type investment planning.

These remarks about the difficulties of investment planning at higher levels of development appear to have some relevance for all planned economies. Additional factors, however, seem to have influenced the Yugoslav decision to abandon investment planning in the economic reforms of 1961 to 1965. The Yugoslavs desired to leave enterprises independent in their daily production decisions but to plan the structure of economic development. Two features made this arrangement fail. First, there appears to have been a gradual breakdown of the national consensus about economic objectives. In order to plan, there must be agreement on the objective to be reached. Centrally planned investment may have become impossible in Yugoslavia because of the absence of political agreement about such planning. The interests of the six republics differed so sharply that no consensus about the objectives of planning or the development strategy was possible. One reason for what appear to be irreconcilable differences over development strategy is precisely the different levels of development. The developed regions saw investment planning as a burden that cut seriously into economic incentives by the high tax rates required, which made grave errors of allocation, and which could be used to transfer resources away from the developed areas. At the same time the less developed regions were convinced that, without investment planning, they were doomed to remain underdeveloped. Thus the decision to abandon or vastly reduce central planning in favor of market determination of investments may indicate that the political decision-making mechanism had failed and that the market mechanism, more "neutral" in its working, was adopted. At the same time, the abandonment of investment planning was considered a defeat for the less developed regions.

The second feature that made the system of investment planning fall apart in Yugoslavia is the difficulty of combining partial planning and partial use of the market. In the effort to leave the enterprises to function independently in response to market signals, while retaining sufficient control of their actions to assure conformity with the national plan, various policy instruments can be used. Financial, quantitative, and persuasive instruments can be applied, generally or selectively. The government can manipulate financial magnitudes to induce firms to move in the desired directions. It can place constraints on their actions by quantitative limits. It can intervene in the decision-making processes by persuading the firms to reach decisions other than those they would have found in their own self-interest in the absence of social intervention. The Yugoslavs never adequately resolved which instruments should be used to guide the enterprises to conform to social objectives, nor how to use the instruments without destroying the rational basis of decentralized economic decisions and without devitalizing the concept of workers' management. In the Yugoslav case, partial planning worked initially but proved to be a disaster in the sixties. Indeed, the economic difficulties in combining independent enterprises and market decisions with central control over investment exacerbated the already tense nationality question and so further contributed to the breakdown of the political consensus.

Thus, in the Yugoslav case, possible ineptitude and rigidity of the planners and higher costs of planning at higher levels of development were secondary factors in causing the collapse of investment planning. The Yugoslav problem (and one that is likely to become prominent elsewhere in Eastern Europe as their own reforms proceed) was to make investment planning compatible with a system of independent enterprises responding to market signals. It was the Yugoslav failure to discover suitable policy means for implementing investment plans, combined with the absence of political consensus (to which the policy inadequacies contributed) that proved crucial in making investment planning fail.

3. Why were charges for the use of social property abandoned? It has been argued that effective group ownership claims over social property have appeared in Yugoslavia and that the concept of social property has proved meaningless. This is one of the most intriguing aspects of the Yugoslav experiment and one that casts doubts upon the viability of decentralized socialist economic systems. Can socialism decentralize and still remain socialist?

The abandonment of investment planning undoubtedly creates a need for an entrepreneur in socialism, a much stronger need than was the case with decentralized production decisions. With only production decisions decentralized, it would probably be possible to induce managers to run the enterprise in the directions desired by the planners. But with investment decentralized there is a need for risk taking and innovative activity that is difficult to promote without a de facto entrepreneur. Once investment planning is abandoned, an entrepreneurial agent becomes truly necessary. In Yugoslavia the workers became the collective entrepreneur. The entrepreneur, in order to make reason-

able economic decisions, must be adequately motivated by
the prospect of gain and by the possibility of loss. Entrepreneurial income, both positive and negative, will appear;
some workers will have positive earnings and some will
have losses from their ventures.

The collapse of social property is more difficult to explain. Although the concept of social property had always
been somewhat vague, this did not create an important
problem until charges for the use of social property were
abolished. Social property thereby became a sort of group
property or collective property of the enterprise members.
The firm supplied its own capital, whether to itself or for
investment in other firms. The troublesome question is
whether the decentralization of investment, which clearly
establishes a need for entrepreneurship and its positive and
negative rewards, also requires "owners" of capital in order to function. On balance, economic factors do not seem
to me to account for the changes in property rights.
I tend to agree with those Yugoslav economists who see no
economic difficulty with charging rent and interest for the
use of social property. For reasons that are not entirely
clear to me, the Yugoslavs did away with charges for socially owned resources, leaving the implicit factor income
to the collective entrepreneur. Although this decision
would appear to be a crucial one, I can offer no really satisfactory explanation. Possibly, it was the result of regional
tensions and the attendant fear that taxes on the enterprise
or other charges would lead to interregional transfers of
funds. Possibly, as the humanists have argued, it is the
successful effort of a new class to guard its privileges by
establishing property rights.

The mere establishment of independent enterprises subject to market forces does not appear necessarily to transform social property into group property nor to prevent
the harmonious development of the national economy
through planning. The Yugoslav experience suggests that

it may be possible to decentralize production decisions without decentralizing investment, although it may not be easy to find the economic instruments to make such an arrangement work satisfactorily. Nor does the decentralization of investment decisions alone appear to lead inevitably to the collapse of social ownership, although it does create a need for entrepreneurs. It appears to be the decentralization of investment decisions, coupled with the elimination of charges for socially owned resources, that seem to make the dire predictions about the erosion of socialism come true.

Finally, the larger the factor income accruing to the enterprise as a result, combined with the increased freedom of the worker-managers to allocate this income among alternative uses, imposes a greater burden on the enterprise collective decision-making apparatus than before. Because of the relatively greater attractiveness of owned than nonowned assets, and because of the costs involved in reaching collective decisions, private savings and owned assets could become the backbone of the capital market.

In this study of Yugoslav events I have been struck by the number of uniquely Yugoslav factors that seem necessary to account for the particular sequence of events. For example, the Cominform Resolution appears to be ultimately responsible for the initial decentralization and for the form it took: workers' management. The tense nationality question played a significant role in the breakdown of investment planning and tipped the balance in favor of the market. National suspicions are also suspect in the abandonment of charges for social property used by the enterprise with the resultant redistribution of rights over social property.

This is not, however, to suggest that the Yugoslav pattern of events has no relevance for other countries. I have also been struck by the extent to which a single change can have broad consequences. For example, a decision (taken for whatever particular reasons) to decentralize production, while retaining control of investment, creates additional needs. An effective management incentive must be established at the enterprise level. The financial signals the enterprise receives must guide it to make the correct decisions. Finally, central planning of investment must be carried out without preventing the incentives or the signals from inducing rational decisions. The Yugoslav experience shows clearly that combining partial planning with partial use of the market, while in principle possible, is no easy task. It demands a sophistication of policy application that very likely exceeds the limited capacities of East European governments and the skills of their economists. As a result, partial planning may well produce a morass from which two solutions are apparent—back to the plan or forward to the market. Which choice would be made would depend on other local factors. Similarly, a decision to decentralize investment also creates needs. The supply and the organization of productive factors becomes essential. An entrepreneurial agent at the enterprise level is required, along with an appropriate incentive system of profits and losses. Decentralizing investment and establishing entrepreneurs may also make it possible, although apparently not necessary, to decentralize "ownership" of social property. Political pressures to that effect may appear, in the name of efficiency, rationality, or regional autonomy.

As more socialist countries attain levels of development at which Soviet-type planning of the classic form no longer seems appropriate, they are likely to experiment with economic reforms. The ultimate consequences of these reforms are not yet known but the Yugoslav experience suggests that the results may be more far-reaching than the reformers either intended or anticipated.

Bibliography

BOOKS

Bajt, Aleksandar. *Marksov zakon vrednosti.* Ljubljana; Pravna fakulteta, 1953.

Bell, Daniel. *The End of Ideology.* New York: Collier, 1961.

Berliner, Joseph S. *Factory and Manager in the USSR.* Cambridge: Harvard University Press, 1957.

Bobrowski, C. *La Yougoslavie Socialiste.* Paris: Cahiers de la fondation nationale des sciences politiques, no. 77, 1956.

Buchanan, James, and Gordon Tullock. *The Calculus of Consent.* Ann Arbor: University of Michigan Press, 1962.

Campbell, John. C. *Tito's Separate Road.* New York: Harper and Row, 1967.

Cerne, France. *Planiranje in trzni mehanizem v ekonomski teoriji socijalizma.* Ljubljana: Cankarjeva zalozba, 1960.

―――. *Trziste i cijene.* Zagreb: Informator, 1966.

Colanovic, B., D. Dimitrijevic, V. Frankovic, B. Horvat, I. Perisin, V. Pertot, V. Stipetic, S. Popovic, V. Trickovic, and F. Vasic. *Uzroci i karakteristike privrednih kretanja u 1961. i 1962. godini.* (The Yellow Book.) Belgrade: Savezni zavod za privredno planiranje, dokumentacioni-analiticki materiali, 7, 1962.

Dickinson, H. D. *The Economics of Socialism.* London: Oxford University Press, 1939.

Djilas, Milovan. *Conversations with Stalin.* New York: Harcourt, Brace and World, 1962.

―――. *Savreme teme.* Belgrade: Borba, 1950.

―――. *The Unperfect Society: Beyond the New Class.* New York: Harcourt, Brace and World, 1969.

Drzavni kapitalizam. Belgrade: Kultura, 1959.

Dzeba, Kreso, and Milan Beslac. *Privredna reforma: sto i zasto se mijenja.* Zagreb: Stvarnost, 1965.

Engels, Friedrich. *Anti-Dühring* (Herr Eugen Dühring's Revolution in Science). 2d ed. Moscow: Foreign Languages Publishing House, 1959.

Engels, Friedrich. *Principles of Communism,* trans. Max Bedacht. Chicago: The Daily Worker Publishing Co., n.d.

Erlich, Alexander. *The Soviet Industrialization Debate, 1924–1928.* Cambridge: Harvard University Press, 1960.

Five Year Plan of the Federal People's Republic of Yugoslavia. Belgrade: Jugoslovenska knjiga, 1947.

Fourth Plenum of the Central Committee of the League of Communists of Yugoslavia. Belgrade: Jugoslavija, 1962.

Granick, David. *Management of the Industrial Firm in the USSR.* New York: Columbia University Press, 1954.

Grossman, Gregory, ed. *Value and Plan.* Berkeley: University of California Press, 1960.

Hoffman, George W., and Fred W. Neal. *Yugoslavia and the New Communism.* New York: Twentieth Century Fund, 1962.

Horvat, Branko. *Towards a Theory of Planned Economy.* Belgrade: Jugoslav Institute of Economic Research, 1964.

Jelic, Borivoje. *Sistem planiranja u jugoslovenskoj privredi.* Belgrade: Ekonomska biblioteka, 1962.

Jugoslavija 1945–1964: Statisticki pregled. Belgrade: Savezni zavod za statistiku, 1965.

Kidric, Boris. *Privredni problemi FNRJ.* Zagreb: Kultura, 1948.

———. *Yugoslavia: Progress of the Five Year Plan.* Washington, D.C.: Embassy of the Federal Peoples Republic of Yugoslavia, 1949.

Kolaja, Jiri. *A Polish Factory.* Lexington: University of Kentucky Press, 1960.

———. *Workers Councils: The Yugoslav Experience.* New York: Frederick A. Praeger, 1966.

Korac, Miladin, ed. *Problemi teorije i prukse socijalisticke robne proizvodnje u Jugoslaviji.* Zagreb: Informator, 1965.

Korac, Miladin, et al. *Analiza ekonomskog polozaja privrednih grupacija.* Belgrade: Savezni zavod za privredno planiranje, Study no. 7, 1964.

———. *Analiza ekonomskog polozaja privrednih grupacija na bazi zakona vrednosti (1962–1966).* Zagreb: Ekonomski Institut, 1968.

Kubovic, Branko, and Vidosav Trickovic, *National and Re-*

gional Economic Planning in Yugoslavia. Belgrade: Federal Planning Bureau, 1961.

Lange, Oskar. *On the Economic Theory of Socialism,* ed. Benjamin E. Lippincott. Minneapolis: University of Minnesota Press, 1938.

――――. *The Political Economy of Socialism.* The Hague: Institute of Social Studies, Publications on Social Change, 1958.

Lavrac, Ivan. *Traznja u ekonomskoj analizi Alfreda Marshalla.* Belgrade: Nolit, 1958.

Lenin, V. I. *State and Revolution.* New York: International Publishers, 1943.

Lerner, Abba P. *The Economics of Control.* New York: Macmillan Company, 1944.

Lichtheim, George. *Marxism, An Historical and Critical Study.* New York: Frederick A. Praeger, 1961.

Maksimovic, Ivan. *Teorije socijalizma u gradjanskoj ekonomskoj nauci.* Belgrade: Nolit, 1958.

Maksimovic, Ivan, and Zoran Pjanic. *Price Problems in Yugoslav Theory and Practice.* Sofia: Bulgarian Academy of Sciences, 1964.

Marx, Karl, *Capital.* 3 vols. Chicago: Charles H. Kerr and Co., 1906, 1909, 1909.

――――. *Critique of the Gotha Program.* New York: International Publishers, 1933.

――――. *The Paris Commune.* New York: New York Labor News Co., 1920.

――――. *The Poverty of Philosophy.* New York: International Publishers, 1963.

――――. *Sochineniia.* Moscow: Gospolitizdat, 1955.

――――. *Value, Price and Profit.* New York: International Publishers, 1935.

McVicker, Charles P. *Titoism, Pattern for International Communism.* New York: St. Martin's Press, 1957.

Meek, Ronald L. *Studies in the Labour Theory of Value.* New York: International Publishers, 1956.

Mesaric, Milan. *Problemi privrednog razvoja i planiranja.* Zagreb: Ekonomski institut, 1966.

Neuberger, Egon. *The Legacies of Central Planning.* Santa

Monica, Calif.: The Rand Corporation, RM 5530 PR, 1968.

Petogodisnji plan razvoja i privredni sistem. Belgrade: Savezni zavod za privredno planiranje, 1960.

Pjanic, Zoran. *Savremene burzoaske teorije vrednosti i cena.* Belgrade: Institut drustvenih nauka, 1965.

Poljski ekonomisti o problemima socijalisticke privrede. Belgrade: Nolit, 1960.

Popovic, Strasimir. *Izbor proizvodne strukture.* Belgrade: Institut drustvenih nauka, 1966.

Privatni rad: Za ili protiv. Belgrade: Komunist, 1967.

Roper, W. C., Jr. *The Problem of Pricing in a Socialist State.* Cambridge: Harvard University Press, 1931.

Sabolovic, D. *Suvremena burzoaska politicka ekonomija.* Zagreb: 1959.

Samardzija, Milos. *Cena proizvodnje.* Belgrade: Nolit, 1957.

Schleicher, Harry. *Das System der Betrieblichen Selbstverwaltung in Jugoslawien.* Berlin: Duncker and Humblot, 1961.

Scitovsky, Tibor, Edward Shaw, and Lorie Tarshis. *Mobilizing Resources for War.* New York: McGraw-Hill, 1951.

Shoup, Paul. *Communism and the Yugoslav National Question.* New York: Columbia University Press, 1968.

Sirotkovic, Jakov. *Planiranje narodne privrede u jugoslavenskom sistemu samoupravljanja.* Zagreb: Informator, 1966.

———. *Problemi privrednog planiranja u Jugoslaviji.* Zagreb: Naprijed, 1961.

Socialist Federal Republic of Yugoslavia. Paris: Organisation for Economic Co-operation and Development. Annual since 1963.

Soskic, Branislav. *Razvoj ekonomske misli.* Belgrade: Rad, 1965.

Soskic, Branislav, et al. *Iz istorije gradjanske ekonomske misli.* Belgrade, 1956.

Spulber, N. *Soviet Strategy for Economic Growth.* Bloomington: Indiana University Press, 1964.

Stalin, J. *Economic Problems of Socialism in the USSR.* Moscow: Foreign Languages Publishing House, 1952.

Statisticki godisnjak FNRJ. Belgrade: Savezni zavod za statistiku, annual.

Stojanovic, Radmila. *Teorija privrednog razvoja u socijalizmu.* 2d ed. Belgrade: Naucna knjiga, 1964.

Sturmthal, Adolph. *Workers Councils.* Cambridge: Harvard University Press, 1964.

Tadic, Ljubomir. *Poredak i sloboda.* Belgrade: Kultura, 1967.

Tito, Josip Broz. *Workers Manage Factories in Jugoslavia.* Belgrade: Jugostampa, 1950.

Trklja, Milivoje. *Kamata na investicione kredite u uslovima drustvenog samoupravljanja.* Belgrade: Institut drustvenih nauka, 1966.

Vacic, Aleksandar. *Uzroci robne proizvodnje u socijalizmu.* Belgrade: Naucna knjiga, 1966.

Vrancic, Ivan. *Problem zakona vrijednosti u prelaznom periodu.* Zagreb: Ekonomski pregled, 1961.

Ward, Benjamin. *The Socialist Economy.* New York: Random House, 1968.

Waterston, Albert. *Planning in Yugoslavia.* Baltimore: The Johns Hopkins Press, 1962.

Weitzmann, Igor. *Das System der Einkommensverteilung in der sozialistischen Marktwirtschaft Jugoslawiens.* Berlin: Duncker and Humblot, 1958.

Wellisz, Stanislaw. *The Economies of the Soviet Bloc:* A Study in Decision-Making and Resource Allocation. New York: McGraw-Hill, 1964.

Wiles, P. J. D. *The Political Economy of Communism.* Cambridge: Harvard University Press, 1962.

Yugoslav Economists on Problems of a Socialist Economy. Radmila Stojanovic, ed. New York: International Arts and Sciences Press, 1964.

Yugoslavia's Way. The Program of the League of Communists of Yugoslavia. Trans. Stoyan Pribichevich. New York: All Nations Press, 1958.

Zaninovich, M. George. *The Development of Socialist Yugoslavia.* Baltimore: The Johns Hopkins Press, 1968.

ARTICLES, PAMPHLETS, PAPERS

Bace, Makso. "O nekim pitanjima kritike i samokritike u SSSR-u," *Komunist* 3, no. 6 (Nov. 1949): 125–67.

Bajt, Aleksandar. "Decentralized Decision-making Structure in the Yugoslav Economy," *Economics of Planning* 7, no. 1 (1967): 73–85.

Bajt, Aleksandar. "Drustvena svojina—kolektivna i individualna," *Gledista,* 9, no. 4 (Apr. 1968): 531–44.

———. "Labor in Marx's Value Theory (An Alternative Interpretation)," forthcoming.

———. "Optimalna velicina investicija iz nacionalnog dohotka," *Ekonomist* 11, no. 1–2 (1958): 79–91.

Bakaric, Vladimir. "Zakon vrijednosti, planiranje i objektivna odredjenost stope privrednog rasta," *Ekonomist* 16, no. 1 (1963): 224–37.

Bicanic, Rudolf. "Centralisticko, decentralisticko ili policentricno planiranje," *Ekonomist* 16, no. 2 (1963): 456–69.

———. "Economics of Socialism in a Developed Country," *Foreign Affairs* 44, no. 4 (July 1966): 633–50.

Bornstein, Morris. "The Soviet Price Reform Discussion," *Quarterly Journal of Economics* 78, no. 1 (Feb. 1964): 15–48.

Campbell, Robert. "Marx, Kantorovich, and Novozhilov: *Stoimost'* versus Reality," *Slavic Review* 20, no. 4 (Oct. 1961): 402–18.

Cerne, France. "Planning and the Market in Yugoslav Economic Theory," Berkeley: University of California, Center for Slavic and East European Studies (July 1962), mimeo.

———. "Pokusaj ekonomsko-logickog testiranje sedam hipoteza iz teorije dohotka," *Gledista* 8, no. 10 (Oct. 1967): 1305–1326.

———. "Otvorena pitanja privatnog sektora," *Gledista* 9, no. 4 (Apr. 1968): 559–66.

Cobeljic, Nikola. "Kriteriji izbora strukture investicija i mehanizam trzista," *Ekonomist* 16, no. 1 (1963): 215–20.

———. "Slabljenje plana i drustvene kontrole—glavni uzrocnici usporenog rasta u 1961 i 1962 godini," *Ekonomist* 16, no. 1 (1963): 62–67.

Dabcevic-Kucar, S., D. Gorupic, R. Lang, M. Mesaric, I. Perisin, J. Sirotkovic, and V. Stipetic. "O nekim problemima privrednog sistema," *Ekonomski pregled* 14, no. 3–5 (1963): 145–567.

Davidovic, Radivoj. "Cena kao faktor drustvene reprodukcije," *Ekonomist* 17, no. 4 (1964): 509–20.

———. "Distribution in the Socialist Economy—Some Principles and Methods," in Radmila Stojanovic, ed., *Yugoslav*

Economists on Problems of a Socialist Economy (New York: International Arts and Sciences Press, 1964), pp. 158–65.

"Development of Forms of Ownership in Yugoslavia," *Yugoslav Survey* 4, no. 12 (Jan.–Mar. 1963): 1673–1689.

"Differentiation of Personal Incomes," *Yugoslav Survey* 10, no. 1 (Feb. 1969): 81–90.

Dirlam, Joel E. "Yugoslav Pricing Policies and the Public Interest." University of Rhode Island, mimeo (n.d.).

Djilas, Milovan. "Aktuelna pitanja agitacije i propagande," *Partijska izgradnja* 1, no. 1 (Mar. 1947): 14–25.

———. "Ljenin o odnosima medju socijalistickim drzavama," *Komunist* 3, no. 5 (Sept. 1949): 1–56.

———. "Na novim putevima socijalizma," speech delivered at Belgrade University, Mar. 18, 1950. *Borba*, Mar. 19, 1950.

Djodan, Sime. "Robna proizvodnja u socijalizmu," *Ekonomski pregled* 17, no. 10 (1966): 600–20.

Djodan, Sime, and Uros Dujsin. "Uzroci i karakteristike privrednih kretanja u 1961. i 1962, godini," *Ekonomski pregled* 14, no. 8 (1963): 657–97.

Djordjevic, Jovan. "A Contribution to the Theory of Social Property," *Socialist Thought and Practice*, no. 24 (Oct.–Dec. 1966): 73–100.

Dobb, Maurice. "The Revival of Theoretical Discussion among Soviet Economists," *Science and Society* 24, no. 4 (Fall 1960): 289–311.

Domar, Evsey. "On Collective Farms and Producer Cooperatives," *American Economic Review* 56, no. 4 (Sept. 1966): 734–57.

Dragicevic, Adolf. "Income Distribution According to Work Performed," *Socialist Thought and Practice*, no. 26 (Apr.–June 1967): 70–89.

Dragicevic, Adolf, and S. Stampar. Book review, *Nase teme* 6, no. 6 (June 1962): 872–94.

Dragosavac, Dusan. "Delovanje zakona vrednosti i trzista," *Socijalizam* 6, no. 4 (Apr. 1963): 3–40.

"Economic Chambers and Cooperative Associations," *Yugoslav Survey* 1, no. 3 (Oct.–Dec. 1960): 325–28.

Erlich, Alexander. "Development Strategy and Planning: The Soviet Experience," in Max. F. Millikan, ed., *National Eco-*

nomic Planning, New York: National Bureau of Economic Research, 1967.

Fleming, J. M., and Viktor R. Sertic. "The Yugoslav Economic System," *International Monetary Fund Staff Papers* 9, no. 2 (July 1962): 202–25.

Furubotn, Eirik, and Svetozar Pejovic. "The Firm: Its Behavior and Property Rights in a Planned Economy," paper presented at the annual meeting of the Southern Economic Association, Washington, D.C., Nov. 8, 1968.

Gatovskii, L. M. "Ob uspol'zovanii zakona stoimosti v sotsialisticheskom khoziaistve," *Komunist,* no. 9 (1957): 39–53.

Gligorov, Kiro. "The Communal Economy," *International Social Science Journal* 13, no. 3 (1961): 408–13.

Gorupic, Drago. "The Investment Decision in Our System of Capital Formation," *Eastern European Economics* 2, no. 3 (Spring 1964): 30–43.

Hadzi-Vasilev, Mito. "Drustveno-ekonomska sustina socijalisticke raspodele prema radu," *Socijalizam* 3, no. 6 (Nov. 1960): 3–99.

―――. "Fenomen privatne svojine u socijalizmu," *Komunist,* May 5, 1966.

Hodges, Donald. "Yugoslav Marxism and Methods of Social Accounting," *Florida State University Slavic Papers* 2 (1968): 40–49.

―――. "Yugoslav Philosophers in the Struggle against Bureaucracy," *Florida State University Slavic Papers* 1 (1967): 77–94.

Holubnychy, Vsevolod. "Recent Soviet Theories of Value," *Studies on the Soviet Union* 1, no. 1 (1961): 47–72.

Horvat, Branko. "Individualno i drustveno vlasnistvo u socijalizmu," *Gledista* 8, no. 3 (Mar. 1967): 335–48.

―――. "Jos jednom o zakonu preteznog porasta i odeljka drustvene proizvodnje," *Ekonomist* 14, no. 1 (1961): 32–39.

―――. "Lekcija is ekonomske teorije A. Dragicevica i S. Stampara," *Nase teme* 6, no. 9 (Sept. 1962): 1318–1333.

―――. "O nekim pitanjima formiranja cene," *Borba,* Jan. 16, 17, and 18, 1963.

―――. "The Optimum Rate of Investment," *Economic Journal* 68, no. 272 (Dec. 1958): 747–67.

————. "The Optimum Rate of Investment Reconsidered," *Economic Journal* 75, no. 299 (Sept. 1965): 572–76.

————. "Prilog zasnivanju teorije jugoslavenskog poduzeca," *Ekonomska analiza* 1, no. 1–2 (1967): 7–28.

————. "Samoupravljanje, centralizam i planiranje," *Pregled* 16, no. 5 (May 1964): 413–44.

————. "Yugoslav System of Self-management and the Import of Foreign Private Capital," in Wolfgang Friedmann, ed., *Joint Business Ventures of Yugoslav Enterprises and Foreign Firms* (New York: Columbia University; Belgrade: Institute of International Politics and Economy, 1967).

"Internal Population Migrations in Yugoslavia," *Yugoslav Survey* 9, no. 2 (May 1968): 1–10.

Jelic, Borivoje. "Some Problems of Planning Systems," in United Nations, Department of Economic and Social Affairs, *Planning for Economic Development,* vol. 2, part 2, Centrally Planned Economies (New York: United Nations, 1965): 261–66.

Jelic, Borivoje, and Albin Orthaber. "Some Characteristic Features of Economic Planning in Yugoslavia," in United Nations, Department of Economic and Social Affairs, *Planning for Economic Development,* vol. 2, part 2, Centrally Planned Economies (New York: United Nations, 1965): 235–60.

Johnson, A. Ross. "The Dynamics of Communist Ideological Change in Yugoslavia: 1945–1953," Ph.D. dissertation, Department of Public Law and Government, Columbia University, 1967.

Judy, Richard W., and Herbert S. Levine. "Toward a Theory of Value in Centralized Economic Planning," paper presented at the Econometric Society Meetings, Dec. 1960.

Kardelj, Edvard. "Nova Jugoslavija u savremenom svetu," speech, Dec. 29, 1950.

————. "O narodnoj demokratiji u Jugoslaviji," *Komunist* 3, no. 4 (July 1949): 1–83.

————. "The Principal Dilemma: Self-Management or Statism," *Socialist Thought and Practice,* no. 24 (Oct.–Dec. 1966): 3–29.

————. "What Is the 'Authentic' Revolutionary Nature of

the Working Class," *Socialist Thought and Practice,* no. 30 (Apr.–June 1968): 10–31.

Kardelj, Edvard. "The Working Class, Bureaucracy and the League of Communists," *Socialist Thought and Practice,* no. 29 (Jan.–Mar. 1968): 3–28.

Kaufman, Adam. "The Origin of 'The Political Economy of Socialism,'" *Soviet Studies* 4, no. 3 (Jan. 1953): 243–72.

Kidric, Boris. "Karakter nase privrede," *Komunist* 1, no. 6 (Nov. 1946).

———. "Karakter robnonovcanih odnosa u FNJR," *Komunist* 3, no. 1 (Jan. 1949): 36–56.

———. "O nacrtima novih ekonomskih zakona," *Komunist* 5, no. 4–5 (July–Sept. 1951): 1–27.

———. "O nekim teoretskim pitanjima novog privrednog sistema," *Komunist* 6, no. 1–3 (Jan.–Mar. 1952): 42–69.

———. "Teze o ekonomici prelaznog perioda u nasoj zemlji," *Komunist* 4, no. 6 (Nov. 1950): 1–20.

Korac, Miladin. "Kreditiranje prosirene reprodukcije u sistemu socijalisticke robne privrede," *Socijalizam* 10, no. 3 (Mar. 1967): 302–24; no. 4 (Apr. 1967): 471–89.

———. "Raspodela prema radu u sistemu socijalisticke robne privrede," *Gledista* 7, no. 8–9 (Aug.–Sept. 1966): 1021–1036.

———. "Socijalisticki robni proizvodjac u procesu drustvene reprodukcije," *Ekonomski pregled* 14, no. 10–12 (Oct.–Dec. 1963): 1027–1075.

———. "Teorija socijalisticke robne proizvodnje," *Nasa stvarnost* 16, no. 12 (Dec. 1962): 563–613.

———. "Teze za teorije socijalisticke robne proizvodnje," *Socijalizam* 4, no. 1 (Jan.–Feb. 1961): 31–51.

———. "Zakon vrednosti kao regulator raspodele dohotka u socijalistickom sistemu robne privrede," *Ekonomski pregled* 17, no. 10 (Oct. 1966): 548–79.

Korac, Veljko. "The Possibilities and Prospects of Freedom in the Modern World," *Praxis* (International ed.) 4, no. 1–2 (1968): 73–82.

Krajger, Boris. "New Economic Measures." Report to the Federal Assembly, reprinted in the *Economic Reform in Yugoslavia* (Belgrade: Socialist Thought and Practice, 1965), pp. 66–89.

Krajger, Sergije. "Dohodak preduzeca u nasem sistemu," *Nasa stvarnost* 7, no. 2 (Feb. 1953): 47–67.

Kukoleca, Stevan. "Osvrt na dohodna cena," *Ekonomist* 17, no. 4 (1964): 770–77.

Lavrac, Ivan. "Competition and Incentive in the Yugoslav Economic System," in Radmila Stojanovic, ed., *Yugoslav Economists on Problems of a Socialist Economy* (New York: International Arts and Sciences Press, 1964), pp. 147–58.

———. "Licni rad i privatna svojina u socijalizmu," *Gledista* 8, no. 6–7 (June–July 1967): 897–907.

———. "Plan i trziste," *Ekonomist* 16, no. 1 (1963): 203–08.

Maksimovic, Ivan. "Ekonomska politika i ekonomska teorija vrednosti i cena," *Ekonomist* 12, no. 4 (1959): 476–85.

———. "Trziste i plan u nasem ekonomskom sistemu," *Ekonomist* 16, no. 1 (1963): 156–67.

Marschak, Thomas A. "Centralized versus Decentralized Resource Allocation: The Yugoslav 'Laboratory,'" *Quarterly Journal of Economics* 82, no. 4 (Nov. 1968): 561–87.

Mihailovic, Kosta. "Prilog izgradnje koncepcije regionalnog razvoja," *Ekonomist* 18, no. 4 (1964): 561–83.

———. "The Regional Aspects of Economic Development," in Radmila Stojanovic, ed., *Yugoslav Economists on Problems of a Socialist Economy* (New York: International Arts and Sciences Press, 1964), pp. 29–45.

Milenkovitch, Deborah. "Reforms in Yugoslav Planning." Paper presented at the National Conference of the American Association for the Advancement of Slavic Studies, Mar. 30, 1967.

———. "Yugoslavia: The Transition from Socialism to Capitalism?" Paper presented at the Northeastern Conference of the American Association for the Advancement of Slavic Studies, Mar. 29, 1969.

Miljevski, Kiril. "Neprivredna potrosnja," *Ekonomist* 16, no. 1 (1963): 53–58.

———. "Possibilities for the Development of Underdeveloped Areas," in Radmila Stojanovic, ed., *Yugoslav Economists on Problems of a Socialist Economy* (New York: International Arts and Sciences Press, 1964), pp. 7–17.

Miller, J. "A Political Economy of Socialism in the Making," *Soviet Studies* 4, no. 4 (Apr. 1953): 403–33.

Mlakar, Cveta. "Drustveno potreban rad u Marksovoj teoriji vrijednosti," *Ekonomist* 15, no. 1 (1962): 111–29.

Montias, J. M. "Economic Reforms and Retreat in Yugoslavia," *Foreign Affairs* 37, no. 2 (Jan. 1959): 293–305.

Neuberger, Egon. "Central Banking in Semi-planned Economies: Yugoslav Case." Ph.D. dissertation, Department of Economics, Harvard University, 1957.

————. "The Yugoslav Investment Auctions," *Quarterly Journal of Economics* 72, no. 1 (Feb. 1959): 88–115.

Orlic, Miodrag. "Licni rad—integralni deo socijalizma ili saputnik," *Gledista* 9, no. 3 (Mar. 1968): 445–52.

Ostrovitianov, K. "Ob osnovnykh zakonomernostiakh razvitiia sotsialisticheskogo khoziaistva," *Bol'shevik*, no. 23–24 (Dec. 1944), 46–60.

Pasic, Najdan. "Critical Survey of Different Conceptions of Self-Management," *Socialist Thought and Practice*, no. 31 (July–Sept. 1968): 32–49.

Pejovich, Svetozar. "Liberman's Reforms and Property Rights in the Soviet Union," *Journal of Law and Economics* 12, no. 1 (Apr. 1969): 155–62.

Pijade, Mose. "Veliki majstori licemerja," *Borba* (Sept. 22, 29; Oct. 5, 6, 1949).

Pirec, Dusan. "Ekonomska teorija planske privrede," *Nasa stvarnost* 16, no. 5 (May 1962): 600–07.

Pjanic, Zoran. "Problem formiranja cena," *Nasa stvarnost* 17, no. 3 (Mar. 1963): 274–97.

Popovic, Milentije. "For the Re-evaluation of Marx's Teaching on Production and Relations of Production," *Socialist Thought and Practice*, no. 19 (July–Sept. 1965): 64–117, and no. 20 (Oct.–Dec. 1965): 62–98.

————. "O ekonomskim odnosima izmedju socijalistickih drzava," *Komunist* 3, no. 4 (July 1949): 98–160.

————. "Povodom diskusije o privrednom sistemu," *Nasa stvarnost* 8, no. 1–2 (Jan.–Feb. 1954): 9–50.

————. "Povodom nacrta uredaba o privrednom sistemu," *Nasa stvarnost* 7, no. 9 (Sept. 1953): 3–33.

————. "Sta drzavni kapitalizam znaci u drustvenom razvitku," *Nasa stvarnost* 7, no. 2 (Feb. 1953): 3–34.

Popovic, Strasimir. "Prilog gradji o ekonomskom sistemu Jugoslavije," *Nasa stvarnost* 17, no. 5 (May 1963): 522–49.

Rakic, Vojislav. "Fundamental Characteristics of the Yugoslav Economic System," in Radmila Stojanovic, ed., *Yugoslav Economists on Problems of a Socialist Economy* (New York: International Arts and Sciences Press, 1964), pp. 123–40.

Rankovic, Slavka. "Yugoslavia's Economic Development," *Socialist Thought and Practice,* no. 14 (Apr.–June 1964): 45–63.

Raskovic, V. "Eticka granica privatnog sektora u samoupravnom sistemu," *Politika,* Jan. 16, 1968.

Rockwell, Charles S. "The Relevance of Illyria for Less Developed Countries," mimeo.

Rusinow, Dennison I. "Anatomy of a Student Revolt," Parts 1 and 2, *Fieldstaff Reports,* American Universities Field Staff, Southeast Europe Series 15, no. 4, 5 (Aug. and Nov. 1968).

Samardzija, Milos. "Odnos vrednosti i cene," *Ekonomist* 12, no. 1–2 (1959): 1–24.

———. "The Market and Social Planning in the Yugoslav Economy," *Quarterly Review of Economics and Business* 7, no. 2 (Summer 1967): 37–44.

———. "Problem cena u socijalistickoj privredi," *Nasa stvarnost* 14, no. 12 (Dec. 1960): 488–515.

———. "Problems of Commodity Production in Socialism and Economic Theory in the USSR Today," *Socialist Thought and Practice,* no. 4 (Dec. 1961): 87–118.

Sefer, Berislav. "Metodoloske karakteristike planiranja licne potrosnje," *Ekonomist* 14, no. 2 (1961): 253–65.

Sen, A. K. "On Optimizing the Rate of Saving," *Economic Journal* 71, no. 283 (Sept. 1961): 479–96.

Shaw, Sin-Ming. "Regional Investment Policies, Capital Formation and Income Equalization in Yugoslavia: 1947–1964." Masters Essay, Department of Economics. Columbia University, 1969.

Sirotkovic, Jakov. "Ekonomski polozaj privrednih grupacija i drustveno planiranje," *Ekonomist* 17, no. 4 (1964): 727–37.

"Sixth Congress of the Yugoslav Trade Union Federation," *Yugoslav Survey* 9, no. 4 (Nov. 1968): 69–84.

Socialist Alliance of Working People in Yugoslavia. "Teza o

licnom radusa sredstvima za rad u licnoj svojini." Adopted by Presidium of the Federal Conference, Oct. 26, 1967.

Socialist Alliance of Working People in Yugoslavia. "Tasks of the Socialist Alliance in the Development of Private Work." Resolution passed by the Federal Conference, Jan. 30, 1968.

Stojanovic, Radmila. "O donosenju investicionih odluka," *Ekonomski pregled* 14, no. 3–5 (1963): 344–49.

Stojanovic, Svetozar. "Social Self-government and Socialist Community," *Praxis* (International ed.) 4, no. 1–2 (1968): 104–16.

Strumilin, S. "Zakon stoimosti i planirovanie," *Voprosy Ekonomiki,* no. 7 (1959): 132.

"Teaching of Economics in the Soviet Union," *American Economic Review,* 34, no. 1 (Sept. 1944): 501–30.

Todorovic, Mijalko. "Current Tasks in the Development of the Economic System and Social-Economic Relations," *Socialist Thought and Practice,* no. 19 (July–Sept. 1965): 13–51.

———. "O nekim pitanjima naseg privrednog sistema," *Socijalizam* 5, no. 6 (Dec. 1962): 3–69; 6, no. 1 (Jan. 1963): 3–38; 6, no. 2–3 (Feb.–Mar. 1963): 3–58; 7, no. 11–12 (Nov.–Dec. 1964): 1387–1444.

———. "A Revolutionary Vanguard—The Abiding Need of Our Self-Managing Community," *Socialist Thought and Practice,* no. 31 (July–Sept. 1968): 7–20.

———. "Some Observations on Planning," *Socialist Thought and Practice,* no. 17 (Jan.–Mar. 1964): 3–48.

———. "Some Questions of Our Economic System," *Socialist Thought and Practice,* no. 9 (Jan. 1963): 17–65.

———. "The Working Man, Capital Formation and Investments," *Socialist Thought and Practice,* no. 22 (Apr.–June 1966): 29–44.

Trickovic, Vidosav. "Strukturne promene u licnoj potrosnji s posebnim osvrtom na rezultate ispitivanja porodicnih budzeta," *Ekonomist* 13, no. 3 (1960): 427–58.

Uvalic, Radivoj. "The Functions of the Market and the Plan in the Socialist Economy," in Radmila Stojanovic, ed., *Yugoslav Economists on Problems of a Socialist Economy* (New York: International Arts and Sciences Press, 1964) pp. 140–47.

Vanek, Jaroslav. "Economic Planning in Yugoslavia," in Max Millikan, ed., *National Economic Planning* (New York: National Bureau of Economic Research, 1967).

Vinski, Ivo. "Rast fiksnih fondova po Jugoslavenskim republikama od 1946–1964 godine," *Ekonomist* 19, no. 1–4 (1966).

Vlaskalic, Tihomir. "Proizvodni proces u socijalistickom preduzecu," *Ekonomski pregled* 17, no. 8–9 (1966): 445–63.

————. "Teoretske osnove i neki rezultati analize ekonomskog polozaja robnih proizvodjaca u nasem privrednim sistemu," *Socijalizam* 7, no. 5 (May 1964): 598–614.

Vracar, Stevan. "Dilema oko drzavne vlasti," *Gledista* 8, no. 5 (May 1967): 771–84.

————. "Partijski monopolizam i politicka moc drustvenih grupa," *Gledista* 8, no. 8–9 (Aug. 1967): 1053–1066.

Ward, Benjamin. "The Firm in Illyria: Market Syndicalism," *American Economic Review* 18, no. 4 (Sept. 1958): 566–89.

————. "From Marx to Barone: Industrial Organization in Postwar Jugoslavia," Ph.D. dissertation, Department of Economics, University of California, Berkeley, 1956.

————. "Marxism-Horvatism: A Yugoslav Theory of Socialism," *American Economic Review* 57, no. 3 (June 1967): 509–23.

————. "The Nationalized Firm in Yugoslavia," *American Economic Review* 55, no. 2 (May 1965): 646–52.

Weiner, Neil S. "Multiple Incentive Fee Maximization: An Economic Model," *Quarterly Journal of Economics* 77, no. 4 (Nov. 1963), 606–16.

Wertheimer-Baletic, Alica. "O nekim aspektima utjecaja ekonomsko-demografskih faktora na formiranje obujma i strukture licne potrosnje," *Ekonomist* 20, no. 1–2 (1967): 246–49.

Wiles, Peter. "Convergence: Possibility and Probability," in Alexander Balinky, et al., *Planning and the Market in the U.S.S.R.: The 1960's* (New Brunswick: Rutgers University Press, 1967).

————. "Imperfect Competition and Decentralized Planning," *Economics of Planning* 4, no. 1 (Jan. 1964): 16–28.

"Workers Management," *Yugoslav Survey* 1, no. 2 (Apr.–June 1960): 9–20.

Zarkovic, Dragoje. "Nacela politike cena," *Ekonomist* 16, no. 3–4 (1963): 646–52.

Zauberman, Alfred. "Revisionism in Soviet Economics," in Leopold Labedz, ed., *Revisionism* (New York: Frederick A. Praeger, 1962), 268–80.

———. "The Soviet Debate on the Law of Value and Price Formation," in Gregory Grossman, ed., *Value and Plan* (Berkeley: University of California Press, 1960), 17–35.

Index

317